PRAISE FOR THE EM

"What a wonderful book!!!! *The E* for everyone who suffers from fear of vomit. This book offers a wealth of information and step-by-step guidance on how to get well. From the strategies, to the chapter on how to manage traumatic childhood vomit memories, and all the QR codes that link to photos and videos, this is brain re-wiring, cognitive-behavioral therapy at its best!"

Elizabeth DuPont Spencer, L.C.S.W.
Author of *CBT for Anxiety* and *The Anxiety Cure*

"I love this book! Ken Goodman compassionately explains the cure for emetophobia with science, humor, and strategy. This book provides everything you need to know about the devastating disorder in an engaging, step-by-step way that includes videos, exercises, and examples. I'd recommend it to anyone suffering from emetophobia."

Maggie Perry, Psy.D.
Huddle.care

"If you struggle with Emetophobia, this is the book for you!! Ken Goodman masterfully lays out the foundation for overcoming Emetophobia and integrates components of Cognitive-Behavioral Therapy, Exposure and Response Prevention and Acceptance and Commitment Therapy.

Tabasom Vahidi, Ph.D.

"This book is your *roadmap to freedom* from emetophobia and Ken Goodman is your expert guide. Not only will you find a wealth of tools, throughout the book are QR codes that when scanned with your smartphone camera, link to videos and images. This really makes the book come alive."

Neal Sideman
Paniccure.com

"Anyone who suffers from emetophobia should read this book. Ken Goodman's expertise and insight provides an easy-to-understand and clear path to recovery. Through his use of metaphors, client examples, and sense of humor, Ken will have you wanting to learn and practice as much as you can, to get your life back from the fear of vomit."

Kimberly Morrow, L.C.S.W.

Author of *CBT for Anxiety*

"This is an incredibly helpful book for one of the most debilitation phobias. *The Emetophobia Manual* is easy to digest, no pun intended, with powerful tools you can use to win your freedom. The videos are terrific with instructions that will encourage and inspire you."

Jennifer Shannon, L.M.F.T.

Author of *Don't Feed the Monkey Mind*

"This wonderful book will educate you on vomit phobia, provide practical solutions and tools, reduce your shame, and offer hope that healing is possible."

Dr. Debra Kissen, Ph.D.

Author of *Rewire Your Anxious Brain for Teens*

"I have suffered with panic attacks and severe emetophobia for over 20 years, but thanks to this book, I am finally FREE and living my life! Ken lays out easy to follow steps, along with QR codes that link to photos and videos. This book frames anxiety in a whole new way; a way in which you actually want to fight it and win. Ken gives winning strategies that make getting better attainable, something I never thought possible."

Ashley

20 year emetophobia sufferer

The Emetophobia Manual

Free Yourself from the Fear of Vomit and Reclaim Your Life

Ken Goodman, L.C.S.W.

ISBN: 978-1-7358891-1-5

Format and design: Sam Goodman
Illustrations: Claudia Cubillos and Jackie Trinidad
Cover: Kerry Watson

This book is intended as a guide and not a substitute for medical or mental health treatment. When dealing with emetophobia or panic disorder it is recommended that you consult with qualified health care professionals. You should not delay seeking medical attention, disregard medical advice, or discontinue treatment because of anything contained herein.

Also by Ken Goodman at QuietMindSolutions.com

The Anxiety Solution Series: Your Guide to Overcoming Panic, Worry, Compulsions, and Fear
A twelve-hour, step-by-step, audio program.

Break Free From Anxiety: The Steps, Strategies, and Secrets to Overcoming Panic, Worry, and Fear
The first coloring self-help book for anxiety.

Stress Free: Relaxation Exercises, Guided Meditations, and More
A download containing six different relaxation exercises.

The Personal Growth Series: Hypnosis for Self-Improvement
Six hypnosis sessions that address confidence, persistence, procrastination, fear, motivation, and achievement.

Sleeping in My Lounge Chair
A download to help people with insomnia improve their sleep.

KenGoodmanTherapy.com
Webinars, articles, and videos on a variety of anxiety related topics.

Dedicated to:

My wife, Cindy, my two boys, Jason and Sam, and my parents, Don and Sally – the greatest joys of my life.

The emtephobes who I have treated and found freedom - we have proven that this disorder can be overcome. Thank you for helping me fine tune the treatment path.

The emetophobes around the world who suffer in silence and yearn to break free - you can beat this!

My colleagues at the Anxiety and Depression Association of America – thank you for your friendship, opportunities for professional growth, and the fabulous work you do for those with anxiety and depression.

TABLE OF CONTENTS

Chapter 1
The Journey Begins: The Roots of Anxiety

Several years ago, I wrote an article about emetophobia for the Anxiety and Depression Association of America (ADAA.org). That article received more responses than any other blog on their massive website. Why would this be? Panic disorder, social anxiety, and claustrophobia are much more common than emetophobia. One would think articles on more common disorders would receive a greater reaction. Unlike these disorders, however, there are few resources on the subject of emetophobia. Emetophobes are starved for information and the number of people suffering with this disorder is greater than most professionals fathom. With so many sufferers and virtually no self-help options, I set out on a course to write this book.

If you read through the posts at ADAA.org you will hear the words of desperate individuals of all ages, sharing how emetophobia has devastated their lives and how they have been unable to find help. Their emotional pain and hopelessness are palpable. Here are two posts from the thousand responses to my article:

I'm 16 and have severe vomit phobia. I started to feel sick every day 10 months ago, but have always had the phobia. I always avoid social situations and even sleep with a bucket by my bed in case I am sick in the night. I feel sick everyday and think I may be sick. This phobia has messed up my life as I had to do exams with it and I probably failed because of it. It has made my friendships more complicated and my family don't really understand. My mum wants met get a job but I've told her how much I struggle but she doesn't understand. Doctors have done so many tests but nothing has come back as an illness. Mum believes I am throwing my life away.

This phobia destroys my life. I obsess over it and it controls me. I don't wear certain clothes because I might throw up if I wear them. I don't eat for days if I feel the slightest bit off. I don't sleep because I'm scared I will throw up. I struggle with anxiety and depression. I've tried almost anything and I don't know what to do anymore.

With years of suffering it's not possible to overcome emetophobia by reading a self-help book. Reading self-help books doesn't work. So don't just read this book. Comprehend it! Collaborate with the material. Take notes. Highlight. Experience the exercises and make healing a priority. Only then will you see the results you desire. Reading passively (not doing the work) is like reading a cookbook in bed. In the end, you have nothing to show for it. You just feel hungry.

People don't make real change by learning new information. They change by living new experiences. In this manual I have carefully laid out an experiential program for conquering emetophobia and panic disorder in an easy to follow, step-by-step format. The road to freedom lies ahead and now it's up to you to rise up and take the brave and gritty steps to happiness. If you believe that it's not possible to get better, it's understandable. Fortunately, you don't need to be confident or hopeful. You just need to work this program with patience and persistence.

Patience and Persistence Are Key

When you learn a language or a complex new skill, the structure of your brain literally changes, but this requires effort and time. Overcoming emetophobia is no different. You will be retraining your brain to not react to your thoughts, worries, and symptoms and to not avoid. As you go through this program step by step, you will feel yourself and your brain changing as behaviors that now feel impossible, become effortless. Do the work, be patient and persistent, and you can change your brain.

In chapters 1 through 14 I lay the foundation for overcoming emetophobia and panic attacks. Bridges require a strong foundation to prevent them from collapsing and in the first fourteen chapters I lay the foundation for your recovery by explaining the perspective, strategy, secrets, and tools to help you build your bridge to freedom. Your quest begins in chapter 4. With each *STEP TO FREEDOM*, I provide clear instructions but it's up to you to take those steps. Follow along exactly as I describe. There is much flexibility in your pursuit, so you can design your recovery to fit your personal needs, situation, and fears. The journey will be challenging but if we work together, you will prevail.

As you read through this book, I encourage you to identify and share certain sections with important people in your life to help them better understand your suffering and what will be required to heal. Feel free to enlist the help of supportive individuals to assist you along the way.

In this book I utilize Quick Response (QR) codes.

A QR code is a bar code with stored information. In this book the QR codes serve as links to photos and videos and can be accessed via your smart phone. Most phones have a QR code scanner built into the camera but if not, you can download a QR reading application for free. **Scan this QR code with your camera to watch an introductory video.**

Open the camera on your smartphone and place the code between the brackets on your screen. Then select the website and wait. A photo or video will appear. Check out the QR code above. If you have trouble go to QuietMindSolutions.com/Emetophobia. Open Q*R Codes Listed by Chapter* to find all the material. Most of the QR codes are in the second half of this book.

The Roots of Anxiety

When my son was seven, I took him out to our garden to pull weeds and plant flowers. I explained, to prevent weeds from growing back you must pull them at the root. This practice applies to the treatment of anxiety as well. To overcome emetophobia and panic disorder you must attack these disorders at the roots. There are two roots to ALL anxiety disorders. The content of all fears and worries derive from two roots:

1. Intolerance of uncertainty
2. Intolerance of discomfort/distress

These are the roots of all anxiety and this is where we will focus. Sufferers of emetophobia cannot tolerate the uncertainty of the possibility of vomit or panic. *Why is that person holding their stomach? Will I get sick if I eat at a new restaurant? What if I get stuck in the subway and throw up? What if there are germs on that handle? If I go into the bar will I see someone puke? What if I have a panic attack? Why am I feeling nauseous? Will this medication make me sick? What if I get the flu? Will I feel nauseous today?* With so much uncertainty, emetophobes can be filled with anxiety from the moment they awake until they fall asleep.

The discomfort that accompanies the uncertainty is typically nausea, but stomach issues, racing heart, lightheadedness, labored breathing, chest pressure, and many other symptoms of panic are also common and cannot be tolerated. Listen for the discomfort and uncertainty in these blog posts:

> *I was having panic attacks because I felt like I was gonna puke. I texted my mom and she helped me but I was shaking like crazy and it was 2 am.*

> *I can't sleep as I'm scared I'm going to be sick. I took an anti-sickness tablet that hasn't worked – my chest is pounding I feel so ill and I don't know if it's my anxiety or I have a bug. I haven't been sick but I've got myself in such a state I could cry.*

Similar to patients who have a fear of starting treatment, you might be anxious to read this book. Why? Because it's uncertain and it might make you feel uncomfortable (the roots of all anxiety). Since this book will focus on the roots of all anxiety, if you suffer with other fears, this book will help those as well. Simply apply the same tools and strategies.

The tools and strategies in this book are based on Cognitive Behavioral Therapy (CBT), the gold standard for the treatment of anxiety. Under the umbrella of CBT falls Exposure and Response Prevention (ERP) and Acceptance and Commitment Therapy (ACT). I utilize the strategies from these modalities and the principles of Mindfulness, all of which have been empirically validated with research as the most effective treatment for anxiety disorders. According to the training manual, *CBT for Anxiety*, "There are over 500 outcome studies on the efficacy of CBT." David Clark and Aaron Beck have performed comprehensive reviews of thirty years of research that show the efficacy of CBT for anxiety and depression. A study by Jokic-Begic demonstrates the neurobiological changes in certain areas of the brain after Cognitive Behavioral Therapy.

> *Hi. I'm not only tremendously afraid of vomiting, but I'm also afraid of the word being said. It's gotten to the point that if a kid throws up near me, or even puts their hands on their stomach, I will scream and start shaking and hyperventilating. It's pretty embarrassing and scary. I've only thrown up once in my life. I don't know what to do. It's consuming my life.*

It would be impossible to write a book on emetophobia without using the V-word. If this word is difficult for you, I encourage you to hang in there and push through your discomfort, so you can learn to overcome this debilitating phobia.

The myriad of euphemisms and ways to verbalize the act of vomiting is fascinating. If you live in England you might want to steer clear of *chunder* or anyone *speaking Welsh*. In South Africa *parking a tiger* has nothing to do with driving or large cats and in Australia, *yodel* is not just a type of singing. If you happen to be in Argentina, you might want to steer clear of a person *throwing a duck away*. To *boak* is something sick people do in Scotland and in the United States, *Ralph* is more than male name and *yak* is not just a wild ox with shaggy hair. This book will help you acclimate to these words and all triggers of anxiety.

How do you acclimate to a cold swimming pool?

The quickest way is to jump in and move around. The temperature of the pool does not change, but by moving your body, you acclimate to the cold. The more you read, hear, and say *vomit, barf, and puke*, the more you acclimate to these words. Accept the discomfort these words produce, keep reading, and soon they won't disturb you. So, whether it's *tossing your cookies* or *blowing chunks*, let's jump in to the material.

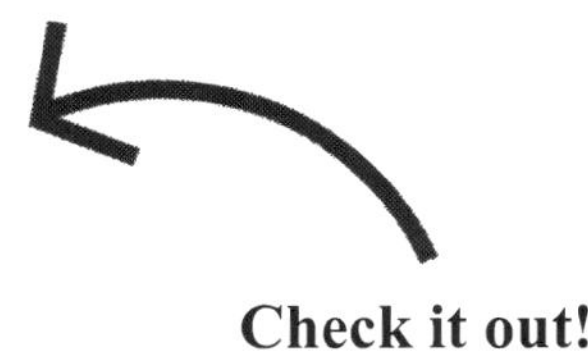

Check it out!

Chapter 2
Why Are Emetophobia and Panic So Debilitating?

Emetophobia is the fear of vomit. It includes a fear of throwing up and/or a fear of others throwing up. There is little research on this phobia and it is unclear how many people suffer from it. One study cited a prevalence of 0.1% (Becker et al. 2007). This estimate is in sharp contrast to the estimates suggested by Kirkpatrick & Berg (1981, cited in Philips, 1985) and van Hout & Bouman (unpublished observations cited in van Overveld 2008) who claim a prevalence of 1.7–3.1% for males and 6–7% for females.

According to the National Institute of Mental Health, 19% of the adult population in the United States suffers with an anxiety disorder and 31% of adults will **suffer** with an anxiety disorder at some point in their life. Unlike many phobias (public speaking, heights, snakes, planes, etc.), the fear of vomit can be pervasive and all-consuming. Most people with phobias can easily avoid the object of their fear and live their life without too much trouble. If you have a fear of elevators, take the stairs. If you have a fear of freeways, drive on the streets. Fear of clowns? Avoid the circus.

A fear of vomit is different however, because it's not something that can be avoided. **All locations carry a risk of vomit**: car rides, doctor's offices, restaurants, amusement parks, being around children at a school, or intoxicated adults at a bar. Wherever you go you must be on guard at all times to make sure you don't get sick and no one around you becomes sick.

The **unpredictability of vomiting** is another factor that causes a high level of relentless anxiety. In the mind of the emetophobe, vomit can occur at any time. This is different from many other phobias. If you suffer from glossophobia and must give a toast at a wedding, you know the exact date you will be giving your speech. If you have aviophobia and must take a flight, you know the exact time your plane will depart. You will only feel anxiety as those dates draw near. **In the mind of an emetophobe, vomit can strike anytime and anywhere.** Because it is a ticking time bomb and you have no idea when or where it will detonate, you must be vigilant in your efforts to prevent the explosion. When a situation becomes precarious, you might experience a panic attack.

A panic attack is a sudden burst of fear and an eruption of physical symptoms which include some or all of the following: racing heart, chest pressure, difficulty breathing, hyperventilation, sweating, lightheadedness, tingling, shaking, jitters, muscle tightness, jelly legs, stomach distress, nausea, and a feeling of being unreal or out of your body. Every year thousands of people race to emergency rooms because they believe they are having a heart attack. They aren't. These attacks can come out of nowhere, for no apparent reason, or be triggered by a thought or situation. There is a fear of being trapped and a worry you won't be able to escape. Often people feel like they are going crazy or dying. According to the Anxiety and Depression Association of America website (ADAA.org) *2-3% of Americans have panic disorder in a given year.* When someone experiences a panic attack, they are often afraid of having more attacks and so they avoid going places where they may be triggered. Later in this book are two chapters on overcoming panic attacks.

Panic disorder becomes severe when you do not leave your home due to your fears and symptoms. This is called agoraphobia. According to the National Institute of Mental Health's website (NIMH.org), an estimated 1.3% of U.S. adults (3.1 million) will experience agoraphobia at some point in their lives.

Emetophobes sometimes appear to have anorexia because they restrict their eating and are extremely thin, but they do not meet the criteria for an eating disorder. Sufferers of anorexia limit eating because they believe they are overweight. People with emetophobia restrict eating because they believe they will vomit.

The final aspect that sets this phobia apart from others is the **vicious cycle that keeps sufferers trapped.** Nausea (and other abdominal symptoms) is the intolerable sensation that constantly leaves the emetophobe afraid they will vomit. In anticipation of going somewhere, anxiety will cause emetophobes to feel nauseous. Once they experience nausea, this triggers further worry about puking or being sick, which causes nausea to worsen and around we go. The discomfort and distress cannot be tolerated and the fear of being sick, puking, being embarrassed, and panicking leaves sufferers trapped in a self-imposed prison.

To play it safe, emetophobes engage in safety behaviors, actions to protect themselves. They might bring medication or water with them whenever they leave their home and utilize other safety measures including eating slowly, not eating, washing hands excessively, eating only familiar foods, not wearing certain clothes, or chewing gum when anxious. They are hypervigilant -- on high alert, constantly looking out for potential threats (sick people, drunk people, spoiled food, etc.). They are avoidant, limiting where they go, what they do, and the distance from home. If they perceive a threat, they will miss work and cancel social plans.

While phobias of heights, closed spaces, and flying are well known, virtually no one has ever heard of the fear of vomit. This makes emetophobia sound strange, and most sufferers keep their disorder a secret from friends and family due to feelings of embarrassment and shame.

The fear of vomiting or others vomiting is constantly on their mind: an ever-present source of worry, shame, and failure and this of course is very sad and can lead to depression. If you are unable to work, limit your social contacts, and have a desire to get married but avoid going on dates because you worry about vomiting, you will experience hopelessness and depression as you forecast a life of isolation and loneliness.

Minimal Research

Research on emetophobia has been minimal. There have been several case studies citing the efficacy of treatment with a single emetophobic patient and there have been a few studies of moderate sample size, researching various aspects of the disorder.

In 2001 Joshua Lipsitz and his team surveyed members of an internet emetophobia support group. Respondents were 50 women and 6 men with an average age of 31. Results suggest that *emetophobia is a disorder of early onset and chronic course, with highly persistent and intrusive symptoms. Emetophobia is implicated in social, home-marital, and occupational impairment and it causes significant constriction of leisure activities. Nearly half of women avoided or delayed becoming pregnant. About three quarters of respondents have eating rituals or significantly limit the foods they eat. Respondents describe other problems such as depression, panic attacks, social anxiety, compulsions, and frequent history of childhood separation anxiety.*

In 2012 a study pertaining to vomiting memories was published in the *Journal of Behavior Therapy and Experimental Psychiatry*. A group of 94 emetophobes was compared to a control group (94 people who did not have emetophobia). Each group completed a self-report questionnaire assessing their memories of their own vomiting and others vomiting. The results concluded that adults with emetophobia *recalled the memories of their own and others vomiting experiences from an earlier age and rated them as significantly more distressing than the control group. The emetophobia group recalled more memories of others vomiting before the onset of the problem. After the age at which the phobia became a problem, they recalled fewer memories of their own vomiting and more memories of others vomiting than the control group.* Researchers concluded that *autobiographical memories of vomiting, that have lost a time perspective and context, are being reactivated with cues for vomiting.*

The results of another internet survey were published in 2013 in *Behavioral Sciences*. Researchers surveyed 131 Germans from an emetophobia internet forum. They calculated a nausea score and grouped participants in either high or low nausea groups and examined the relationship between nausea and characteristics of the fear of vomiting. They concluded that *participants in the high nausea group had significantly higher ratings of subjective fear and significantly longer duration of fear of vomiting. Additionally, the high-nausea group contained more participants with a body mass index below 19 than the low-nausea group.*

The first randomized controlled trial evaluating the protocol for Cognitive Behavioral Therapy for emetophobia was published in 2016 in the *Journal of Anxiety Disorders*. Twenty-four participants were randomly assigned to either twelve sessions of CBT or a waitlist. *Six (50%) of the participants receiving CBT achieved clinically significant change compared to two participants (16%) in the waitlist group.*

In the next chapter I will address the antecedents and recovery of emetophobia through the writings of a former sufferer.

Chapter 3
How Did I Get this Way and Can I Prevail ?

Each person's road to emetophobia and panic is different but the stories are similar and usually begin with a trigger. I asked one of my emetophobia patients if she would be interested in writing about the origins and development of her phobia and the depth of her despair. She granted me permission to share her writing in this book.

Here is the beginning of her emetophobia story in her own words:

I'm currently 31 but my emetophobia story started when I was little, very little. I had always thought it started the night I got violently ill in 3rd grade, but as I was thinking about writing this, I actually realized it started one year earlier.

A classmate of mine got sick and the teacher filed us out of the classroom. While my group of friends were outside, we were all talking about what had just happened. I brought up to the group that I had never gotten sick, at least not to my memory. One girl said a statement that stuck in my subconscious so deeply and triggered my obsession with vomit. She said, "If you don't get sick, you will die." I found this to be incredibly shocking and terrifying. Here I was, so young, and faced with the reality that I was going to die because I had never gotten sick. I remember going home that day and asking my mom if I had ever gotten sick. She replied, of course, when I was a baby. I was momentarily relieved, but my obsession about getting sick started to grow. I became so curious about this. Why hadn't I gotten sick yet? I didn't want to die.

That summer, a friend of mine slept over and during the night she got sick. I remember asking her so many questions about it as I had slept through the incident. She told me what happened, and I even remember telling her, I want to get sick. My obsession grew more. Then a year later, the fateful night that is so imprinted in my memory, it still feels like it happened yesterday.

It was a warm summer night and I was so excited to eat a Jack In The Box burger. It was delicious and a rare treat. That night my stomach began to hurt like nothing I had really felt before. My mom gave me some Pepto Bismol and I laid in our guest bedroom. No matter what I did my stomach ache would not go away. I would try and think about all the things I loved in life: soccer, my friends, horses. None of it made that pain go away.

I finally fell asleep, then awoke in sheer panic in the middle of the night. I was violently ill all night long! It was the worst feeling in the entire world. I was absolutely terrified of what my body was capable of. I had never felt anything like it and never wanted to feel anything like it again. Now I had finally experienced it and I hated it.

I started to do everything in my power to make sure that feeling never happened again. I didn't want to go to school. I started to not eat. I was terrified to eat. I mean, food is what caused this horrible sickness right? And what if it happened at school? I couldn't bear the thought. I lost so much weight that my parents took me to see a stomach specialist. I had to drink one of those radioactive shakes so the doctors could see my insides There was absolutely nothing wrong with me. Still, that didn't calm my nerves.

Towards the end of the school year, my 3rd grade teacher pulled me aside after class and talked to me. She told me if I didn't start coming to school more she was going to have to hold me back a year. She confided in me that when she was in college, she was scared to face the future. Somehow, this resonated with me. I also didn't want to leave all my friends and watch them go ahead while I stayed behind. The talk clicked with me, and I began to live again.

I started eating and going to school, and my phobia and obsession quieted down for a long time. I was able to live pretty much phobia free except for the occasional scare when I would go to parties as a teenager and others would get sick due to drinking too much. I was able to be around it. I never drank too much in fear of getting sick, but other than that I didn't really think about it often. While I experienced anxiety in different forms, I was able to live rather freely. I traveled the world, lived my dreams, and lived completely independently in new cities all the while falling in love and making a real life for myself. My phobia would creep in maybe once or twice a year when I would eat too much, or drink too much. Nothing too bad, just a whisper.

Then around age 25 I began working more, eating less, stressing out, and experiencing more anxiety. That's when my phobia started creeping in. It started out just when I would travel. I convince myself that I would get motion sickness, even though the only time I felt motion sickness was on a boat in Hawaii. Even then, I didn't actually throw up but it triggered a thought that it could be possible. Around the same time my friend got pretty sick riding in a plane. I put those two experiences together and convinced myself it was only a matter of time before it actually happened to me. This awakened my phobia deeply.

I began to not eat 12 hours before I would travel. This worked for a short time but soon I began to experience intense anxiety at the thought of getting sick while traveling. It became paralyzing. I talked to a doctor and was prescribed anti-anxiety medications to take when I traveled. These were like a miracle pill. They took away every irrational thought I had, relaxed me, and I was able to fly, at least for a while.

Soon though, I began experiencing anxiety in more places. I put so much intense pressure on myself to be the best always. As an actress, I needed to book every job, be on TV, make films, win awards, just be the best, nothing less. This created even more anxiety. Every audition and class became a life or death situation. I convinced myself that I would get sick before auditions and jobs due to the amount of anxiety I experienced, so I stopped eating 12 hours before which completely drained my body.

The ups and downs I put myself through were exhausting. I began to hate my work. Hate the self-imposed hell I was putting my body through. When I would work, I would be terrified I would get sick on the job in front of everyone and it was all I could think about. The amount of anxiety, plus not eating in fear of getting sick was starting to become too much for me. This is when I started to avoid. And man, oh man, did it feel good. To say no to an audition, to say no to a job, to say no to eating out with friends - it took all the anxiety and fear away in an instant. I could stay home, relax, and feel safe. It was the best drug out there. When I did make plans I usually canceled. As I started to withdraw, my fear grew bigger. I soon didn't want to do much of anything. And if I did, the amount of fear and anxiety I would put myself through was excruciating. I knew I was traveling down a dark path but I didn't know how to stop it.

My emetophobia progressively worsened and then exploded beyond belief in November 2017. I experienced some sort of stomach flu or food poisoning. I woke up in the middle of the night and started to gag. I began to sweat profusely. I knew what was coming. I was somehow able to control my body and not let sickness happen. I still don't know how I did it. I hardly ate anything for a week.

Then Thanksgiving arrived and the morning of my three-hour drive to San Luis Obispo. My pre-travel rituals weren't working. I took my medication and it was like I had taken a mint. I felt nothing but absolute fear. I took another. Then I took a motion sickness pill. Still fear. As my husband drove, I experienced the worst panic attack I ever had in my entire life. Convulsions, gagging, gasping for air. I thought I was dying. I was in absolute terror the entire drive. I thought I would have to call an ambulance on the side of the road. Somehow, I managed to make it to San Luis Obispo, and played it off to my family, saying I got car sick and had to lie down for the night.

No one but my husband knew the extremity of my fear. Two days later, we returned home. The morning before we left, I began having the same physical panic attack symptoms while I was getting ready. I hid them from everyone. I was gagging uncontrollably in the bathroom, terrified of getting sick. I loaded myself up with medication to the point of sedation and was able to calm down enough for the drive home. I knew I was at a breaking point. It was my breaking point. When I got home I wasn't able to leave my bed. I was constantly nauseous. I stopped eating and lost 10 pounds seemingly overnight. I was terrified of going outside. The fear and phobia ate me alive.

I went to the emergency room because of my non-stop panic attacks. They pumped me with more drugs and an appointment to see a psychiatrist. I lost track of reality. I was so malnourished that my brain wasn't functioning properly. I honestly can't even remember periods of that time. After the new year I was able to see a psychiatrist and I told her about my emetophobia. She was the first person other than my husband that I confided in. I was put on more medication with the possible side effect of vomiting. At this point, I had no choice. I was taking so much Ativan daily, I was like a zombie anyway. I took the plunge and really tried to give the medication a chance. Due to my fear of getting sick, it took me a month just to get up to 5 mg (20mg is a therapeutic dose). The night I took my first 5mg pill, I awoke with the same fear I felt in 3rd grade - body sweating, heart pounding, nausea. I knew what was about to happen but this time I was able to control it. I did not get sick. But that was it, I stopped the medication immediately.

I began seeing a therapist weekly. For the first time I was able to open up and really express the pain I felt dealing with my emetophobia all these years. It was liberating. Unfortunately, my phobia had such a strong hold on me, I was only able to make tiny steps - able to eat a little more, see some friends once in a while, and have my family come visit me. I was still very thin and not eating much. I felt nauseous all the time. Due to my immense fear I was not able to drive more than two miles away from home. I could not work. I rarely saw friends. I never ate at restaurants. I could not use public restrooms. I didn't go to the movies. I wasn't living. I lived in fear all day even while confining myself in my apartment. That's when I reached out to Ken.

Perhaps this story triggered emotions or thoughts about your own journey. Perhaps you can relate to how her emetophobia began and took hold. The recipe is a combination of an anxious predisposition, a trigger, repetitive thoughts, regular feelings of nausea or stomach distress, hypervigilance, safety behaviors, and avoidance. Mix continuously day after day, and *voila*! you have created a giant pot of emetophobia and panic. In the next chapter we will take a closer look at these ingredients. But before we do, let's take a glimpse into my patient's current life, two years after our first appointment. I asked her if she would write about her progress and she was happy to share:

What a journey this has been. I first reached out to Ken what seems like a lifetime ago. I reached out to him two years ago in a last-ditch effort to get my life back. I was so sick back then I could barely get out of bed and eat more than 800 calories a day in fear of vomiting. I was a skeletal ghost on the brink of death. I was so sick and it was my mind that was the sickest of all.

I will never forget the first time that I reached out to Ken. My mind was so consumed with thoughts of vomiting I was literally going crazy. I couldn't go more than 10 seconds without the crippling fear of vomit. I was so terrified, even just talking to him on the phone the first time because I was convinced that just talking about my fear of uttering the words "vomit" or "puke" would make me throw up. I had such panic and anxiety during our first few sessions that I wasn't sure I would be able to continue with treatment. Every time we had a session I would wake up in terror hours before, convinced that this time, this session would be it - the moment vomiting would finally happen. Despite the terror, I kept going and I'm so thankful I did.

The work was the hardest work I ever put myself through in my life. Countless times I wanted to give up. During my journey of recovery there were so many road bumps and relapses that my journey looked more like a corkscrew than a line, but each time I wanted to give up, Ken's voice was always there telling me to just keep going. So I would brush myself off and tell myself that I was doing this work so I wouldn't have to suffer like this for the rest of my life. When I felt like giving up, Ken would always say to me, "keep doing the work. You don't have to believe you will get better, you just have to do the work." So every single day, I would show up for myself. Some of those days would be filled with such intense panic and anxiety I would cry and fall to my knees in mercy, but after my cry, I would blow my nose and just keep going.

I look back at all the things that I couldn't do and it breaks my heart thinking about that girl imprisoned with emetophobia. Back when I was sick, I would write in my journals about all the things I dreamed about doing, unsure if those things would ever happen. I can now say, I am living my life in ways I never dreamed possible.

In so many ways I wasn't living before. I dropped out of college way back when because my anxiety about vomiting in class was so severe, I couldn't concentrate. I am proud to say I am now a full-time college student working towards transferring to my dream university. I used to call in sick to work all the time when there was any inkling that my stomach might be upset and if I did go into work, it would be a long, arduous, torturous day, filled with anxiety and panic. I finally had to stop working. Now I am back working on projects that fill my soul and fulfill me in ways work never did before, mostly because I am able to concentrate 100% at the task at hand instead of my stomach and my fears.

The freedom I feel in my everyday life is a freedom I have never felt before, and something I couldn't even imagine just a few short years ago. I used to avoid going out to eat with friends and family in fear I might vomit during the meal. Now I eat out with friends and family all the time. I don't worry about what I am eating or if it is prepared safely or if I will get sick. I purely just enjoy the time spent with loved ones over food.

I used to starve myself for days. Now I eat three meals a day. I used to not eat anything before I left home. Now I eat whatever I want, whenever I want with ease. I used to surf through the day on an empty stomach and caffeine to keep the hunger pains away. Now I eat full meals before any and all appointments, dates, interviews, you name it. I eat outside my apartment at restaurants and friends' homes without even the slightest inkling of thoughts about vomiting. I used to pick at my food at restaurants, with vomit thoughts plaguing me the entire outing, always taking my meal to go, telling those I was eating with that "I wasn't hungry" or "I just ate" to cover the fact that inside I was reeling with such intense anxiety I couldn't even take a bite of food in fear of vomiting in front of them.

I used to have to go to the bathroom countless times during a meal at a restaurant, just to calm myself down enough to get through the experience. I'm sure people I was eating with probably thought I was either doing drugs or bulimic because I was so thin and would barely eat. Now I eat at restaurants with such ease I don't even think about throwing up. I am immersed in conversation and the enjoyment of the moment. If I do get a pesky thought about throwing up while eating out, I say to myself "well, too late now, nothing I can do about it", and I keep eating.

I used to be consumed with thoughts about throwing up, I mean a never-ending torture machine of thoughts plaguing me twenty-four hours a day, seven days a week. Now, I go days, weeks, without a mere thought. I used to spend hours online searching forums, websites, groups, anything for reassurance. Now I never search out anything vomit related online. I try new foods, and foods once deemed dangerous. This past year has tasted SO good. I didn't eat tomato or chocolate products for years in fear that they would aggravate my acid reflux and cause me to vomit. Now I eat pizza and chocolate regularly. I don't check expiration dates religiously anymore, and eat leftovers with ease.

I have been under weight since my teens. I have gained twenty pounds and I feel and look healthy. I don't feel weak, faint, or nauseous from not eating all day. I now know what it feels like to be energized from food, not from an addiction to caffeine. Compared to before, I rarely experience symptoms of IBS or acid reflux and when I do, I don't freak out about it.

Before seeking treatment with Ken, I could travel no more than two miles in the car. I was trapped in my neighborhood unable to escape it. I could barely walk around the block without having a severe panic attack. Ken and I worked on this one step at a time. Just going up the street to the market took me months to conquer. Driving to Target and walking around the store was something that brought me such dread, Ken had to come to my apartment to help me navigate staying in the store without fleeing, while having the most intense panic I was sure I was either going to die or vomit.

With a lot of hard work, Ken's strategies, and medication, I can now drive more than two hours from my home by myself. I drove to Santa Barbara by myself with periodic traffic. This was the first time I have spent the night away from home in more than three years. It was incredibly liberating.

I meet up with friends all the time now and I don't arrive late. In the past I cancelled dates with friends all the time and if I didn't cancel, I would arrive late because the anxiety and stomach problems were so severe, I couldn't leave my apartment on time and I would have to stop at public bathrooms along the way. I now show up early or on time, and eat while in the presence of new and old friends alike. I can go to movie theatres, hair salons, and malls, places that would terrify me because I felt like I couldn't escape. I now shop for hours without the stabbing fear of suffocation and the images of being swallowed whole by the mass of people around me.

I can go into tall buildings and take the elevator to the top floors without having panic so severe I cry and hyperventilate at the thought of being trapped at the top level unable to escape. The first few times I met my psychiatrist I met with her outside the building because her office was on the eleventh floor. Even though I was filled with anxiety, it was an amazing accomplishment when I finally made it to her office. Friends, too, always had to meet me outside because the fear of going in an elevator was so severe that I wouldn't even be able to step foot inside. That is now gone. Completely gone. I now travel up and down in elevators with ease.

I exercise harder than I have in years. I run so hard, something that I remember from when I was a teen and played soccer competitively. My heart rate goes higher than I have ever allowed it while exercising. I push myself constantly to get stronger physically. Before treatment, I hadn't exercised in years, terrified that if I worked out too hard, I would throw up.

I don't monitor how I am feeling constantly, checking my body for symptoms on how I feel, asking myself if I'm nauseous or how my stomach is doing. I honestly never even think about it unless a random symptom like a headache shows up. And when I get a random stomach symptom or heart burn or diarrhea, it doesn't trigger anxiety any more. I had so many setbacks in my recovery because of these symptoms. It was a living hell.

I had a stage in my recovery where I was afraid to let go of my fear It had been with me since I was ten years old and it was just a part of me - who I was. I would ask Ken, "who will I be without my fear of vomiting? What will I think about? Would I be me?" I couldn't even imagine a life without crippling fear plaguing my every thought. I felt that in a way my fear of vomiting was keeping me safe all these years; that if I gave up my fear then I would just start magically throwing up everywhere. It took me a while to let go of these fears; to let go of the abusive security blanket I had been carrying with me since a child. But once I let go, I felt a liberation that is indescribable; freedom I am unable to convey with words.

Ken would always tell me that I would be the same person I am, just without the fear and anxiety anymore. Meaning I could do and think about FUN things, like my goals, dreams, vacations, daydreams, family, and friends. He couldn't have been more right. I am so glad I put my trust in his words and learned to let go of my fear. Life is SO much better without an all-consuming crippling fear. I truly hardly ever think about throwing up, and when I do, it just isn't that big of a deal anymore. I know I will be okay when it happens. These are words I thought I would never be able to utter. I truly believed I would take emetophobia with me to the grave.

This brings me to my biggest achievement. I had a migraine a few weeks ago. I have had them sporadically throughout my adult life and I have felt nauseous a few times from some really bad ones. Well, I went to sleep to numb the pain and woke up around three A.M. feeling very woozy. I felt sick to my stomach and started gagging. I had never gagged from a migraine before. This was it. This was the moment I told myself I was going to vomit. So I calmly went to the bathroom and sat by the toilet and gagged some more. I was finally ready for it...but nothing happened! While I didn't throw up, I couldn't believe how well I had handled it. This was proof that all of this work that I had done these past two years was worth it. I had broken free from emetophobia and knew I was going to be okay.

So here I am, a completely new person; a person I couldn't have dreamed of because I could have never imagined the freedom I feel now. It's strange to think there was a time I was afraid to get rid of my fear. I was afraid because this fear had been with me since I was ten years old, and I was afraid of who I would be without it. Well, I can confidently say, I had nothing to fear. I absolutely love the person I am without it. I am finally me, the real me.

People in my life constantly say how much I have changed, how much happier I seem. They feel like they got their friend back, their daughter back, their wife back. I feel like I got me back. The me I was before fear took over my life. Life doesn't have to be painful. Life doesn't have to be terrifying. I now know I don't have to fight every day just to live. I can take life as it comes, and let it happen. I don't have to control every second of my life. Bad things will and can happen, and I know I will be okay. I will survive. I will cope. I can now finally give back all the love given to me in a way I could never give before. I am living my life, completely free from the fear of emetophobia, and I couldn't have done it without hard work, grit, or the exceptional support and guidance from Ken.

It's not necessary to believe you will get better but it helps to know that it's possible. And now you know it's possible.

Chapter 4
Breaking Down the Fear of Vomit into Small Chunks

Let's examine the elements that make up emetophobia and the vicious cycle that keeps the disorder in perpetual motion.

Anxious Predisposition

Common sense tells us that everyone is born with gifts and liabilities which are enhanced or reduced by one's upbringing. Some individuals are naturally funny while others are born with a shy personality. Some people are born with greater intellect or athletic abilities than others. I know people who have been risk takers since childhood. Some people are naturally calm, while others are born with an anxious temperament. All of these innate characteristics are influenced by the person's upbringing, experiences, and the people they meet. Take, for instance, two 13-year-old boys with social anxiety. They both play video games but the mother of one puts her son in a magic class. He loves it and takes more classes. Magic not only becomes a hobby he enjoys but it gets him performing in front of people and talking to other magicians. Over time his social anxiety vanishes while the other boy continues to play video games in isolation.

Neither one of my children was born with athletic prowess. They both played sports and did fine but were clearly not gifted and eventually found other interests. They both started piano at the same age. Only one of them became a musician. With a little social anxiety on my side of the family and some generalized anxiety on my wife's side, both sons were born with an anxious predisposition which manifested differently. Whenever one son went somewhere for the first time (kindergarten, skiing, basketball camp, sleep-away camp) he would vomit.

Last August my wife and I flew with him to Emory University in Atlanta to help him get settled for his first year of college. On the flight, he was so nervous he went into the bathroom and puked. He sat back in his seat and did not mention it until we visited months later. For my son, vomiting is not a big deal. It's how he experiences intense anxiety and he accepts it. His anxiety is not debilitating because he is not afraid to throw up, does not worry about it, and does not allow it to dictate his life.

Now that you have learned it's possible for anxiety to cause vomiting, you might be worried this could happen to you. Let me give you some good news. Everyone experiences anxiety differently and **if you don't vomit due to anxiety, you won't. That's NOT how YOU experience your anxiety.** Think back to all the times you felt panic. Did you vomit? Usually people with emetophobia rarely vomit and that is why they are so afraid of it. Most emetophobes manifest their anxiety via nausea, stomach distress, and terrifying thoughts— not vomiting. So, let me repeat: if you don't vomit due to anxiety, you won't.

The Trigger

There is usually something that triggers an anxious predisposition and sets emetophobia in motion. The trigger can be anything, including a loss, health issue, a news report, a scary thought, or a vomiting trauma. I treated a woman whose emetophobia began in elementary school when she heard her mom vomiting violently in the bathroom. During lunch, as she ate the sandwich, her mom prepared for her, she began to worry: *What if my mom contaminated my sandwich? What if I vomit in class? What if people laugh at me?* She started to feel sick and went to the nurse's office convinced she caught her mom's illness. Although she felt better when she got home, she felt sick the next morning and did not go to school. Why did she insist on staying home? Because of the meaning she attributed to feeling sick.

The Meaning We Attribute to the Trigger

My patient attributed her nausea to the flu. Let's look at another example. You're getting ready for a peaceful night sleep when you see something moving on the floor next to your bed. **A spider!** You yell for your braver-half to kill it. Your hero jumps into action. The shoe slams down on the hardwood. Thank goodness! Then you see the spider scurry under the bed. *NOOO! You missed! I can't sleep in here tonight.*

Your poor aiming hero tries to convince you that it's a small spider who is more afraid of you. But you don't see it that way. *What if he crawls on me when I'm sleeping?* Your partner thinks you're overreacting and climbs under the covers. *Come on. It's just a little spider.*

You're horrified! *Aren't you afraid it's gonna bite you?* You point to your mouth. *It could crawl into your mouth when you're asleep.* With a roll of the eyes, your knight in shining armor turns in for the night… while you sleep on the couch in the living room.

Why is it that two people can experience the same trigger, but react so differently? Because the meaning each gives to the trigger is different. Anxiety is based on our perception. It is a protective mechanism meant to keep us safe and is activated when we attribute a scary meaning to our external and internal world. One spouse perceived the spider as a threat and the other did not. It's not the trigger but the meaning you attribute to the trigger. A young emetophobe might perceive a tummy-ache as a potential catastrophe while another young person with a similar tummy-ache, but no anxiety, does not.

Repetitive Worries

Thoughts can be triggered by anything, including a friend announcing they were sick, an upcoming drive, or stomach noises after a meal. "What if" can then become catastrophic, automatic, and repetitive, as the anxious mind dwells and the fear transforms from possibility to probability.

Thoughts come so quickly we tend not to recognize them. We just think. Intrusive recollections of a past vomiting experience or anticipation of a disgusting puking episode can replay like a scary horror movie in your mind, resulting in relentless fear. It's normal to worry, but the worries of an emetophobe are constant, particularly because much of life centers around food and the body's need for regular nourishment. When the mind and body are occupied with something pleasant, those thoughts tend to go to the background. Unfortunately, they don't stay there for long. Start paying attention to your thoughts. What are you thinking right now?

Nausea and Stomach Distress

With dwelling on worries comes symptoms of anxiety, and the primary symptom of emetophobia is nausea or some form of stomach distress (pain, butterflies, bloating, gas, indigestion, diarrhea, constipation). These sensations can feel horrible and cause an explosion of fear. Once a person begins to *feel* nauseous or stomach distress, they begin to worry they will vomit. The worry in turn causes more anxiety and more nausea. Remember, if you have never vomited due to anxiety, then vomiting is not how you experience anxiety. Nausea yes, but not vomiting.

Disgust Sensitivity

Although no one enjoys puking or witnessing others toss their cookies, emetophobes see it as torturous, painful, and intensely disgusting: essentially the worst imaginable. Whereas most people roar with laughter during the diarrhea and vomit scene in the movie *Bridesmaids*, emetophobes find it revolting and vile, and close their eyes. The same exact scene causes opposite reactions in different people.

A study published in the *Journal of Anxiety Disorders* in 2008 examined whether emetophobic participants display elevated levels of disgust. *A group of emetophobic members of a Dutch website on emetophobia (n = 172), and a control group (n = 39) completed an internet survey containing an Emetophobia Questionnaire, Disgust Propensity and Sensitivity Scale, and a Disgust Questionnaire. Results showed that the emetophobic group displayed significantly elevated levels of both disgust propensity and disgust sensitivity.*

Not too long ago I was flying to Washington, D.C., to give a presentation at the annual conference of the Anxiety and Depression Association of America and on the descent into D.C. I vomited into a barf bag. How would you have reacted if you had been sitting next to me? Anxious? Nauseous? Incredibly disgusted? The man to my left patted my shoulder as I was retching into the bag. I'm sure he didn't enjoy the experience but he was not grossed out. Emetophobes have a heightened sensitivity to vomit and view it as the most disgusting thing imaginable.

Hypervigilance

In Israel, where terrorism has been a dangerous problem, residents of the country are on high alert for unaccompanied backpacks, containers, and boxes. They are hyperaware and authorities are alerted if a suspicious item is spotted. When there is a possibility of danger, we look out for it. If teddy bears were dangerous, we'd be on the look-out for teddy bears. Because vomit and vomiting are the worst things imaginable, you're on guard for anything related to these possibilities. As you endeavor to keep yourself safe, you are prepared to flee if you sense danger. Hypervigilance strengthens emetophobia. The more you look out for it, the more it's on your mind, and the more anxious you feel. It's common for emetophobes to analyze their body for warning signs as they ask themselves a series of questions: *How am I feeling? How's my stomach today? Am I nauseous? Am I hungry? Is that my stomach growling? What does that mean?*

Safety Behaviors

Safety behaviors are meant to help you *feel* safe and include the following: asking others if they are sick, checking expiration dates, throwing away food before the expiration date, smelling food, not eating, eating slowly, eating only inside your home, sitting in the front seat of a car, sitting in the aisle of a movie theater, waiting an hour after eating before leaving the house, eating only familiar foods, paying in advance at a restaurant, cleaning tables with wipes, sleeping with a bucket by your bed, chewing gum when anxious, researching rates of food digestion, and having certain items with you at all times (anti-nausea medication barf bag, water bottle, gum, hand sanitizer, surgical mask). Some emetophobes have elaborate eating rituals: only eating certain foods, at certain times of the day, in a specific way, and in specific places. They must control their eating to keep themselves safe. It is also common to constantly ask loved ones for reassurance (*Do you think I'm sick?*) and this can put a strain on the relationship. Safety behaviors reduce anxiety temporarily but maintain the disorder and eventually cause more anxiety. One of my patients took pretzels with him wherever he went and desperately consumed them when he experienced an urge to gag. This reduced the possibility of gagging but caused increased anxiety with the anticipation of grad school interviews (you can't munch on pretzels during an interview at Harvard).

Ironically, behaviors that are meant to keep you safe not only perpetuate the disorder, some behaviors make anxiety and nausea worse. For example, chewing gum excessively causes you to swallow air pockets which can cause abdominal bloating and stomach discomfort, particularly if you have IBS. Also, Sorbital, an artificial sweetener in many sugarless gum, can act as a laxative which may cause cramping, digestive distress, and diarrhea. One of my patients needed to take an antibiotic for an infection. She decided to play it safe and not take the medication with food as was directed. This resulted in an upset stomach which escalated her anxiety and increased her fear of eating.

Avoidance

If vomit and vomiting are so disgusting, scary, and embarrassing, why doesn't everyone avoid situations where puking is possible? Because of our perception of the degree of the disgust and the likelihood it will happen. If you believe it's vile, terrifying, and likely to occur, then you must avoid.

Common places and activities emetophobes avoid include unfamiliar foods, bars, restaurants, hospitals, doctor offices, airplanes, boats, windy roads, the back seat of a car, theaters, public restrooms, or any situation where it could lead to you or someone else to barf. Emetophobes will also avoid anything that might trigger nausea, worry, or anxiety.

Does your family help you avoid? Do they open doors for you so you don't have to touch the handle? Do they only go to restaurants you want to eat? Avoidance keeps you safe from your fear but at what cost? What have you missed out on in life?

Avoidance might be the fastest way to prevent and reduce anxiety, but it's only temporary, and makes all fears worse. By avoiding, anxiety sufferers learn that they cannot handle their fears. As they avoid more triggers, their fears grow over time. Vomiting is a natural experience, which rarely happens but **avoidance has strengthened your emetophobia**. Many of my emetophobia patients avoid eating due to a fear they will vomit. This often leads to hunger pains, which are misinterpreted as nausea, which in turn causes **more** anxiety and more food restriction. **Avoidance increases anxiety**.

As a safety precaution some emetophobes do not eat for several hours before they leave the home. Others eat *safe foods* beforehand so they can use the *I'm not hungry* excuse to avoid eating unknown foods at social gatherings. Food is also avoided when any form of stomach distress is noticed. This leads to gastrointestinal noises and hunger pains which are misconstrued, resulting in more worry, hypervigilance, and refusal to eat. Emetophobes may not eat for days at a time due to their fear.

In extreme cases, emetophobes stop eating for weeks and experience significant weight loss. They can be misdiagnosed with anorexia and then unsuccessfully treated in an eating disorder program. If you are underweight, it's vital to seek a team of professionals to help you: a therapist who specializes in anxiety disorders, a psychiatrist who can prescribe medication, and a registered dietitian who is willing to learn about emetophobia (most are uneducated about this disorder). If you are malnourished you might need to be admitted to a residential treatment center or a partial hospitalization program that specializes in the treatment of anxiety disorders exclusively. In extreme cases of malnourishment, the body can become medically compromised to dangerous levels and admission to a medical hospital is required for stabilization.

Exertion of Control

Emetophobes utilize safety behaviors and avoidance in an effort to prevent themselves from vomiting. By controlling as much as possible they are under the impression that their strategy is working. After all, you rarely vomit, right? It must be working. All that effort is paying off. Or is it? Might this all be an illusion? (More about this in an upcoming chapter.)

Compulsions

Only a percentage of emetophobes have compulsions. A compulsion is a repetitive behavior meant to stop an obsession, reduce anxiety, and prevent the fear from happening. Common compulsions associated with emetophobia include excessive hand washing, overuse of hand sanitizer, checking for expiration dates, asking for reassurance, and excessive cleaning of surfaces. The frequency, duration, and intensity of compulsions can vary and can also be performed mentally. A common mental compulsion is repetitively reassuring yourself that you'll be okay. Like avoidance, safety behaviors, and hypervigilance, compulsions help you feel safe and reduce anxiety temporarily but ultimately they make emetophobia worse. Later in the book is a chapter on obsessions and compulsions.

Once anxiety is triggered it becomes self-perpetuating. No further stressors are needed to keep the anxiety going. It takes on a life of its own as safety and avoidant behaviors, symptoms, and the fear of those symptoms drive the phobia.

The Cycle of Emetophobia:

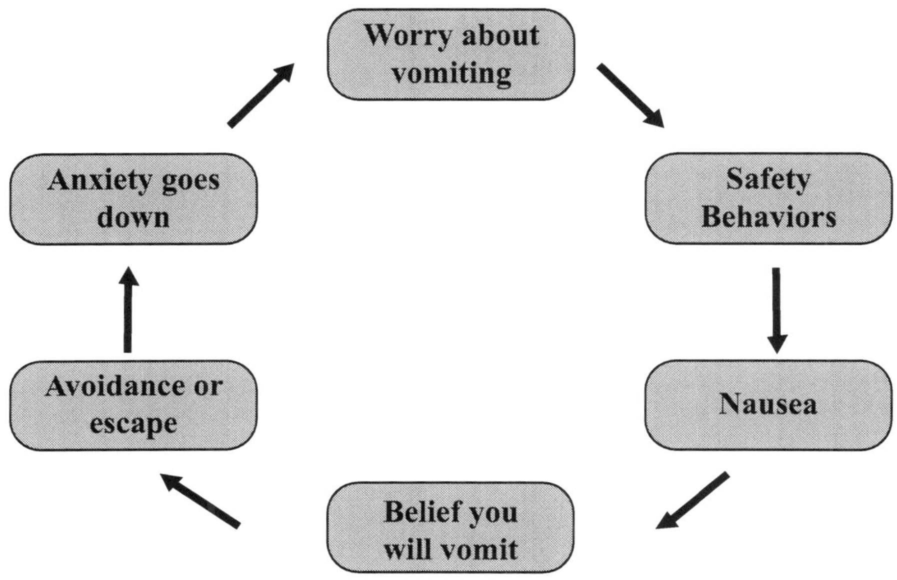

Is it possible to break the cycle and cure emetophobia? The answer is, ***yes, it's absolutely possible***. No one who suffers with anxiety believes this, however, especially when they've made multiple attempts at treatment. All patients have doubts. Fortunately, you don't have be confident or hopeful to get better. You just have to implement the strategies you will learn and take the steps. People that work the program **correctly**, every day, can free themselves of emetophobia despite their disbelief.

If you can get to the point where you are not afraid to vomit and you don't try to stop yourself from vomiting with avoidance, compulsions, hypervigilance, and safety behaviors, you are free from this debilitating phobia. This begins by viewing the fear from a different perspective, which I will address in the next chapter.

STEPS TO FREEDOM

Going forward, most chapters will end with Steps to Freedom, the steps you must take to beat emetophobia and panic. Make them a priority and you will prevail. Here is your first Step to Freedom:

Safety & Avoidant Behaviors: Make a list of all the things you avoid, your safety behaviors, and any compulsions. Identify all the ways anxiety changes your behavior. Start paying attention to your behaviors and add to the list as you go through your week.

By the way, the magician I referenced in the beginning of the chapter was me. Check out this photo.

Chapter 5
Looking at Anxiety from a New Perspective

> to free yourself from debilitating fear
> worry, and panic you must look at the problem
> of anxiety from a completely new perspective

The text written in the box above appears to be in a language we cannot comprehend. However, if you look at the box in a mirror, you will be able to understand its meaning. Your ability to understand a problem depends upon your point of view, how you look at the problem.

Anxiety sufferers try to solve the problem of their anxiety from the same perspective that created it. This does not work. To beat anxiety, you must look at the problem in a completely different way, from an alternative point of view. That is what we are going to do in this book. I am going to help you look at your anxiety from a new perspective. Instead of struggling with your anxiety, you are going to heal your anxiety by doing something different.

Many years ago, at the Magic Castle in Hollywood, I watched David Avadon invite four gentlemen in suits and ties onto the stage. He proceeded to ask them questions about their lives. They had no idea why the audience was laughing because they did not see what we saw. From our perspective, we witnessed David pick pocketing these volunteers without their knowledge. We roared with laughter as they were completely unaware that he was stealing their wallets, keys, combs, handkerchiefs, breath spray, and even their neckties! Only from the audience perspective could one see clearly what was actually happening. They were clueless. To heal your anxiety you must begin to look at anxiety from a different point of view.

YOUR CURRENT PERSPECTIVE IS ONE OF INNER TURMOIL AND INNER STRUGGLE:

- You struggle internally with the uncertainty of not knowing if your nausea is the flu, food poisoning, or anxiety.
- You struggle with whether or not to take any type of medicine.
- You experience inner turmoil of "what if" worries about the possibility of vomiting or other people vomiting.
- You struggle to control everything to make sure you don't puke.
- You struggle with the decision to go to a restaurant with friends or family.
- You experience an inner battle with whether or not to keep your phobia a secret and how to hide unusual behaviors.
- You struggle to avoid as much as possible (planes, restaurants, bars, doctor offices, movie theaters) as you make excuses for why you are canceling.
- You are tortured by the guilt of how your disorder has impacted your family.
- You are tortured by the prospect of having a panic attack as you struggle with whether or not to leave your comfort zone.
- You struggle with repetitive washing, cleaning, and wiping to ensure you're safe.
- You struggle to maintain close proximity to loved ones just in case you feel sick or overwhelming panic and need their assistance.
- You struggle with shame, doubt, hopelessness.

Struggling with yourself gets you nowhere. Let's look at anxiety from a different perspective.

Instead of struggling with yourself, you will be playing a game with anxiety – a mental game.

The exact nature of your opponent, what it looks like, and where he's from will be revealed in the next chapter, followed by the game itself.

"Problems cannot be solved with the same mind set that created them."
Albert Einstein

STEPS TO FREEDOM

Victory Journal: Obtain a notebook. In this notebook you will be tracking your victories and realizations. It will **not** be a journal of your feelings or struggles, only your successes and the realizations you have from your experiences and from reading this book. People with anxiety tend to focus on the negative and don't realize their progress. You're about to climb a mountain with a backpack full of rocks. Now is your opportunity to join the thousands of former emetophobia sufferers who have reached the top. Looking up will be daunting. Instead, put your head down, take one step forward at a time, and celebrate your accomplishments by documenting your progress in a Victory Journal. **All steps, large and small, are worthy of an entry.** Your only homework now is to obtain a journal or notebook.

Chapter 6
Nausea, the Brain, and Your Opponent

Before I explain the game and introduce you to your opponent, let's begin with a brief discussion of the body, brain, nausea, and imagination.

The Body

Right above each of our kidneys are three-inch-long glands called adrenal glands which produces the hormone adrenaline. The nickname for adrenaline is *the fight-or-flight hormone* and its purpose is to give us power and energy to respond to emergencies. To simplify a complex process, if a fire breaks out in your home, your brain will send signals to your adrenal glands and your adrenal glands will secrete adrenaline. Adrenaline makes you fast and strong so you can put out the fire or run. This is why it's referred to as the *fight-or -flight hormone*. It gives you the energy to run towards the danger and fight, or run away from it and flee. It's what you need in an emergency.

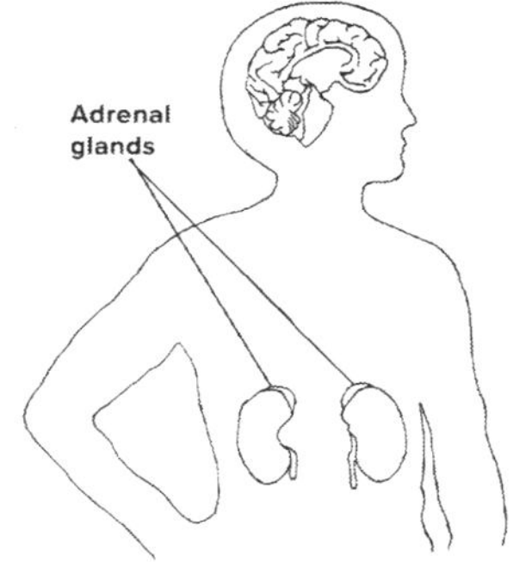

Adrenaline (along with Cortisol) is a necessary hormone **but** it also causes symptoms of anxiety: chest pressure, racing heart, muscle tension, labored breathing, lightheadedness, sweating, stomach distress, an out-of-body feeling, hot flashes, and NAUSEA.

Nausea

Nausea is a symptom of many conditions (motion sickness, food poisoning, influenza, pregnancy, menstrual cycle, intoxication, and many medical conditions). But nausea is also a symptom of anxiety and it's triggered when the brain signals the adrenal glands.

The process is predictable and it's similar to other substances.

What happens to a person who drinks a bit too much alcohol? Their speech slurs, their thought process slows, and their balance becomes unstable. You could predict it. What happens if a person drinks a lot of coffee? They feel jittery and restless. This too, is predictable. Depending upon the substance you put in your body, your body will react accordingly. Although you are not drinking adrenaline, it's similar. It's as if you drank five shots of adrenaline and then began to feel nauseous, sweaty, and anxious. If you could drink it, you would realize the connection: *I'm feeling this way because I just drank all that adrenaline*. Because the process is happening internally, outside of your awareness, you don't think of it in that way. Similar to substances you drink, adrenaline causes a reaction in the body and it begins with the brain.

The Brain

The brain is amazing. It calculates thousands of things at the same time but it tends to do what it's programmed to do, similar to a computer. If someone reprogrammed your computer 2 + 2 = 5, what would happen the next time you pushed 2 + 2? That's right. It would equal 5, even though it's wrong. A similar process takes place between your imagination and your brain. If your imagination tells your brain something scary (even if it's wrong) your brain will signal the adrenal glands to secrete adrenaline. With years of practice, your brain has become programmed to react to the scary thoughts of your imagination.

Your Imagination

Your imagination can take over at any time: *What if I feel nauseous when I'm taking my test tomorrow? What if I vomit in class?* Since vomiting in class is an emergency, your brain will signal your adrenal glands, just because you had the thought. Your adrenal glands will then secrete adrenaline and you will begin to feel nauseous way before a potential emergency Once nauseous, your imagination cries out again: *I'm feeling sick. This might really be the flu. How can I take my test tomorrow?* The fight-or-flight response is now fully activated. Every time your imagination declares an emergency, your brain signals your adrenal glands to secrete adrenaline, resulting in symptoms of anxiety.

Here is the flow:

Imagination says something scary.
Brain reacts sending signals to the adrenal glands.
Adrenal glands secrete adrenaline.
You become anxious.

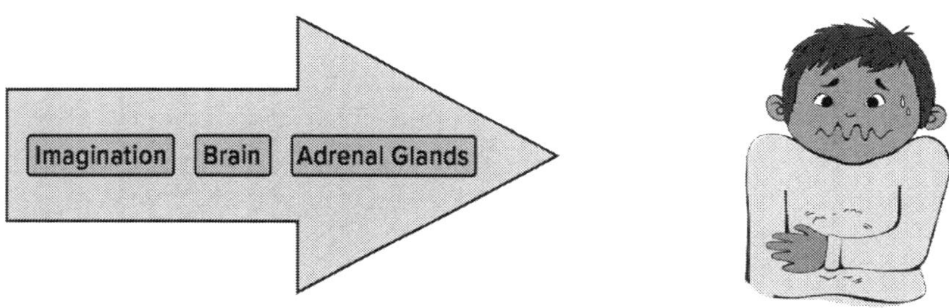

Now that you have a basic understanding of the brain and the body, I will explain the game you will be playing with your anxiety. Like all games, this one has an opponent. Because the process begins with your imagination, we have identified your opponent as...

The Anxiety Monster in Your Imagination.

Instead of waging a battle within and struggling with yourself, you will view the problem of emetophobia and panic as a mental game against an opponent. Your opponent is anxiety and you create its form and expression.

This process is called externalization and personification. We are taking the struggle out of you (externalizing it) and putting the source of anxiety in a creature (personifying it). Battling an opponent instead of yourself will make the process of overcoming anxiety easier.

Like an avatar in a video game, you construct the antagonist of your choosing. It can be anything or anyone: someone scary (Pennywise, Darth Vader), an alien, an emoji, an angry baby, a silly creature, an insect (a bee, spider, or gnat), an animal (octopus, laughing hyena, elephant, snake, lizard), a cartoon (Megatron, Plankton, Roger Rabbit, Chicken Little, Cruella de Vil), a character from the movies (Wicked Witch of the West, BeetleJuice) an iconic figure such as the devil, or something you create. If you choose something abstract like a black cloud, add facial features. It can be anything but you! (I will explain why later.)

Although it may sound silly, playing a game against an opponent instead of struggling with yourself changes your relationship with anxiety and will make it easier for you to prevail.

Below are a few examples of opponents created by the thousands of patients I have treated over the years. Some drew their own and others downloaded images from the internet.

I asked a few of my patients who overcame their anxiety how creating an opponent was helpful. Here is what they said:

> *"The Anxiety Monster is that inner-voice that you have, your worries, your imagination making you crazy. Once I was able to separate my anxiety monster from my own brain it really helped me to not feel like I was beating myself up any more. By being able to blame the thoughts on someone else, essentially this monster, it helped me to minimize the voice that I would hear, the thoughts."*

"Creating a monster made my anxiety more tangible and when it's tangible it's easier to fight and deal with."

"The Anxiety Monster I think is sort of a physical embodiment of my critical self-talk. The metaphor for the Anxiety Monster helped me push it away because when you're repeating these things to yourself that are negative or irrational it's hard to see what it actually is, which is negative self-talk. It was a helpful way to imagine what it would look like if an actual person was saying the things that I was saying to myself and how horrible it would be."

"It's the monster. It's not me. It's someone else tempting me to do things. When it's just yourself you can't stop it but when it's something outside of you, you're able to say no and fight it easier. It gives you something to blame and something to defeat."

"I don't like when people tell me what to do, so having a creature outside of myself, whose sole purpose is to make me miserable, made me determined to defy him and beat him. It also helped me see that he doesn't know what's going to happen."

This anxiety monster was created by a former patient with emetophobia.

Chapter 7
The Mental Game

To beat anxiety, stop struggling with yourself and look at your problem from the perspective of a mental game against an opponent. Here is what the game looks like: You are in the *Land of Misery* and to win you must find your way to the *Land of Freedom* (freedom from fear, worry, panic, and barfing). A giant maze separates these two lands and to win you must drive a bus through the maze.

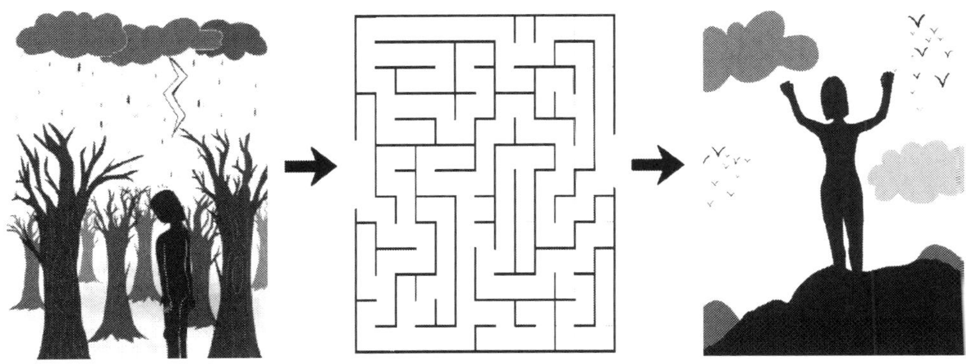

Although the maze is confusing, it will not be your most difficult challenge. You have a much larger problem. In fact, an enormous one.

THE ANXIETY MONSTER IS ON YOUR BUS!
And his goal is to keep you trapped in the Land of Misery!

The Anxiety Monster in your Imagination is in the back of the bus shouting various threats, demands, and questions…

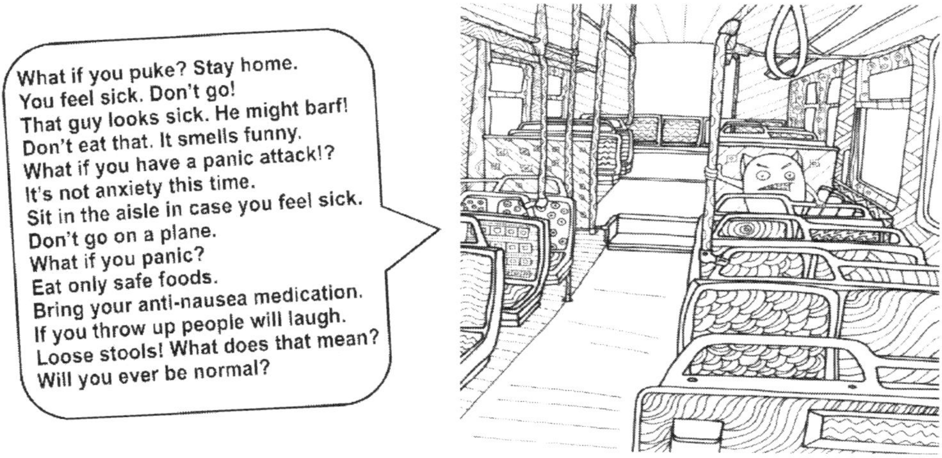

What if you puke? Stay home.
You feel sick. Don't go!
That guy looks sick. He might barf!
Don't eat that. It smells funny.
What if you have a panic attack!?
It's not anxiety this time.
Sit in the aisle in case you feel sick.
Don't go on a plane.
What if you panic?
Eat only safe foods.
Bring your anti-nausea medication.
If you throw up people will laugh.
Loose stools! What does that mean?
Will you ever be normal?

Your opponent seems to have a lot of scary demands and questions. **Now I have some questions.** What are your options? What can you do about your opponent in the back of your bus? Think creatively. Use your imagination. **This is your bus!** What would you like to do to the annoying guy sitting in the back?

Throw him off the bus is how many of my patients respond. Others say they would go to the back of the bus and tell him to shut up. Other answers include play loud music, build a wall, kill him, put duct tape over his mouth, and ignore him.

These are all great answers! This game, however, is a *mental* game, not a *physical* one. You cannot throw your opponent off the bus, kill him, or build a wall. You also can't put an apple in his mouth and shove him under the seat.

THIS IS A GAME OF STRATEGY.
You must outsmart your opponent by doing what he does not expect.

Here's the good news. Although you cannot kick anxiety off the bus, he cannot kick you out of the driver's seat. Which means you always have control of the steering wheel, gas pedal, and brake.

YOU control the bus.
THIS IS A HUGE ADVANTAGE!
YOU decide the direction you go, where to turn, and how fast you drive.
You are in control!

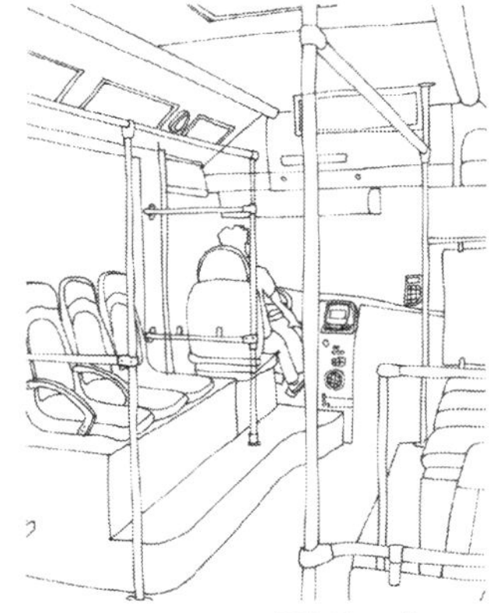

Unfortunately, your opponent has an advantage too, a BIG advantage…

The Anxiety Monster in your Imagination possesses the map.

He can see the correct road to the *Land of Freedom*. You can't. You don't have a map and you don't have a GPS, which will make getting through the maze confusing and tricky.

Your anxiety monster has a key advantage but so do you. **If you use your advantage wisely, you will win.** But you must have a good strategy. To win any game, whether it is a game of chess, backgammon, or a video game, you must have a plan to outsmart your opponent. Currently, your anxiety monster has an excellent strategy and, unfortunately, you do not. This is about to change!

The first step in this mental game is to understand you opponent's strategy and then to develop a strategy of your own. Fortunately, your opponent only has two strategic moves. Only two! But they are powerful and clever. In the next chapter, I will divulge your monster's first strategic move.

"Sometimes you find yourself in the middle of nowhere, and sometimes in the middle of nowhere you find yourself."
– Unknown

Chapter 8
Anxiety's First Strategic Move

Although you control the bus, people with anxiety do not feel in control.

- Physical symptoms of panic are so severe, every day thousands flee to local emergency rooms believing they are having a heart attack.

- The chronically lightheaded do not go anywhere without their spouse for fear of passing out and not having anyone to help them.

- Anxiety sufferers with IBS and unexpected diarrhea are fearful to leave their home and must always know the location of the nearest bathroom.

- Panic attack sufferers do not venture into unfamiliar territory or leave their comfort zone alone due to a fear of having a panic attack.

- Those with emetophobia are consumed with fears of vomit, particularly when they eat, leave their home, see someone puke, or experience nausea.

These out-of-control physical symptoms, and the worry that accompanies them, can result in avoidance, decreased work performance, shame, and restricted freedom. It can limit one's enjoyment of life, stress out family, and cause depression. You may be in the driver's seat but you are not in control of your vehicle – YET.

Your anxiety monster is winning because he has an excellent strategy. As you drive your bus through the maze in search of the *Land of Freedom*, you encounter hundreds of forks in the road and at each fork you will be making an important decision.

As you leave the land of misery, the first decision comes up quickly. You must decide which direction to go. Both roads look exactly the same and you have no idea how to proceed. What would you do?

Perhaps you would explore your options. You drive slowly to the left to survey the situation. You quickly discover that something feels off. You feel unsettled and uncomfortable. You back up the bus and drive slowly to the right. This way doesn't feel so bad. In fact, it feels pretty good. Now you have a little more information. Which direction would you drive? To the left or the right? The uncomfortable road or the comfortable road? When I ask my patients, they always reply, *the comfortable way*.

Here is an aerial view of the same fork as you drive your bus out of the *Land of Misery*.

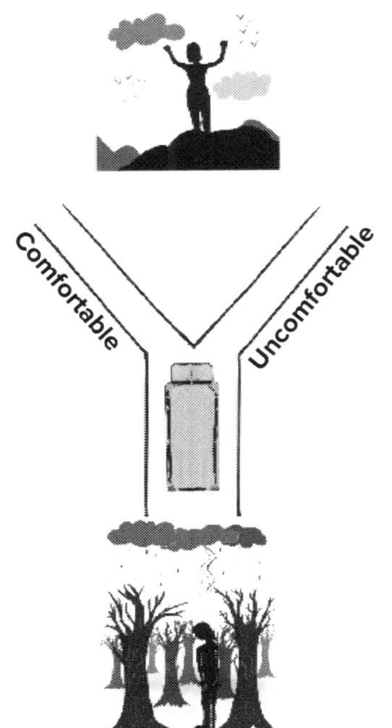

Your anxiety monster is in the back of the bus and he is holding the map.

What I am about to show you is what your opponent sees. You will never see this because you do not have a map.

Look at what your monster sees. Remember, you don't see this…

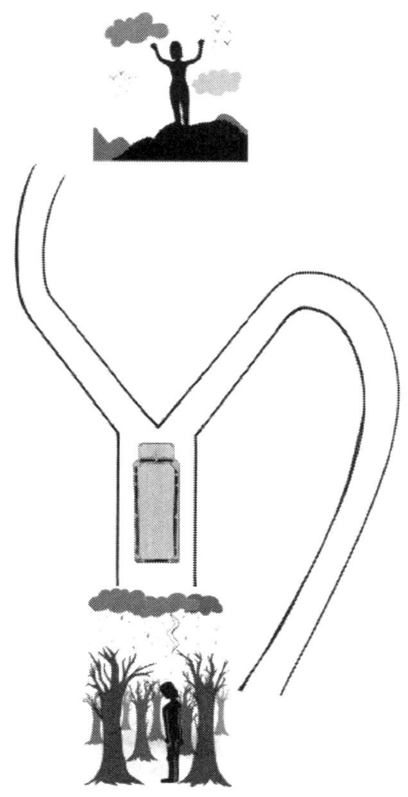

What do you notice? One direction leads to the *Land of Freedom*, while the other circles back to the *Land of Misery*. If you suffer with emetophobia, one of the reasons why you might be stuck in *Misery* is because you keep choosing the wrong roads. You repeatedly select roads that circle back. But how does this happen?

By looking at the map your anxiety monster sees the direction he wants you to go. To win, he needs you to take roads that circle back to the *Land of Misery.* But because he does not control the bus, he has to be clever. So, what does he do?

He tricks you by **lying**.

To make sure you head in the wrong direction, your imagination will scare you with disastrous predictions and frightening questions. He fools you by declaring that one road will be horrible and you won't be able to handle it. **But it's all a LIE! None of it is true!** Your imagination lies, catastrophizes, and distorts. This is the bane of all anxiety sufferers of **all** ilk. Believing the deceptions in your imagination is why you are suffering.

As you go through the maze of life, your opponent will say anything to get you headed down the wrong road:

- He will exaggerate risk and confuse possibility with probability.
- He will tell you the worst possible outcome is the most likely.
- He will claim you can't, when you can and don't bother trying.
- He will state you are sick when you are just anxious.
- He will tell you that you will puke when you haven't in years.
- He will convince you to rearrange and limit your life to prevent a fear that almost never happens.
- He will tell you that vomiting is catastrophic and must be avoided at all cost.
- He will tell you that he is trying to keep you safe when all he is doing is making you miserable.
- He will tell you not to eat even though you are emaciated.
- He will claim that the pains in your stomach are warnings not to eat.
- He will claim that the medication that has been prescribed to help you will make you vomit.
- He will tell you to avoid doing things unless you are 100% certain.
- He will tell you that all of your efforts to prevent vomiting are the reason why you have not puked and you must continue to follow his safety measures to prevent disaster.

All of it is a lie! A trick! A scam!

To get you headed in the wrong direction, he will outsmart you with verbal trickery, intimidation, questions, and threats. He has to. He does not control the bus… YOU do!

One of my emetophobe patients had the opportunity to go on a weekend cruise with her closest friends. She wanted to go but there was a lot of uncertainty. Her anxiety monster constantly reminded her of the possibility of getting motion sickness even though she never had it previously (lie #1). Before having emetophobia, she enjoyed plenty of roller coasters with no queasiness. Her monster warned her about the massive amounts of food and alcohol and the probability of food poisoning (lie #2) and passengers puking (lie #3).

Anxiety's objective was to make her miserable by getting her to choose the road of certainty and comfort, which in this case meant staying home. My patient's thoughts created so much anxiety she felt nauseous the morning of the cruise. That's when anxiety grabbed its megaphone and began shouting more fabrications and ridiculous questions: *You might have the flu* (lie #4). *Is this anxiety or the flu?* (lie #5) *What if you're nauseous and sick for the next three days?* (lie #6). *You'll be trapped on the boat in a state of misery* (lie #7). *It's safer to stay home!* This final statement is actually true. It's always safer to do what anxiety commands, but always doing what's safe means you will retain your disorder.

She texted her friends, *I'm sick. I think I have the flu. I'm sorry.* She chose the certain and comfortable road. Several hours later, after the cruise departed, her nausea disappeared. She did not have the flu. Although she had an anxiety-free weekend, she missed out and spent three days alone, feeling miserable, depressed, and ashamed. She asked her friends about the cruise when they returned. Not only did they have a great time but the water was calm, no one got food poisoning, and no one threw up. Her anxiety monster achieved its goal of making her miserable by lying. Nothing she feared actually came true (but they might have come true and this is where all anxiety sufferers get stuck).

Emetophobes are not the only ones being tricked. Everyone with anxiety falls for lies. It's difficult to think clearly when you're feeling anxious and your mind has convinced you that the worst outcome is guaranteed. People who suffer with claustrophobia believe the elevator doors will not open and they will be stuck for hours. People with illness anxiety believe they have cancer, ALS, or some other tragic illness whenever they experience an uncertain physical symptom. Mothers who fear for their children's safety sometimes believe their children will be kidnapped. I treated a woman who worried every time a family member drove on the highway because she believed they would die in a car crash.

Recently my wife called me in a panic because she received a phone call from the Department of Water and Power stating that we did not pay our bill and if we did not send payment in the next thirty minutes our water and power would be turned off. I told her not to pay anything because it was a scam. She called the DWP and sure enough, it was. She believed the scammer's lie and because she was overwhelmed with anxiety, she could not think clearly. Whether the lie comes from an outside source (the DWP) or your own imagination, the reason you are anxious is because you are believing a lie – that the worst possible outcome will likely occur.

Is it possible that a lie could come true? However remote, it is. There are no guarantees. Your opponent is clever and will usually predict calamities that could happen. My patient might have puked on the ship or saw others vomit. A child could get kidnapped. A person could get cancer. And a relative could die in a car crash. There is no absolute certainty. And because there is no absolute certainty, emetophobes are constantly being fooled. They want a 100% guarantee. The problem is you can't be 100% certain and be emetophobia free.

To be free from emetophobia and panic, you must accept a degree of uncertainty. When people fly on planes, drive in cars, try new medication, shake stranger's hands, they accept some uncertainty. They sacrifice 100% certainty for freedom. You can't have both. You must let go of 100% certainty to overcome anxiety, all forms of anxiety – panic, emetophobia, fear of elevators, worries about loved ones dying – all anxiety.

How is your opponent so tricky?
Because it's easy to not see things clearly.

Here is an example: How many "F's" are in the sentence below? Read the sentence **out loud** and count the number of F's.

FINISHED FILES ARE THE RESULTS OF YEARS OF SCIENTIFIC STUDY COMBINED WITH THE EXPERIENCE OF YEARS.

How many "F's" did you count? Your anxiety monster says, *there are three Fs in the sentence above.* We know he lies. Use your QR code reader for the answer. Most people only see three or four F's. How can we miss something right in front of our eyes? Because we don't see things clearly. This is why it's easy for anxiety to fool us. Sometimes things feel dangerous but they are not. When claustrophobics stand in an elevator, it **feels** like the walls are closing in. Obviously, they are not. Sometimes we think we cannot do something but we can.

Sometimes we think that our efforts to keep us safe are necessary but they aren't. When you have emetophobia your perception of yourself and your world is influenced by your thoughts (The Anxiety Monster in your Imagination, whose objective is to keep you miserable).

How many times have you thought you were going to vomit when you did not? How many times did your opponent claim you were sick when you weren't? How many times has nausea led to vomiting? If you are similar to most emetophobes, you have been fooled by anxiety thousands of times over the years. When we misperceive, it's easy to be fooled and make the wrong choice.

Approximately how many times a day do you believe you are going to vomit but don't? Multiply that by 365 and then by the number of years you have had emetophobia. This is how many times you have been fooled by just one of your opponent's lies. Other lies include all the times you avoid as well as when you engage in safety behaviors.

In the next chapter I will explain why it's so easy for anxiety sufferers to fall for the same lie repeatedly. But before I do, let's apply a real-life example to the mental game you are playing.

Brad has been invited to a party with all of his friends. He wants to go but he suffers with emetophobia and is ambivalent about attending. He sits in the driver's seat, at another fork in the road. He can choose the comfortable and certain path which consists of staying home and watching videos on YouTube or he can choose the uncomfortable and uncertain path and go to the party. His anxiety monster has the map and its goal is to keep him miserable. It knows that if he can get Brad to do what's comfortable and certain, he will never overcome emetophobia.

Because anxiety does not control the bus, it must lie and threaten to get him to stay home. It tells Brad that people will be drunk and someone might vomit. It tells him that he might get food poisoning. It reminds him that one of his friends who has been sick will be there and she might still be contagious. Each time Brad's opponent shouts a threat from the back of the bus, Brad's brain signals his adrenal glands to secrete adrenaline causing his anxiety to rise. He soon feels nauseous at which point his monster declares that he is sick and should not leave his house. By keeping him focused on the worst-case scenario and his symptoms, the anxiety monster can get him to choose the path of comfort and certainty instead of going to the party. Brad has not thrown up in ten years and believes that this is all due to his efforts to avoid unsafe situations.

Brad chooses to play it safe and stay home. This is what is comfortable and certain. He sends a text apologizing for not being able to make it – again. As he watches videos on his laptop, he notices he no longer feels nauseous. *I guess I wasn't sick after all.* His anxiety is soon replaced with depression as he focuses on the state of his life. Brad feels like he is not where he should be professionally and socially, and is not living the life he desires and deserves. He feels like a failure and imagines others think he is a failure too. He mopes around his apartment in sweat pants while his monster celebrates his misery and another victory.

Anxiety is a disorder of perception: The perception of the likelihood of a catastrophe and your inability to handle that perceived catastrophe.

There is also a perception that you can control what you cannot (this will be discussed later). If you have a fear of elevators, it is likely due to your perception of elevators being unsafe and your inability to handle being stuck inside should it break down. *What if it breaks and I'm trapped?* It's uncertain. To be trapped inside might result in a panic attack. Although there is a possibility of getting stuck in an elevator, the perception of those who are not afraid is that they are "safe enough." These fearless elevator riders also believe that if they do get stuck, they would be able to handle it.

We don't have to be 100% certain to live a happy life. What activities do you engage in where certainty is not 100%? Driving? Dental cleanings? Public speaking? Physical activities? New medication? Swimming? Bike riding? Are these activities safe enough? If you required 100% certainty, you could not engage in any of them.

Consider this question: Suppose you had an appointment in a tall office building. Before you enter the building, a man wearing a chicken costume urges you to stay out: *Sometime in the next hour a meteor is going to hit this building. Don't go in!* How would you react? Picture this scenario in your mind. What would you do if you encountered such a man dressed as a chicken? Would you go into the building? And if you did, would you be worried about meteors? Many of my patients (but not all) answer they would go into the building and they would not be anxious. If you are similar, how do you explain the absence of fear? Why would you not feel anxious going inside despite the threat of a meteor hitting the building?

Answer: Because you would not believe the man dressed as a chicken. If you don't believe the lie, you tend not to be anxious and you don't avoid. On the other hand, if you believe the lie, you will feel anxious, and it might affect your behavior. Perhaps you would avoid entering the building or you might compulsively check online for meteor warnings. Your anxiety (your feelings and behavior) is based on your perception – what you believe; not what is real. Earlier in this chapter, how many F's did you perceive?

When you suffer with emetophobia and panic attacks, you are constantly believing the lies of your imagination and every time you do, your brain signals your adrenal glands to secrete adrenaline causing nausea and other symptoms of anxiety, which results in more anxious thoughts and more adrenaline.

Why You Cannot be the Anxiety Monster

Some people struggle with the concept of an anxiety monster. They feel it's silly or have difficulty separating themselves from their anxiety.

This is normal. You have viewed yourself and anxiety as one in the same for years. Consider this. You and your anxiety are very different. Your anxiety monster lies, bullies, and threatens. Is this how you describe yourself? Most people with anxiety are not liars or bullies, and most are not mean or threatening. This is why you cannot be your anxiety monster.

The suffering that emetophobes endure is serious and the battle they face to overcome is challenging. To some, the metaphor of a mental game against a tricky opponent seems silly, and indeed, it is. If it were not so effective, I would only teach it to anxious children. It just so happens, externalizing anxiety and personifying it, works! It works because it makes the problem more tangible and therefore easier to manage.

Anxiety sufferers are creative, kind, artistic, and intelligent people with active imaginations who take their imaginations very seriously. If these are your natural gifts then let's use those gifts to help you improve your life. Although you might feel the metaphor of a mental game against an opponent is silly, a bit of silliness can bring a tad of levity to a dark and scary problem. So, take a leap of faith and work the program, even if you are skeptical.

What would the anxiety monster in your imagination say about the picture in this QR code? He would say, *the top square is darker than the bottom square*. This is a lie! Place your pointer finger on the line between the two squares and you will see they are the same shade of grey. Sometimes things *appear* a certain way but are incorrect. Sometimes things *feel* catastrophic but they are not.

STEPS TO FREEDOM

Write in your Victory Journal: Make a journal entry about what you have learned so far. Do not write about any doubts, fears, or anything negative; write only what you have learned and any positive thoughts.

Chapter 9
The Amygdala, Prefrontal Cortex, and Your Core Beliefs

Because anxiety begins with your imagination, we have identified your opponent as the *Anxiety Monster in Your Imagination.*

As I stated previously, every time your anxiety monster asks a scary question or spouts off a lie and you take it seriously, your brain signals your adrenal glands to secrete adrenaline. Your adrenal glands are set off when there is an actual emergency *but* also when an emergency is perceived. If that's not bad enough, your adrenal glands will also secrete adrenaline when you **don't** perceive an emergency. For instance, if I show an arachnophobe a picture of a spider, he may instantly feel anxiety even though there is no danger. It's just a picture. Why does this happen? Oftentimes people with anxiety can't understand why they feel anxiety when there is no logical reason. An explanation of two parts of the brain may help: the **Prefrontal Cortex** and the **Amygdala**.

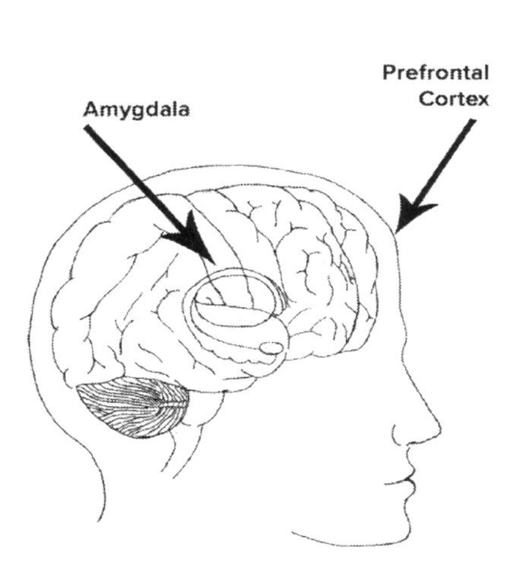

The prefrontal cortex is in charge of logical thinking and reasoning. The amygdala is in charge of emotional reactions. The amygdala is called the primitive brain because, like a lizard when it hears a loud noise, it just reacts (it does not think). Since the **amygdala processes information faster than the prefrontal cortex**, if an emetophobe sees a picture of a cartoon character vomiting, his amygdala hijacks his entire brain, overriding the prefrontal cortex. He will then react with emotion, even though it is just a silly picture. When the prefrontal cortex is captured by emotion (disgust, fear), it can't do its job, which is to think rationally. This is why people with anxiety, who consider themselves to be logical, can't understand why they are behaving so illogically.

When you were in fifth grade and there was a fire drill, did you get scared? On the contrary, if you were like most children you were happy because it meant getting out of class. Most children do not get scared because they know it's a drill and there is no danger. The alarm system of the **building** is blaring but there is no emergency. This is the same for emetophobes and people who suffer with panic. The alarm system in your body is blasting (nausea, racing heart, etc.) but there is no emergency. It is a **false adrenaline alarm**. It is just your anxiety monster pulling the alarm and watching chaos ensue.

Children remain composed during a fire drill because the teacher calmly announces, *We are having a drill. Everyone please line up quietly.* Imagine their reaction, however, if the teacher yelled, ***FIRE, FIRE!*** They would be terrified! The combination of a blaring **alarm** and a **scary message** is overwhelming and this is what sufferers of emetophobia and panic disorder experience. Their body's alarm system is engaged in the form of nausea, throat constriction, jitters, lightheadedness, etc., while at the same time scary thoughts are being repeated in the mind. When your body's alarm system activates there's an assumption that there is a real emergency and what you are thinking is true. The physical symptoms make the thoughts feel believable. After all, why would your body react this way if there wasn't an emergency?

The purpose of the amygdala is to protect us from danger. It operates in the background, constantly on alert, making sure we are safe. Similar to a faulty car alarm that goes off when a person simply walks by, the amygdala can be exceedingly reactive and when it signals the adrenal glands, resulting in nausea or stomach upset, it's easy to believe you are going to vomit, even when it never happens.

Like a Secret Service agent protecting the president, constantly on the lookout for danger, your amygdala is relentlessly on guard. To do their job properly, Secret Service agents see everyone and everything as a possible threat. This is exactly how your anxiety monster views the world. For emetophobes, the threat is vomit and panic, and you must be on high alert every waking second. Wow. That's exhausting.

As you look at your life through the lens of potential vomit disasters and panic attacks, your amygdala's motto is "better be safe than sorry." If you react to every perceived threat with a dinosaur sized dose of adrenaline, there will be many anxiety attacks, unnecessary behavior, and missed opportunities. Once your amygdala realizes there is no danger, it begins to settle down, but this is challenging when you take the lies of your imagination seriously.

Core Beliefs

Perhaps it will be helpful to examine how other types of anxiety sufferers view the world through a different lens than yours.

If you happen to see two people laughing, what do you think? People with social anxiety often think, *They're laughing at me. They think I'm a loser.* They believe that people are talking about them, staring at them, and don't like them. As you fear vomit, they fear embarrassment, judgment, and rejection.

One of my previous patients with social anxiety shared, *If I was standing in the mall, I would imagine people wondering, "Why is that person just standing there? What's wrong with her?" If I was talking on my phone, I would imagine people thinking, "There's another person talking on their phone."* **It was all based on her core beliefs**: *People are judging me. People think bad things about me. What people think about me is important. Everything is embarrassing.* Some socially anxious students won't walk across a classroom to turn in an assignment because of these core beliefs, and if they do, it causes a great deal of anxiety.

Core beliefs often stem from childhood or adolescence and are ingrained so deeply they are **felt** as absolute truth and not questioned. Just because something feels true does not mean it is.

Is talking on a phone or walking across a classroom embarrassing? Are people really judging and are those judgments important? If your core belief is that people are judging you, you will feel anxious and embarrassed, even if the core belief is false. Before a socially anxious student leaves her seat, the amygdala will fire off, adrenaline will instantly secrete into her body, and then physical symptoms will ensue as she scurries across the room staring down at the ground to avoid classmates' perceived stares.

Let's take another example. If a person has a core belief that *bad things always happen to me,* everything they experience will be filtered through this lens. A decade ago, my neighborhood was evacuated in the middle of the night due to a large and severe brush fire. Thankfully the brave firefighters prevented all homes from destruction. Last night the temperature in Los Angeles was pushing 100 degrees and the winds kicked up: a recipe for another fire disaster. I went to sleep hoping everything would be okay but my neighbor, who has a belief that bad things always happen to her, packed her car just in case an evacuation was necessary and stayed up all night worrying and monitoring the news. No fire started. Nothing happened. Preparation is important but if you have a core belief that bad things always happen to you, your imagination will keep you on high alert as you look at the world through the lens of expected disaster.

What would you think if you experienced a few headaches in one week? Sufferers of illness anxiety might believe they have a brain tumor. They look at their body through the lens of medical disasters and when they notice something small, calamity is what they perceive. Because of their false beliefs, they are on high alert, compulsively scanning their body and checking online for information about their symptoms. What do you think they find online? Disaster! As they read about the worst possibilities, they get caught in the web, and their anxiety soars.

What are your core beliefs, your perceptions, and the lens through which you view the world?

Emetophobes see vomit and vomiting as the worst thing imaginable. Vomit is disgusting but is it the worst thing imaginable? Can you think of worse? Being bitten by a large dog on your face? How about being in a severe car crash on a highway or being diagnosed with ALS? Is a child being kidnapped worse? How about being trampled by an elephant?

The Illusion of Control

Elephant jokes spread across the United States in the early 1960s People loved sharing and there were hundreds of them, including this one:

> Two men are sitting on a bench reading a newspaper in New York's Central Park. Periodically one man pats the top of his head three times in a row. The other man is perplexed.
>
> *Excuse me. I'm curious as to why you are patting your head.*
> *It's trick I learned in Africa. It keeps the elephants away.*
> *But there aren't any elephants in Central Park!*
> *Yes. Works quite well, doesn't it!*

The illusion of control is an overestimation of the ability to control events. It occurs when people believe they can control or influence outcomes which they cannot. This belief system was identified by Dr. Ellen Langer, a professor of psychology at Harvard and Yale. Through her research at Yale in the 1970s, Langer demonstrated how people often behave as if chance events are due to personal control. She defined this illusion as *an expectancy of personal success probability inappropriately higher than the objective probability would warrant.*

Most emetophobes rarely vomit and they believe that this is a direct result of their efforts. They believe they have successfully prevented themselves from vomiting because of their avoidance, hypervigilance, and defensive tactics. But is this really true? Are you really preventing anything? After all, most people rarely vomit without any effort. Perhaps this is an illusion, cultivated and then cemented into a core belief, due to your hypervigilance to prevent vomit and a parallel life of not vomiting. With years of extraordinary effort in puke prevention, and only a few vomiting episodes, a correlation develops: *I have successfully averted puking because of my efforts. I am controlling the situation.*

This core belief is an illusion -- another lie.

Your extraordinary efforts might be lowering the odds slightly but everyone will vomit at some point. It's going to happen. Food poisoning and the stomach flu are rare, but when they occur, there is absolutely nothing you can do to prevent yourself from throwing up. In fact, vomiting is your body's way of aiding the healing process and helping you to feel better.

My emetophobe patients avoid boats, roller coasters, windy roads, and airplanes because they might get motion sickness and vomit, yet most of them admit that this has never happened because they don't get motion sickness. They might feel nauseous on roller coasters, planes, and boats but not due to the motion; due to their anxiety. Which is why emetophobes also try to avoid anything which might trigger anxiety, nausea and stomach distress, an impossible endeavor, especially if you desire any sort of life. In later chapters you will learn how to deal with symptoms you cannot control, manage them, and ultimately reduce them significantly.

Ask yourself the following: *Are my efforts to exert control really preventing anything and do they help me feel happy and make my life better? What is the price I am paying for my efforts to control and is it necessary and worth it?* The illusion of control has become a core belief and is reinforced each day by a sense of victory.

Some emetophobes feel a sense of accomplishment when they make it through the day without throwing up. It often feels like a personal triumph worth fighting for until you realize how much it has impacted your life.

Emetophobes also have another core belief: *I can't handle anything to do with vomit. I can't handle seeing it and I can't handle vomiting.* This may be true now but this book will teach you differently.

STEPS TO FREEDOM

Make a list of your core beliefs, your perceptions, and all of your worrisome thoughts. In other words, all the cruel things your anxiety monster says to you. Write them in **the second person**, as if your opponent is speaking to you. Instead of *"***I** *have the flu"* write, *"***You** *have* *the flu."* Instead of *"What if **I** have a panic attack?"* write, *"What if **you** have a panic attack?"*

Here are examples:

- **What if worries:** *"What if you can't find a bathroom?" "What if you have a panic attack?" "What if you vomit in class?" "What if you have the flu?"*
- **Threats:** *"If you go you will puke!" "If you eat that you might get sick." "You will never get over this."*
- **Orders:** *"Eat slowly!" "Don't go!" "Wash your hands!" "Don't eat!" Go home!" "Check the expiration date!" "Find a way out!"*
- **Exclamations:** *"Oh my God!" "Oh no." "This is so embarrassing!" "Your heart is racing!!!!" "You're nauseous!!!!"*
- **Put Downs:** *"You're a loser." "You'll never amount to anything." "You're a failure." "You're an embarrassment."*
- **Mind Reading:** *"They think you're weird." "If you puke they will think you're disgusting" "No one likes you."*
- **Existential Questions:** *"What is the purpose of life?" "Why is there so much suffering?" "Why did God choose you to have anxiety?"*
- **Futile Questions:** *"Will you ever be normal? "Why do you have these thoughts?" "Why are you nauseous?" "How are you feeling?"*
- **When Nausea or Stomach Upset Begins:** *"This is it." "You're gonna puke!" "You're really sick this time." "Don't eat."*
- **Disastrous Predictions:** *"You will have morning sickness for 9 months!" "You will never find a partner and be happy."*
- **Confidence Busters:** *"You can't do it." "You won't be able to handle it." "You'll never be better." "It's too risky – don't try."*

After you make a list of everything your opponent says in the **second person** (all of your thoughts), identify or create an opponent. Who is your Anxiety Monster? What does it look like? Search for one on the internet or draw a creature that represents anxiety. Give it an expression. Even though I call it a *monster*, it does not have to be scary. Your opponent can look silly, weird, annoying, or sneaky. A cartoon, politician, male, female, or an abstract figure with a face. Any creature you can visualize. Once you've identified an opponent, write all his threats, demands, put-downs, and questions around your picture.

The picture on the next page was drawn by an emetophobe who chose a scary creature as her opponent. She could have written much more. Start paying attention to your thoughts, including what you think when you experience symptoms and the thoughts that affect your behavior.

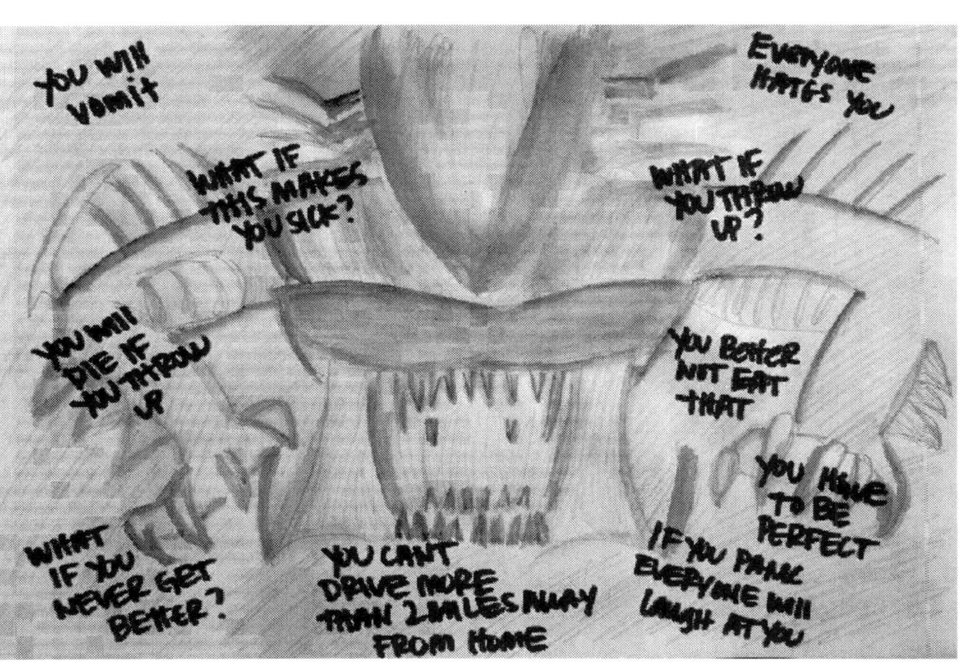
YOU WILL vomit
EVERYONE HATES YOU
WHAT IF THIS MAKES YOU SICK?
WHAT IF YOU THROW UP?
YOU WILL DIE IF YOU THROW UP
YOU BETTER NOT EAT THAT
YOU HAVE TO BE PERFECT
WHAT IF YOU NEVER GET BETTER?
YOU CANT DRIVE MORE THAN 2 MILES AWAY FROM HOME
IF YOU PANIC EVERYONE WILL LAUGH AT YOU

Chapter 10
Your Opponent's Second Strategic Move

Before I explain your monster's second strategic move allow me to repeat this important message. To overcome emetophobia and panic disorder:

1) Take action by completing the assignments in this book.
2) Change your perspective by looking at your fears and worries through the prism of a mental game against a tricky, mean opponent whose objective is to keep you miserable by lying.

Your anxiety monster has only two strategic moves. The first one is to lie. By lying he can get you driving in the wrong direction. It's easy to fall for the lies because of your body's faulty, overly sensitive alarm system. It's all based on your perception and core beliefs. Eventually you must demand reality.

Your opponent's second strategic move is to ask a provocative question or make a provocative statement. These questions and statements are so compelling you can't help but go to the back of the bus to respond. Why is this strategic? Anxiety knows the longer he can engage you in a conversation, the more anxious you become. Whenever you are dwelling or analyzing a situation you are in the back of the bus conversing with your opponent. Each time your imagination says something scary, your brain signals your adrenal gland to secrete adrenaline, and the longer the conversation, the more anxious you feel. And it all begins with a provocative statement or question. It's how your opponent baits you.

Not only do you feel more anxious the longer you dwell, but something else is occurring. If you are engaging with your imagination in the back of the bus, what are you **not** doing? **Answer**: Driving.

And if you are not driving, you are not living your life and you are not moving forward to the Land of Freedom. Provocative questions and statements are intended to make you anxious and stall you.

Questions are common: *What if you're really sick this time? What's your plan if someone at the party gets too drunk? The food you ate tasted funny – do you think it was spoiled? What if you puke at dinner in front of everyone? Do you think you have the flu? What if another passenger gets motion sickness? Do you think if you let your guard down and relax you might puke? How are going to prevent catching the flu when you go to the doctor's office tomorrow? Will you ever get better? Should you take the medication? Do you think you will you ever get married? What if you panic? What are you going to do if you can't get out?*

When you ask a scary question, you are going to get a scary answer.

And those answers can linger for a long time. There is a tendency to dwell on questions and replaying worst case scenarios in your mind. Your anxiety monster shouts from the back of the bus, *What if the chef at the restaurant has the stomach flu?* Suddenly, the two of you are in the back of the bus watching a scary movie on his laptop about you catching the flu and vomiting. When the movie is over, he whispers in your ear, *in case you might have missed something, let's watch it again.* And as you sit there staring off, watching the horror movie in your imagination for the third time, you go deeper into the depths of anxiety. By the time you have watched the movie for the fourth time, you decline your friend's invitation for dinner. If that's not bad enough, you spend the rest of the night cuddling with your monster, as he tells you how much of a loser you are and how you will never get better.

Your anxiety will attempt to get you in the back of the bus at any opportunity. Anticipatory anxiety is the worry people experience before facing a fear. If you have aviophobia and have a flight in June, you might start worrying about it in May. As the event draws near, the dwelling worsens and the anxiety rises. Any time you are experiencing anticipatory anxiety, you are in the back of the bus with your opponent.

Needless dwelling can also occur after an event. It's common for emetophobes to beat themselves up on the drive home if they leave an event too early or if they cancel plans with an excuse. Being alone is the perfect opportunity for your imagination to engage you in a lengthy conversation about how pathetic you are and how you will never turn your life around. By the time you are home, you feel more hopeless than ever.

Being alone is a common time for your opponent to make a threat or ask a question but he's audacious enough to interrupt you at work and at social gatherings. My patient who worked in a hair salon had difficulty focusing on the job when her monster asked her questions. If a customer shared that her child was sick, my patient would wonder the rest of the day if she was contagious. Because her co-worker sometimes brought interesting smelling foods for lunch, my patient worried all morning if the smell would make her feel nauseous and vomit. She found it challenging to cut hair when entangled in conversations with her imagination.

In addition to fears of vomit and panic, you might have other worries about life, your family, your health, or anything else uncertain. Provocative statements to get your attention include thoughts about the future and the past, as well as philosophical questions about the meaning of life, what happens when you die, and the tragedies of the world and the expanding universe. **Watch out for unanswerable questions,** such as, *What's the purpose of life? Are people really happy? Why is this happening to me? Will I ever get better? What's going to happen to those starving children in Haiti? Do people hate you? How are you going to get better? What if this is all a dream?* It doesn't take much for your monster to get you to the back of the bus and once you're there, it's difficult to return to the driver's seat and carry on with your life.

Ignore all unanswerable questions!
Their only purpose is to engage you in a conversation.

One more truth to keep in mind. Sometimes the monster's predictions will actually come true. At some point in your life you will throw up. At some point you will see or hear someone vomit. And eventually you will see a barfing scene in a movie or on television. This does not mean you should take your imagination seriously. As they say, even a broken clock is right two times a day. Ask yourself this question, *would you go to a psychic, take her seriously, and follow her advice if she* *was wrong 90% of the time?* Of course not. Well, guess what?

Your opponent is wrong 99.9% of the time.

You can't stop thoughts from popping into your head, **so do not try**. They come too quickly. You can't prevent the content of your thoughts. **Everyone** has anxious, weird, sexual, and violent thoughts. EVERYONE. But if you do not suffer with anxiety, those thoughts will vanish quickly. Only when you dwell on them, do they feel important. ***Thoughts only have as much power as you give them and the more you dwell, the more power they have.***

Your opponent's second strategic move is a potent one, but as you go through the chapters of this book you will learn effective moves to prevent mindless dwelling in the back of the bus. In the meantime, beware of your opponent's intentions: he wants to engage you in meaningless discussions because the longer you interact, the more your brain signals the adrenal glands, and the more anxious you become.

If you were home at night, alone, sitting in front of the television, channel surfing, what would you do if a scary movie popped onto the screen? If you're like many people, you would change the channel **immediately**, because you know that watching would make you anxious. The same is true for the scary thoughts in your imagination. In upcoming chapters, you will learn how to change the channel in your mind and disengage when a frightening thought or a provocative question tries to engage you. The scary thoughts in your mind are as unimportant and insignificant as the scary movies on your television. Only when you focus on them do they FEEL important, significant, and scary.

Counterproductive Thinking Disguised as Productive

It is common for anxiety sufferers to believe certain types of thinking are helpful when they are not. Anticipating problems, problem solving, preparing, and planning ahead are all important ways we successfully manage upcoming events. This, however, is not useful in all situations if you suffer with anxiety. Planning and preparing for a panic attack or a vomiting emergency might seem like a good idea but the consequence is more anxiety. Sufferers can spend hours thinking about how they will respond should a panic attack occur in a given situation or what to do if they began to feel nauseous. In reality, this form of preparation increases anxiety as you focus on the worst-case scenario.

Throughout the day your anxious mind searches for uncertain situations, the possibility of vomit and panic, and then feeds you ways to resolve the uncertainty and solve the problem. Has following the suggestions of your anxiety monster lead to a productive and happy life? The only preparation needed will be the strategies laid out in this book. There is no need to figure out anything by having a discussion with your anxiety monster in the back of the bus. Anxiety will also try to derail you with images of past vomiting traumas or panic attacks. I discuss how to heal yourself from trauma in a later chapter.

I asked an emetophobe patient to write about how creating an opponent has helped in her recovery:

> *Externalizing and personifying my anxiety has helped immensely. I will admit that at first it was hard and seemed somewhat silly. For so long it felt like I was fighting against myself, which is a horrible way to live. Constantly mad at myself, hating myself, angry at myself, all for having feelings that I couldn't help. Once Ken told me that it wasn't me, it was my monster who was trying to trick me into staying sick, I jumped on board. I didn't want to fight myself anymore.*
>
> *Not only that but I saw how my monster lies and tricks me by telling me horrible things! He would say things like "you are worthless, no one loves you, you are going to vomit, don't eat that it will make you puke, if you vomit you will die!" I realized I would never say things like that to myself or anyone. They are awful! And worst of all I had been listening and believed the lies for years. This made me sad and angry, and it made me want to fight - not me, my monster. This process makes me feel like I am fighting a battle and there is someone I am beating. I imagine him to be gross and with an annoying voice. It helps to not take him so seriously. I know his agenda is to get me to fall for his lies because I have done it so many times, and I know where it leads me- absolute misery.*
>
> *It's a game and every time I don't listen to him or I do something that he tells me not to, he gets a little smaller. He is not nearly as threatening now. I know he is a liar and sometimes I still fall for his tricks because he knows me so well, but he is almost gone. I don't think I would be nearly as confident overcoming my anxiety if this entire process was me fighting myself. I do believe I have a monster, and I know he is losing, because for the first time I am winning. I am getting bigger, and I am trusting* ***me*** *again, not him. And it feels great.*

Now that you understand your opponent's two strategic moves, the following chapters will focus on **your** strategy for conquering emetophobia and panic.

STEPS TO FREEDOM

Give your opponent a name: All villains have names –Joker, Darth Vader, Lord Voldemort, General Zod, Doctor Octopus, Baron Zemo. Use your creativity and invent a name for your opponent: Trick Monster, Hoax, Megaphone, Lord Liar.

Notice each time your opponent shouts something provocative: In other words, be aware of your thoughts and reframe them as coming from a tricky opponent trying to lure you to the back of the bus with questions, threats, and lies. Pay attention to your thoughts and respond out loud: "*I see what you're doing. You're trying to mess with me by telling me...*" Complete the sentence with whatever your worry or question happens to be.

Coloring: The next page is an adult coloring illustration from my book *Break Free from Anxiety*, the world's first coloring, self-help book, a step-by-step guide for all types of anxiety. Many find coloring to be relaxing and meditative. To help reinforce the concept of not going to the back of the bus, color the following page. To find adult coloring books as well as *Break Free from Anxiety*, visit ColoringBookZone.com.

Don't
Go
to
the
Back
of the
Bus

Chapter 11
Creating Motivation to Win Your Freedom

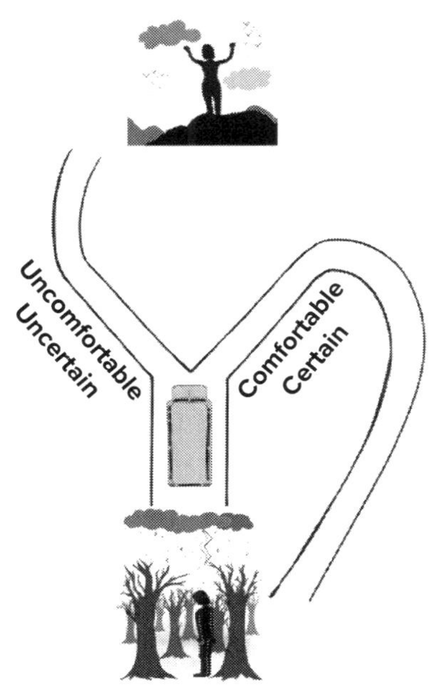

QUESTION:
Look closely at this map. If an emetophobe were to **LOSE** this mental game, which direction would he have to go: uncomfortable and uncertain or the comfortable and certain?

ANSWER: The comfortable and certain way is the losing road. Which means:

If you are **un**comfortable, anxious, and u**n**certain, you are **WINNING**!

What? Usually when you're winning you feel great. Not in this game. Feeling uncomfortable, anxious, and uncertain is how you know you are on the correct road. It's how you know you are headed in the right direction. It's your compass. Perhaps an example might help.

One of my emetophobic patients was progressing nicely but had yet to fly on a plane. Unlike yours truly, he did not suffer with motion sickness but he was afraid someone like me might be sitting in the next seat. He was offered and accepted a promotion at work in spite of the requirement to periodically fly. One day he arrived at a session very anxious after being told he would have to travel at least once a month beginning in three weeks. He was not sure he could do it and contemplated rescinding his acceptance.

He was at a fork. He could choose to take the comfortable and certain road and return to his previous position. This would mean no extra income or elevated status and a continued fear of flying. (Look at the map again. The comfortable road takes you back to the Land of Misery.) Or he could take the promotion and go down the path of discomfort and uncertainty.

Anxiety sufferers seek out my services to help them stop their anxiety, but beating anxiety is the **long-term goal**. This is what happens when you reach the *Land of Freedom*. To get there, however, you must drive your bus through the maze of life, choosing roads of discomfort and uncertainty, which will **cause** anxiety. Therefore, the short-term goal is NOT to stop anxiety. Let me repeat, the short-term goal is **NOT** to stop anxiety.

The short-term goal is to learn how to respond to anxiety in a better way and not let it have power over you.

This is what I'm going to teach you. Instead of white-knuckling and praying as you face your fear, or avoiding it all together, I'm going to teach you how to form a new relationship with anxiety.

Cultivating a new relationship does take time, so be patient.

Your opponent wants to remove all doubt and distress and create solutions to help you feel better immediately. He says, *you're justified in trying to prevent something bad from happening and stopping anxiety as quickly as possible.* Ask yourself this question: Has choosing easier, comfortable, and certain roads given you a better life?

Along with gratitude, purpose, and meaningful relationships, what makes people happy are the pride and fulfillment of mastering a new skill, accomplishing a task that takes effort, and bravely facing a fear. If these don't produce an immediate sense of satisfaction, they will serve as steps to happiness in the long run. When your mindset is to do what is certain and comfortable, and avoid any action that requires effort and struggle, achieving happiness will be challenging to attain. Base your decisions on what you value (family, friends, career, religion, and your pursuits and dreams) not what you fear.

Identify a fear you are no longer afraid of or something that once caused discomfort but now is comfortable: a recent fear or even something from years ago. How were you able to overcome it? In the space below, write about how you triumphed over discomfort and anxiety.

What would your life be like if you had not overcome this fear and discomfort? Prior to beating it, were you confident you would prevail? You don't have to be confident to beat emetophobia but you must be motivated. Ask yourself, *Why put so much effort into beating emetophobia?* To successfully navigate the maze of discomfort and uncertainty, you must be motivated.

Are you so sick and tired of emetophobia that you are willing to do whatever it takes to get rid of it?
What is going to motivate you to stay focused and push through discomfort and uncertainty?

One of my patients, at the beginning of our third session, shared that her childhood friend in New York was dying of cancer. My patient wanted to be there but she was experiencing panic attacks and was terrified to fly.

Her dying friend, who understood her fear, told her it was fine not to visit: *You don't have to come. I understand. It's okay.* But my patient was **not** okay with this. As quickly as her anxiety rose at the thought of flying, it diminished with her determination to be there for her friend. She would not let her anxiety get in the way and was going to be there no matter what. She made this decision based on her values, not on her fears. She got on the plane despite her discomfort and uncertainty and flew to New York. By the end of the year, she had visited two more times and her fear of flying had greatly diminished. To increase your motivation to beat anxiety, identify what emetophobia has cost you.

How has emetophobia and panic impacted your life?

How has emetophobia and panic affected your dating life or marriage?

How has emetophobia and panic hurt your family?

How has emetophobia and panic hurt your friendships?

How has emetophobia and panic impacted your career?

How has emetophobia and panic hurt you financially?

What have you missed out on because of emetophobia and panic?

What will the Land of Freedom look like?

____

____

____

____

____

Reread what you wrote above and complete the following **declaration**:
I will give 100% and do whatever it takes to beat emetophobia because...

____

____

____

____

To help keep you motivated, read your declaration every day. If part of the reason you are going to fight is for someone else, get a picture of that person and place it next to your declaration. You can also put a picture of something you will do once you beat your anxiety. For instance, if you want to take a trip to Hawaii but are too afraid to fly, find a beautiful photo of Hawaii and place it next to your declaration.

STEPS TO FREEDOM

Read your declaration out loud: To help keep you motivated, read your declaration and your answers to the questions in this chapter several times a week.

The STEPS TO FREEDOM are not **suggestions**. They are **requirements** to beating your opponent. You must be determined to win even if you do not believe it's possible. Many of my patients do not believe they can overcome their fears and that's okay. As I stated previously, belief is not essential to prevailing but taking action is.

Chapter 12
The Winning Mindset

I'm about to blow your mind so be sure you're sitting down. The powerful strategy you are about to learn in the next few chapters will take some time to **fully** digest and comprehend. It will seem odd at first. You might not get it. But once you have all the pieces in place and begin to implement the strategy, it will make sense. Be patient and open. Remember, you are looking at this problem in a new way, from a different perspective. You are playing a mental game against a lying bully in your imagination whose goal is to keep you miserable.

I have explained that to overcome emetophobia and reach the *Land of Freedom* you must choose roads of discomfort and uncertainty despite the threats by your opponent. In other words, you must go **in** to anxiety to get **out** of anxiety. The patient I wrote about from the previous chapter who flew to New York three times in a year, experienced high levels of anxiety prior to her first flight and during take-off. The second trip to New York wasn't as scary and her third flight even less so. The high anxiety she initially experienced, dissipated with **repeated exposures**.

Most emetophobes seldom face their fears and when they do, it's usually because they have no choice. They do it reluctantly, with a great deal of fear. They walk into anxiety's territory unwillingly, tentatively, cautiously, terrified, and praying that their worst fears do not come true. Their mind set is defensive and they seldom face the fear again and if they do, it's in the same manner.

There are plenty of instances of people confronting their fears repeatedly, yet **never** overcome debilitating anxiety. For example, an emetophobe who goes to restaurants a few times a week, yet remains anxious each time. With all the practice, why doesn't this brave soul get better? It's true that eating out several times a week is good practice, but if you're white-knuckling it, using safety behaviors, eating the same food slowly, and praying you do not panic or puke, all you are doing is practicing being anxious and strengthening your anxiety.

You must not only go down the path of discomfort and uncertainty on a frequent basis, you must do so with a particular perspective and mindset.

Several years ago, my mother was diagnosed with breast cancer. She was told that if she did radiation and chemotherapy she might live. The doctor explained that the treatment would make her feel nauseous and vomit and she would lose her hair. Without hesitation she replied, *If that's what I have to do to live, I'll do it. When can I start?* She had a certain mindset, a *bring it on, is that all you got?* mentality.

The mindset of all anxiety sufferers is defensive. As an emetophobe you must be **on guard** for things that might disgust you, **overly prepare** for every possible catastrophe, be on the **lookout** for diseases that might cause you to be sick, and **protect** yourself from uncertainty with compulsive rituals, all while **avoiding** situations that might cause embarrassment, disaster, and panic. **Anxiety requires you to live in a defensive posture at all times.**

But remember, you are playing a *game*, and like all games you can't win if you are only playing defense. Can a basketball team win if it only plays defense? Never! What about a soccer or baseball team? Absolutely not. **You can't win ANY game ONLY playing defense**, including the mental game against your Anxiety Monster.

To win you must go on the offense, which requires an offensive mindset: a ***"bring it on, is that all you got?"*** *mentality.*

In 1974, Muhammad Ali had a championship title fight against George Foreman. The fight took place in Africa and was called, *Rumble in the Jungle.* At the time Foreman was the champion. He was younger, bigger, and stronger than Ali, *and* he was the heavy favorite. Most people did not believe Ali had a chance. When facing an opponent who is bigger and stronger, you must have a good strategy to win and that is exactly what Ali had. In round one Ali came out swinging with a flurry of punches. In rounds two through seven he did what he called, the *rope-a-dope.* He covered his face and body with his gloves, leaned back against the ropes and taunted Foreman, *Hit me fool. You can't hit me.* What do you think Foreman tried to do? For the next six rounds as Foreman punched away, Ali protected his face and body with his gloves, absorbing the impact of the punches as he bounced against the ropes, all the while taunting Foreman, *Is that all you got, George? They told me you could hit.* By the eighth round, Foreman was so tired from punching, he could barely keep his arms up. That's when Ali went on the attack, knocking Foreman to the ground, winning the fight and the championship.

How did Ali outsmart Foreman?

- He invited the hit.
- He took the hit.
- He responded to the hit.
- He attacked!

That is an offensive mindset.

You are up against an opponent who is bigger and stronger, which means you have to be cunning and clever in order to defeat him. **You must outsmart your anxiety monster by doing what he does not expect.** He will not expect you to *invite the hit* but that is exactly what you need to do. It's clear what *inviting the hit* means in regards to Ali and his opponent, but how does it pertain to you and your opponent? *Inviting the hit* is the opposite of your natural inclination to stop or run from anxiety. It reflects an offensive mindset of purposely **seeking out** discomfort and uncertainty and **demanding** to be anxious.

I know. It sounds crazy. *Seek out anxiety? Make myself anxious! Are you kidding? If you're afraid of anxiety, why would you seek it out? That makes no sense.* Hear me out. If you want to beat anxiety, you must go down roads of discomfort and uncertainty which means you will feel anxious and nauseous. Walking into anxiety's territory, praying you don't become nauseous or anxious is unrealistic and sets you up for failure. It's like jumping into a swimming pool hoping you don't get wet. If you're going to get wet, you might as well invite it. In most games someone makes the first move. Why not you?

Bring on the anxiety. I can handle it.

Making the first move by inviting anxiety is strategic in three ways:

1) It shows your opponent that you are not afraid (even if you are).
2) By doing the opposite of what anxiety expects, you will catch it off guard.
3) You are creating the attitude and energy needed to push through discomfort and uncertainty.

How you invite anxiety is vital to your success and it begins with putting on a *game face*. What is a *game face*? It's a face that reflects a determination to win, even when you are uncertain. It's stern, serious, and tough. It's not just expressed in your face; it extends through your body with your posture and movement. It's not timid or hesitant. It's quick, decisive, and hard-hitting. You mean business.

Put on your *game face,* demand uncertainty and discomfort, and act as though you got this – to win, break free from anxiety, and be happy! That is an offensive mindset.

Trust the process and begin with small steps. Before facing discomfort and uncertainty put on your game face and say out loud:

Bring on the anxiety! I can handle it! This is a wonderful day to do hard things!

Say it like you mean it. Demonstrate to your opponent a determination to beat him. Exclaim out loud:

Bring on the discomfort and uncertainty. This is hard but I'm going to do it anyway. I can handle it! (even if you're not sure)

Exposure Therapy

When teenagers learn how to drive a car, they usually start in an empty parking lot, not on a highway. Similarly, you will start by taking small steps into anxiety's territory. These steps are called exposures. You are purposefully exposing yourself to what makes you anxious. Each emetophobe's path into anxiety's territory is different. While a certain exposure might be easy for you, it might be difficult for someone else. For instance, on a scale of one to ten (ten being the most difficult), how would you rate your fear of looking at a cartoon character vomiting? Give it a number: ___. Would it be easy? Disgusting? Scary? Circle all that apply.

Exposure therapy begins with the least anxiety producing stimuli. The psychological process of repeating an exposure until it becomes relatively comfortable is called habituation. Think about your own life and recall a challenge that was initially uncomfortable and how with repeated exposure, it became comfortable. Here are a few examples of things that are initially scary, uncomfortable, or challenging, and then become easier with repeated practice:

- Driving a car
- Changing a baby's diaper
- Getting an injection
- Lighting a match
- Cooking a recipe
- Sleeping in the dark
- Staying home alone
- Giving a speech
- Performing any physical activity (rollerblading, swimming, dancing)
- Doing a certain job or job duty

Compare the first time doing something challenging with the most recent. With repeated exposure and practice it becomes more comfortable, as long as you are using the correct mindset. If you don't have the correct mindset and you don't practice enough, you may not habituate.

Exposures are challenges, experiments, and opportunities. They are **challenges** because they are not easy. For emetophobes, looking at a photo of someone vomiting is difficult, scary, and disgusting. You might feel nauseous. Remember what underlies all anxiety: An intolerance of discomfort/distress.

Intolerance of uncertainty is the second root of all anxiety, which is why exposures are also **experiments**. We don't know the outcome. It's uncertain. You might think that eating a bite of food in a restaurant will make you vomit but you don't know until you try. The uncertainty makes the exposure scary. With repeated exposures you begin to understand that what you fear would happen, does not. Even if you are 90% sure that you won't barf, that 10% is enough to cause avoidance. Frequent exposures push you towards that 99% threshold, which increases confidence and ends avoidance.

Finally, exposures are **opportunities** to grow. By doing exposures, you are retraining your brain to perceive these situations as nonthreatening and learning that you can handle the discomfort and uncertainty. With frequent practice, what was once difficult becomes tolerable and eventually easy. Exposure therapy won't make you **feel** better but it will make you **be** better.

Planned and Spontaneous Exposures

A planned exposure is a challenge that is done on purpose to create discomfort and uncertainty for the practice of tolerating it. Watching a video on YouTube of a cartoon character barfing is a planned exposure. A spontaneous exposure is a challenging situation which you did not expect (while watching a movie an unexpected vomiting scene appears on the screen). Both types of exposures are important. The planned exposures will be laid out in this book and you will have the opportunity to tackle them one at a time. That comes later. During the course of your day spontaneous exposures will present themselves unexpectedly and you will have additional opportunities to grow. Look at them as opportunities.

You won't feel ready for any of them, so don't wait to feel comfortable and certain. Adopt the attitude, *I'm afraid, but I'm going to do it anyway!* You will always have doubt when you face a fear. Anxiety will not let you be confident.

The goal is to live your life, not to be comfortable or certain.

One planned exposure on your journey through the maze to the *Land of Freedom* will be watching videos of people puking. What is your opponent telling you now? *There's no way you'll be able to watch vomit videos. They will make you sick. What if you can't do it?* Don't engage with your monster. Don't answer his questions. Just keep reading. For most emetophobes, this video exposure is terrifying and difficult but thankfully this is not where you will start. Much easier exposures will be tackled first and you will work up to videos.

You decide the order of the exposures and go from the least difficult to the most. You must be able to handle **pictures** of cartoon characters vomiting and **photos** of people puking before watching **videos**.

Many exposures can be broken up into smaller steps if necessary. For instance, if looking at a photo of someone vomiting into a toilet is too triggering, first look at it from a distance and then gradually move closer. If watching a puking video is too scary, begin by watching with the sound off. If driving after eating a meal is too frightening, start by taking one bite of food and then drive down the block. The exposures in this book begin with the least anxiety inducing and lay out a specific strategy for walking into your opponent's territory. It begins with an offensive mindset.

Invite Your Monster to Play

Before facing any exposure or fear, put on your game face and invite your monster to play. Say one of the following invitations out loud:

Bring on the uncertainty. Make me uncomfortable. I can handle it.
Let's do this. I'm going to win and you can't stop me!
Try to trick me. I'm ready. Bring it.
Make me nauseous. I dare you.
Bring on the anxiety! I can handle it.
I want my freedom. Bring it on.
I'm excited to do hard things. Let's do this.

In chapters to come I will discuss how to face exposures and the best way to respond to discomfort, uncertainty, anxiety, and nausea.

STEPS TO FREEDOM

Create a *Winning Mindset Page*: In an earlier chapter you created an anxiety monster and wrote the horrible things he says to you. Now you will be creating your responses. Print a photo of yourself on a piece of paper and write your two favorite invites from the list above. Feel free to make up your own. You will be adding other responses to this *Winning Mindset Page* in the coming chapters.

*In case you were wondering, my mom went through treatment, beat cancer, and is alive and well.

Chapter 13
Responding to Anxious Thoughts

After you make the first move, *Bring on the anxiety. I can handle it*, your opponent will counter with his move in the form of: A) a worrisome thought B) an anxious sensation (nausea, racing heart, lightheadedness, etc.); or C) both. In this chapter I will address worrisome thoughts.

Remember, the worries are all lies. They may **feel** real but this is just a feeling. When symptoms of anxiety (nausea) accompany worrisome thoughts, the thoughts feel true but they are not. Because your anxiety monster does not have control of the bus, the only ways he can win are to lie, threaten, and engage you in a conversation. And because he desperately wants to win, do not count on him shutting up any time soon. Your opponent will not be quiet, at least for right now. Talking is his only means of winning. You can't stop your thoughts, so don't try. They come too quickly. Many sufferers make the mistake of trying to stop their thoughts.

Instead of trying to quiet your monster, you must outsmart him. You can take away his power by being more clever or more intense.

Reacting to the worries, threats, and demands will not work. Instead of going to the back of the bus, doing what he tells you to do, or **reacting** with a fearful reply, you will be **responding** to your thoughts shrewdly in a way that anxiety does not expect. Your responses must surprise your opponent and take him off guard. Your responses (to your thoughts) will be unconventional, prepared, and calculated. As you begin the process of cultivating a new relationship with anxiety, you will no longer be submitting to his intimidation, lies, and tricks.

Each time your opponent uses his bullhorn from the back of the bus to bully you, you will have a **winning response he won't expect**. It will not be easy at first. Anxiety is a deceitful trickster who will always win if he can engage you. Therefore, you have to be ready with a quick response that will prevent engagement and get you moving down the winning road.

The new relationship you are forming with anxiety takes time. It begins with changing how you respond to the bully. Like a school yard bully, he wants to get a reaction (a startled response, tears, wincing, shaking) and he expects you to follow his commands. Imagine how perplexed he will be when he tries to scare you with, *It's so disgusting! What if you puke?* And you respond:

Thanks for sharing. Have a nice day. I can handle it.

That's not a response your opponent expects. He expects you to freak out. Now you're the one in control. Since you will not be able to stop your anxious thoughts, do not try. **The purpose of a clever response is to help you not take it seriously and not engage.** Remember, this is a mental game. Your opponent will make a move (anxious thought) and then you will make a move (clever response). He will make another move and then you will respond again. This is a move-by-move game. **Refuse to submit to your opponent each time he makes a move and tries to scare you.**

Your thoughts are only as powerful as you perceive them. The less seriously you take them, the less power they have over you. You will learn to frustrate your monster with your wits, overpower him with toughness, and outsmart him with the unexpected.

Chris Webber, a National Basketball Association (NBA) All-Star, shared a story on the Dan Patrick radio show about playing against John Stockton, an NBA All-Star and a member of the Olympic Dream Team. If you are not familiar with these players, Webber is big, powerful, and 6'10" while Stockton was one of the shortest guys in the NBA standing at 6'1".

Webber: *Stockton was one of the toughest guys I ever played against. We had a series in the playoffs and we were playing against Utah and the great Malone and Stockton… I told coach Adelman before the game, "the first play of the game I'm gonna lay Stockton's ass out." …. I laid him out. One of the best screens I ever did. I got my shoulder in his head area too, made it a little dirty.*

Use your QR code reader app to watch the video and see how Stockton responded to the hit.

The next time anxiety tries to trick and bully you with *Don't go. You're really sick!* You respond: *Nice trick.*

And then slap anxiety on the butt and do the opposite of what he says.

You must back up your statements with action by choosing the path of discomfort and uncertainty, otherwise your responses are meaningless. Responding in a clever way to your thoughts will help you face your fears but like learning any new skill, it will take practice. Planned exposures will give you that practice and prepare you for unexpected exposures, like an unanticipated Uber ride with a driver who has body odor or hearing that a friend you saw yesterday has the flu.

Since doing exposure therapy is necessary for beating emetophobia, your opponent will try to scare you into not doing the work: *Don't do it. What if you throw up?* You need to have a response ready. How about this one? *You're a liar. I'll handle it.* And then put on your game face and do the exposure.

Worrisome thoughts diminish and disappear ONLY when you stop avoiding. That's the **only** way to stop your thoughts. Until then, your task is to not take the thoughts seriously and not engage. Think of something you no longer avoid. Do you worry about it any longer?

When faced with the task of doing daily exposures, your anxiety monster is going to recommend that you do it later. Multiple times a day you will be sitting in the driver's seat, faced with a decision: Do I take the road of discomfort and uncertainty or the road of comfort and certainty? Your monster knows that doing exposure therapy is the path to victory so he will do everything he can to convince you not to practice:

Don't do it! It's gonna make you nauseous.
What if you throw up?
What if it makes you so anxious you can't eat?

What if you have a panic attack?
Do it later. You don't have time. You can do it tomorrow.
If you do it you will obsesses about it the entire day.
It's too gross. You can't do it.
It's too hard. You can't do it.
You're not feeling well. Do it later when you're feeling better.
This won't work. How is this going to work?
You'll never beat this.

Your anxiety will try to thwart your intent to heal yourself. Beware of his threats, lies, and orders. You can't stop your thoughts, but you can respond with something clever that anxiety does not expect.

Using the exact same response every time you have an anxious thought is extremely effective because it prevents you from engaging with your thoughts. Every time anxiety asks a question, respond *I'm not answering the question*. And if it fits your personality, add *asshole!* at the end. This will prevent you from accidentally slipping into a meaningless conversation.

Opponent: *Does the food smell bad?*
You: *I'm not answering the question, asshole.*
Opponent: *What if it's spoiled?*
You: *I'm not answering the question, asshole.*
Opponent: *What if you get sick?*
You: *I'm not answering the question, asshole.*
Opponent: *Should you eat it?*
You: *I'm not answering the question, asshole.*

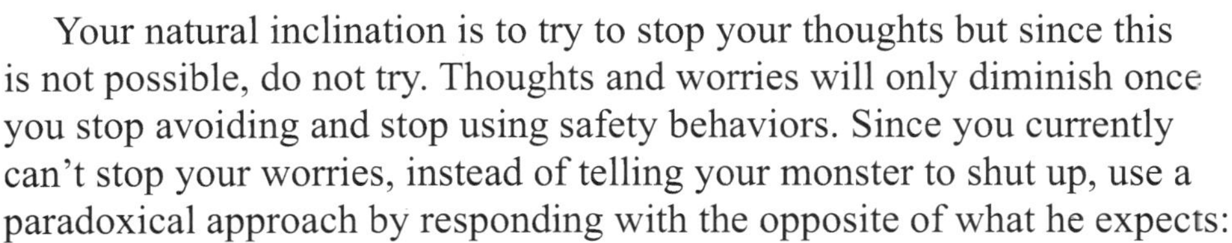

Your natural inclination is to try to stop your thoughts but since this is not possible, do not try. Thoughts and worries will only diminish once you stop avoiding and stop using safety behaviors. Since you currently can't stop your worries, instead of telling your monster to shut up, use a paradoxical approach by responding with the opposite of what he expects:

Opponent: *Don't go. You might get nauseous.*
You: *Keep talking Big Mouth.*
Opponent: *What if you barf?*
You: *Keep talking Big Mouth.*

As you become better at responding over the course of weeks and months, your monster will become quiet. In other words, the frequency of your worries will diminish as you learn to dismiss them and not avoid. When your opponent tells you something scary, respond with a quick and clever comeback. From the list below, identify responses that suit your personality:

Thanks for sharing. Have a nice day.
Keep talking Big Mouth. I'll be fine.
Junk mail. Click bait. Not going there.
You're a liar. I refuse to believe your crap.
I don't know if it's true or not, so whatever.
I need uncertainty to be free, so keep it coming.
I'm certain enough. I'll handle it.
Just meaningless noise. Fake news! I have no time for you.
I see what you're trying to do. I'm not falling for it.
Thanks for this opportunity to practice. Is that all you got?
I'll figure it out. I can handle it.
It's in God's hands. Not yours.
I'm choosing uncertainty to be happy. I can handle it.
I will not exaggerate my problems.
I will not underestimate my abilities.
You're a loser and people think you're weird.
You have nothing new to say. You're boring.
You're out of your mind. What's wrong with you?
I'm driving the bus. I'm in control now.
I'm taking my life back so you can stick it!
It doesn't matter what you say. I'll figure it out.
Whatever! So what? It is what it is.
I'm not answering the question.
Cool. Keep the lies coming. I love it.
Just a thought. No comment. Move on.
I love it when you talk dirty. Keep it coming.
Are you trying to mess with ME? Not going to happen!
Up your butt with a coconut.
That's a good one. You almost got me. High five.
Not taking the bait.
Just a thought, period.

By adding the word "period" you end the conversation, preventing you from attaching to the thought. Feel free to create your own responses. Make sure they are short and to the point. Do not try to debate your opponent or try to convince him that he's wrong. He can easily lure you into a conversation with provocative questions, so keep your comebacks brief. By responding in this way, you are putting some mental distance between you and your anxiety. Repeat your chosen responses with every threat, question, and order, all day. This is a move-by-move game and in the beginning of treatment it feels like an extended game of Monopoly – very long.

Because your worries are lies, we hit them hard. Like a professional baseball pitcher, your monster is throwing lies at you with intense velocity. If you want to change the direction of those lies, hit them hard. It's basic physics. To change the direction of a moving object, it must be hit with a powerful force moving in the opposite direction. Don't bunt. *Swing for the fences!* Knock your anxiety off balance with profanity if that fits your personality: *F-off* is a classic. Every time he asks a question, gives an order, or makes a threat: *Eat shit and die!*

Instead of trying to stop your worries, you are going to make your voice louder and more dominant. Instead of trying to stop anxiety, summon forth a competing emotion – anger. Getting angry can override your anxiety. Direct your anger towards your opponent for lying to you, tricking you, and messing up your life. Do not get angry at yourself -- only your monster. He's the bully causing you pain. It's time to stand up to the bully and let your voice be heard. If anger does not fit your personality, I will discuss other competing emotions later in the book. In the meantime, try to be assertive and stern with your opponent.

To beat anxiety, you must match his intensity.

STEPS TO FREEDOM

Add responses to your *Winning Mindset Page*: Add your favorite responses from the list above to the *Winning Mindset Page* from the last chapter (the page with the photo of yourself). Feel free to create your own responses. Don't write *shut up* because he won't and don't write *go away* because he has no intention of leaving.

Visualization: Think of a time in your life when you were tough, angry, or assertive. Close your eyes and think about it. Allow yourself to remember and if possible, feel the emotion. Then replace the object of your anger with your anxiety monster and visualize yourself telling him, *You will NOT win! I will be free. F-off.* Do this exercise at least one time a day. There are many steps to freedom. Take them seriously and often and you will reach the goals you desire.

Chapter 14
Responding to Physical Sensations

Anxious thoughts can be worrisome, time consuming, and scary but when you also experience physical symptoms like nausea, stomach distress, heart burn, or loose stools, it can be **terrifying**! In addition to normal body sensations everyone experiences (stomach noises, bloating, headaches, loose stools, diarrhea, indigestion) as an anxiety sufferer, you also experience physical symptoms of anxiety (jitters, labored breathing, nausea, lightheadedness, out-of-body sensation, racing heart, tingling, hot flashes, etc.). These symptoms can build gradually or hit hard suddenly. They can be chronic or episodic. They can come out of nowhere or be triggered by something specific (an event, person, place, thought, or time of day.) They can even occur suddenly when you're feeling calm and happy. Just noticing you're feeling good can trigger anxiety.

As you feel physical symptoms you will also experience thoughts about these symptoms. **Start paying attention to your thoughts. What is your monster telling you when you begin to have symptoms of anxiety or any physical symptom?** Perhaps something like: *Oh no. What does this mean? Why is my stomach making noises? Am I nauseous? What if*

I get nauseous? I'm not going to eat now. Is there anything else wrong? Why does this keep happening? What if it gets worse? I'm not going out. I can't deal with this. Will this ever stop? Instead of reacting with these types of thoughts, I'm going to teach you how to respond in an effective manner.

Your ultimate goal is to **stop** nausea and the fear of vomiting but as I've stated previously, this is the **long-term goal**; it's what occurs when you reach the *Land of Freedom*. Since you must choose roads of discomfort and uncertainty to reach this destination, you are in essence choosing to feel anxious. Therefore, the short-term goal is not to stop anxiety. The short-term goal is to learn how to respond to your anxiety in a better way so it does not have power over you.

By choosing anxiety and responding to your anxiety in a clever way, you will reach the Land of Freedom.

Imagine driving your bus through the maze of life. It happens to be a wonderful day and you're relishing the scenery and feeling fabulous. You don't notice your anxiety monster tiptoe to the front of the bus. You glance in the rear-view mirror and see him directly behind you! ***BOOO!*** You instantly feel a shot of adrenaline. ***YIKES!*** You react by pushing your anxiety away. This is a normal reaction. When you feel anxiety there is an urgent desire to stop it, to push it away with urgent desperation. What you don't notice is that your opponent is sitting in a swing (the kind of swing you would find in a park).

What happens when you push a swing? If you said, *it comes back*, you would be right. And what happens when you push a swing harder? Yep. It comes back harder. This is also true for anxiety. When you try to push away anxiety with urgent desperation, it comes back with full force. When you push, struggle, and beg your symptoms to stop, they worsen.

Your best move is paradoxical -- to do what is unnatural -- to let anxiety sit there (in his swing) and not push it away. We treat symptoms differently from thoughts because the symptoms are real while the thoughts are distortions. Therefore, we hit the lies hard and accept the symptoms instead of fight them.

We must accept what we can't control. My niece was born with vision in only one eye. At age ten she had surgery which made the situation worse, resulting in double vision. She now sees double of EVERYTHING! This was difficult and scary. How do you hit a softball when you don't know which ball to aim at? How do you avoid bumping into people when you don't know which image is the real person? Her eyes were fooling her and she had to learn what was real and what was not. It took her a couple of years to fully accept her condition and figure out how to live with seeing double. She returned to playing softball. She graduated from school and went to college. She even DRIVES! The fake images try to fool her but she ignores them. She told me, *it doesn't bother me anymore. I just accept it.* **This is your task – accept what you can't control and not get fooled by the tricks of your mind.**

My niece has been able to live a full and happy life, not because her condition improved but because she was able to accept her condition and focus on living. Anxiety sufferers have an advantage because with acceptance, **symptoms of anxiety diminish significantly and fade away for long periods of time.** Anxiety is normal so expect symptoms periodically. When they return, welcome them back. Urgent desperation to make them stop only intensifies them.

Like a river, let the anxiety flow through you. If you try to stop a river's flow with a giant boulder, the water must work around it, which intensifies the force.

Instead of **reacting** to symptoms, with urgent desperation for them to cease, **respond** by doing the unimaginable – welcome the symptoms and ride them out: *This is exactly the feeling I need right now. Keep it coming. I got this.* This response is counterintuitive but if you have ever escaped from a Chinese finger trap, you understand how a counterintuitive approach is the only successful way out.

Watch this video: A paradoxical response to physical symptoms will reflect the beginning of a new relationship with anxiety. Responding with a different emotion other than panic **will take practice.**

Dr. Les Greenberg, professor of Psychology in Canada, talks about facing fears with a competing emotion: *People try to change emotion by not feeling it.... The best way to change an emotion is with another emotion.* He teaches patients to use anger in the face of fear: *The anger is going to change the fear.... It undoes the fear.... You can't run away and thrust forward at the same time... Very deep emotions are impenetrable to reason. You can't change them through reason. So the best way to change an emotion is with a new emotion.*

When your anxiety tries to mess with you, respond with toughness: *Is that all you got punk!* Or try an excited response: *Hip, hip hooray! You're back!* Your tone is more important than the words you use, so declare these statements with a feeling of toughness or excitement.

Perhaps a calm response is what you prefer: *I'm okay. I'm doing fine. I can ride this out.* Say it repeatedly in a **calm, slow tone of voice** as if you are trying to calm an anxious child. If you say it to yourself with a fast, frantic tone it will not help. Imagine a friend trying to calm you down but using a fast, frantic, and loud tone of voice, ***You're okay! You're fine! You'll be okay! You're fine! YOU'RE FINE. IT'S OK.*** This would agitate you more. Now imagine your friend saying the exact same words **very slowly and calmly.** Try it. The same words feel much different.

Say your response out loud when you can, otherwise think the response and imagine the tone. In an upcoming chapter I will discuss in depth how activating a competing emotion will help you move through anxiety more easily. Here are suggested responses for when you **feel** anxious, when you experience nausea or other physical symptoms:

Good. I'm winning. More points for me.
(You're winning because you're on the winning path)
Thanks for the adrenaline. I'm living my life.
(The goal is to live your life, not to be comfortable)
Welcome back. Stay as long as you like.
(Exaggerate the welcome to confuse your opponent)
Is that all you got? Bring it on. I can handle it.
(Like Ali, you are inviting the hit)
I need this because I want my freedom.
(You don't want it but you need this feeling to be free)
It's okay. I'm doing fine. I'm riding it out.
(Say it very calmly and slowly and keep repeating)
Hip, hip hooray! You're back.
(Acting with excitement shows you are not intimidated)
Just riding the wave. I can handle it.
(You can't stop the wave but you can surf it out and it's temporary)
False adrenaline alarm.
(Say it five times fast. It's a tongue twister!)

Hi sexy. I see you. - Then blow him a kiss.
(The ultimate disrespect)
Nice to feel you again. Can I get you a glass of lemonade?
(It's really urine)
This is exactly the feeling I need right now. Keep it coming.
(The opposite of trying to stop it)
Give me more nausea. It doesn't matter. I can handle it.
(The less you care about being nauseous, the more it will go away)
This is exactly the feeling I need to retrain my brain.
(You are literally rewiring your brain)

Instead of **reacting**, you will be **responding** to the weird and uncomfortable sensations that emerge in your body. Your monster will lie and tell you there's an emergency but it's just adrenaline or heartburn or acid reflux or diarrhea. It's your signal to use one of the above responses and keep driving down the correct road, in other words, keep living your life. (You can also do *Three-by-Three Relaxation Breathing*, which I will explain in the next chapter).

As I noted previously, think of the anxiety monster as similar to a middle school bully. He wants to get a reaction from you: to startle or embarass you, or make you cry. He expects to scare you. Instead, respond with something that will take him off guard and demoralize him, like John Stockton. He won't expect it. This is how you deal with nausea (and other symptoms) brought on by the bully.

Remember we treat symptoms differently from thoughts. The symptoms are real and something we must accept but the thoughts are lies and distortions (the nausea is real but the worry you will vomit is a lie). Therefore, we welcome the symptoms but **we hit the thoughts hard.**

Volleyball players are familiar with the concepts I am teaching. To change the direction of the ball they hit it hard, SPIKING it with such force, their opponent has difficulty returning it. When a person is new to volleyball, hitting the ball comes with excruciating pain. Although it stings, the coach pushes new players to keeping swinging hard, even though the hand and wrist have turned red. They put on their game face and hit one ball after the next. By the time the first practice is over, each new player has hit over 100 balls and they show up the next day for more. They accept the pain and eventually, within one to two weeks, the pain stops. **To get to that point, players must put on their game face, go on offense, and accept the pain.** Treating your emetophobia in a similar fashion, will reap the same results.

If you have ever lifted weights or worked out regularly you understand this concept. No pain. No gain. Athletes aren't just tolerating the pain, they want it. They view pain and burning muscles as a positive because this means their muscles are growing. The pain eventually subsides until they push themselves to the next level.

Beware of your monster's attempts to deflate you and your efforts:

You can't do it. You suck. Everyone thinks you're a loser. You're a failure and you always will be. You're such a disappointment to your family. You're weird and everyone knows. Just give up. Stop trying. You won't be able to do it. Don't even try. What's the point?

When you experience these types of thoughts, hit them hard like a volleyball spike and walk away: *F-off A-hole.* And then go about your business. Don't engage or you'll end up in the back of the bus.

Focus on where you have influence (your behavior and thoughts) and accept what you cannot control (your physical symptoms).

Since at this time you cannot stop anxiety, go one step beyond accepting it: **Welcome it! Demand it! And encourage more!** *This is exactly the feeling I need right now. Keep it coming.* The good news is, by using this paradoxical approach consistently, over time your anxiety will diminish significantly.

As you **encourage more** anxiety, be aware of your subconscious desire to **stop** anxiety. It's common for anxiety sufferers to respond. *Keep it coming, give me more*, with the real hope that their symptoms subside. In other words, they don't mean what they say. You must want anxiety so you can learn to tolerate it, not let it have power over you, and ride it out. New volleyball players are not trying to stop the pain of hitting the ball. They are learning to tolerate it. Stopping the anxiety is not the goal. Once you retrain your brain that you can handle the symptoms, you will stop fearing them, and then anxiety will reduce in frequency, intensity, and duration.

When your monster says: *This isn't working. You're still nauseous.* Respond by saying: *That's cool. Give me more. I can handle it. I'll be fine.* Monster retorts: *What if this doesn't work?* And you respond: *I'm not answering the question. Give me more anxiety. I can handle it.*

Accept the situation and feelings that already exist. Resisting reality will escalate your emotions. When you feel nauseous don't fight it and don't try to figure out why. Attempting to ascertain *Why is this happening* not only depletes your energy, it's unproductive and escalates your emotions. Why? Because now you're in the back of the bus talking to anxiety.

One of my emetophobe patients reacted with fear each time she experienced *diarrhea*. Upon further questioning we decided she was actually experiencing loose stools. She believed that if anxiety could cause loose stools, it could also cause her to vomit. Another emetophobe patient believed that her loose stools were due to food poisoning. Each were preoccupied with having loose bowel movements and believed the lie told by their anxiety monsters. I had to explain that loose stools are normal and one of the most common symptoms of anxiety. The goal is not to stop loose stools, rather, to stop them from triggering fear. This is what you will learn in chapters to come.

When your amygdala fires off you will feel physical sensations, followed by an instinctive and instantaneous impulse to stop your anxiety as quickly as possible. Asking for reassurance, escaping, avoiding, engaging in safety behaviors, or doing a compulsion is the quickest way to reduce your fear and, with a lot of practice, this process has been programmed into your brain. Thankfully, reprogramming your brain does not require surgery, just a lot of hard work. What you will learn in coming chapters is how to ride out the symptoms.

We are not trying to stop your automatic thoughts, physical sensations, and impulsive reactions. They come too fast. Your work begins immediately after. Your effort will be focused on what to do next. Whether you respond to your opponent out loud or in your head, **reply with passion and enthusiasm.** After experimenting with various responses, choose one or two that you like the best and use them each time. **Keep it simple.** It's too difficult to come up with different responses each time your monster threatens something scary or you experience a symptom. Repeating the same responses will prevent you from engaging.

STEPS TO FREEDOM

Responses to symptoms: Identify a few responses from the list above and add them to your *Winning Mindset Page* from the previous two chapters. Your photo will then include three types of responses: 1) Inviting uncertainty and distress, 2) responding to worrisome thoughts, and 3) responding to physical symptoms. Experiment with the responses and memorize the ones you prefer. You will have plenty of time to practice using them in the coming chapters.

Identify a theme song: When my UCLA football team charges into the Rose Bowl, the crowd rises up and claps to the Bruin fight song, pumping up themselves and the team. When Luke Skywalker fights Darth Vader, the audience hears John William's powerful instrumental reflecting the intensity of the battle and the drive for good to prevail over evil. In the video game, *Legend of Zelda*, gamers hear a moving theme song as they strive to save the princess and save Hyrule. Most protagonists in film battles, sporting events, and video games have theme songs. You could use one too. Music can enhance motivation, generate energy to defeat the bad guy (your Anxiety Monster) and help you move through anxious situations more easily. You can choose an instrumental piece: *Indiana Jones, Gladiator, Rocky, Star Wars*, or your own college fight song. If you prefer lyrics, how about Pat Benatar's "Hit Me with Your Best Shot" or Survivor's "Eye of the Tiger" from *Rocky*. (Can you tell I'm stuck in the last century?) Prefer songs in this century? "Fight Song" by Rachel Plattea, "Roar" by Katy Perry, "Unstoppable" by Sia, or "Titanium" by David Guetta. Once you identify your song, play it as much as you can so it gets stuck in your head and listen to it before facing a fear. Athletes use music to power through strenuous workouts and you can use it to help you push through exposures.

Watch my niece's video about living a happy life with double vision:

Chapter 15
3 by 3 Breathing, Mindfulness, and Relaxation Exercises

Think about something you do well. How did you become good at it? Perhaps you have a natural ability but more likely it was by learning, practicing, and doing it repeatedly. If you want to be a better chef, you cook. If you want to be a better batter, you bat. And if you want to be a relaxed person, you must practice relaxation. You've become an expert at worrying because of years of practice, perfecting the skill. In this chapter, I present three activities you can start today and do every day to help you become a calmer person.

Emetophobia is a disorder of the mind that is experienced physically in the body, and acted out behaviorally with avoidance, safety behaviors, and compulsions.

Take a look at the vicious cycle:

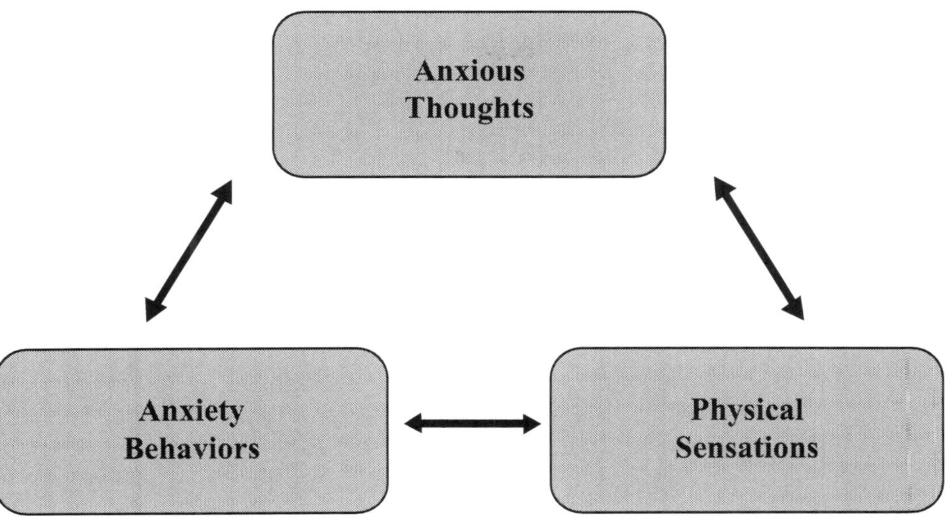

The arrows go both ways. A behavior can lead to a physical reaction which causes an anxious thought, and an anxious thought can cause a physical reaction which leads to an anxious behavior. The best places to break the cycle are at the weakest links: behaviors and, to a lesser degree, thoughts. It is at these points where you have the most influence. Although you have little immediate impact over physical symptoms, those symptoms will diminish significantly (and often disappear) as you change your behavior and refuse to believe the lies in your imagination.

You can also reduce physical symptoms of anxiety, including nausea, by other means as well: Three by Three Relaxation Breathing, Mindfulness, Guided Meditation (and Physical Exercise which I do not address in this book but is very important). By practicing these three therapeutic modalities on a daily basis (along with the other strategies outlined in this book) you will notice your symptoms reduce over time and for some, the reduction is immediate.

Three by Three Relaxation Breathing

Breathing is an automatic and instinctive process we seldom think about. Unlike reading, we do not have to be taught how to breathe. **Or do we?** Put one hand on your chest and the other on your stomach. Now inhale and observe what rises. Does your chest or stomach rise? Perhaps both. Try again if you are not sure.

In *The Anxiety and Phobia Workbook*, Edmund Bourne, PhD cites studies that have demonstrated that anxious people tend to breathe from their chest, while those who are more relaxed breathe more slowly from their abdomen. If you breathe from your chest and through your mouth, you might be creating an imbalance of oxygen and carbon dioxide in the bloodstream, which can result in symptoms such as rapid heartbeat, dizziness, and tingly sensations. Pay attention to your breathing the next time you are anxious. Perhaps you will notice your breathing accelerates or you're not breathing much at all.

Picture in your mind the breathing of a person having a panic attack. Their **chest** pumps **rapidly**. Their breathing is **loud**, as air rushes in and out of their **mouth**.

The opposite of panic breathing is *3 by 3 Relaxation Breathing*: It is **slow**, **silent**, with the **stomach** and through the **nose**. This might be difficult if you're a chest or mouth breather, but it is well worth the practice. **Many of my patients have told me that 3 by 3 Relaxation Breathing was a key element to beating their anxiety.**

Before I explain how to do 3 by 3 Breathing, use your muscles and push your stomach out, **without breathing**. Push it out. Then let it fall back. Try this a few times.

Try this now ***slowly***. Without breathing, push out your stomach slowly and then bring it in slowly. If you're a chest breather, your stomach muscles might be weak. Develop those muscles by practicing daily.

To learn how to do *3 by 3 Relaxation Breathing,* watch this video and follow along.

To reinforce what you learned in the video, read these instructions.

A. Inhale **slowly and silently** through your nose while using your muscles to **push your stomach out** (like a balloon inflating). Then exhale **slowly and silently** through your nose as your stomach falls. Your breathing should be silent. No sound. Try this several times. If you are a chest breather this will feel awkward and uncomfortable. Keep practicing. Some might feel lightheaded. Don't worry. Once you have it, move on to step B.

B. Repeat step A and add a **three-count pause** after you inhale. Inhale, pause for three and then exhale. I call it *3 by 3 Relaxation*

Breathing because of the three-count pause after you inhale and because you take three consecutive breaths. Practice this now, doing one set of three breaths, pausing for three counts after you inhale. Then move on to step C.

C. What your mind is doing is just as important as your breath. If you are breathing correctly but you are thinking about vomiting, the breathing will not relax you. When people are anxious, the various systems of the body tend to race: pulse, blood pressure, thoughts, breathing. As you slow down your breathing, you will also be slowing down your mind by focusing on a calming or motivational thought. **As you inhale, think the first half of the phrase very slowly. Pause for three. Then exhale with the second half of the phrase.** Any short phrase works:

1. *I can* (hold for 3) *relax.*
2. *Bring it* (hold for 3) *on.*
3. *Stay* (hold for 3) *strong.*
4. *Let go* (hold for 3) *let God.*
5. *Keep* (hold for 3) *going.*
6. *Live* (hold for 3) *life.*
7. *I can* (hold for 3) *handle it.*

Think the words as slowly as you can. Practice this now.

D. If you do not **practice *3 by 3 Relaxation Breathing***, it will not work when you need it. You must practice when you are not anxious for it to work when you are, otherwise you won't even remember to do it. **Practice five to ten times a day, no more than six breaths at a time – which is about one minute of breathing**. Start off by practicing alone with your eyes closed. Once you get the hang of it, practice with your eyes open in a variety of public locations (park, restaurant, car). Because the breathing is silent, no one will notice. Frequent practice will keep you calmer throughout the day, prepare you for sudden anxiety attacks, and over time, you will breathe correctly, from your abdomen, naturally, without thinking about it. One of the reasons smokers find smoking relaxing is because they are taking breaks from their day and they are breathing. You'll be doing the same without inhaling toxins. Since *3 by 3 Relaxation Breathing* is not in your daily repertoire, you won't remember to practice unless you **create reminders**.

Leave notes in various places and put reminders on your cell phone. Practicing six breaths, five to ten times a day, will be essential to your success.

E. **Use breathing as a tool for managing anxiety and stress.** When you practice *3 by 3 Relaxation Breathing* six breaths are sufficient. But when using it to deal with symptoms of anxiety, breathe for as long as necessary. It takes time for adrenaline to leave the body, so be patient. The higher your anxiety, the more the adrenaline, and the longer it will take to subside. Do not rush the process. Doing so will only escalate your symptoms. Since it is easier to reduce symptoms when they are mild, start breathing as soon as you begin to feel anxiety rather than waiting until your anxiety level is high.

F. **The correct mindset** is vital to your success, and managing expectations is key. View breathing as an umbrella in the rain. The umbrella is there to help you through the storm, not to stop it. Think of *3 by 3 Breathing* as a tool to help you through anxiety. **Accept your symptoms, declare you can handle them**, and then use *3 by 3 Relaxation Breathing* to contain the anxiety and prevent symptoms from escalating. **By accepting your symptoms and breathing, your anxiety will often diminish but if it doesn't, affirm that you will persevere regardless.** The more you practice breathing (in conjunction with the other strategies you are learning), the more effective it becomes.

Use *3 by 3 Breathing* a) before and during an exposure, b) when anxiety hits gradually or unexpectedly, c) after resisting a compulsion, and d) for practice.

Mindfulness

Mindfulness-Based Cognitive Therapy is a modified form of cognitive therapy that incorporates mindfulness practices such as meditation and breathing exercises. Using these tools, therapists teach clients how to break away from negative thought patterns that can cause a downward spiral. Mindfulness is an expanded awareness of your internal and external experience from a nonjudgmental and compassionate perspective. In this state, we are fully awake to the present moment, as opposed to hanging out in our heads—in the future or the past where anxiety resides.

When you are mindful, your thoughts are focused on what's unfolding around you. You observe everything taking place in the moment from a neutral perspective, without judgment. Instead of trying to understand your thoughts, you notice them without judgment and let them drift from your mind without attaching meaning to them.

You can use mindfulness when doing 3 *by 3 Relaxation Breathing.* Focus on your breath, noticing the sensations as you breathe. Notice your stomach rise and fall. Notice what you are hearing around you. If you notice an unpleasant sensation (lightheadedness) or your thoughts wonder, just notice them without labeling it as good or bad.

Studies show that mindfulness helps reduce anxiety. Stefan Hoffmann and his colleagues conducted a meta-analytic review. They identified 39 studies totaling 1,140 participants who received mindfulness-based therapy for a range of conditions, including cancer, generalized anxiety disorder, and other psychiatric conditions. They concluded that *mindfulness-based therapy was moderately effective for improving anxiety.*

Let's experiment with mindfulness. Find something small to eat—no more than what fits in the palm of your hand (trail mix, a piece of fruit, chocolate, three different kinds of crackers). In a moment, you will close your eyes and eat **mindfully**. You will notice, without judgment, what it **tastes** like on your tongue, what if **feels** like in your mouth, what you are **hearing**, your breath, as well as your thoughts. *I notice it tastes sweet. I notice the sound of the crunch.* Notice it all with compassion and without judgment. If your cell phone rings, rather than think, *that's so annoying*, just notice the ring and what it sounds like without judgment as you continue to eat: *I'm noticing my phone ringing.* If you feel nauseous, notice the feeling without a reaction: *I notice I'm feeling nauseous.* Then move your attention to other sensations. Try this exercise now.

Try to engage in two mindful activities a day (brushing your teeth, walking in your neighborhood, smiling at a stranger). When you wash dishes, notice with all of your senses the soap and sponge, the food being washed away, the running water, the sensation of the food in your belly, and the sounds around you. If you accidentally get wet or break a dish, notice everything with self-compassion and without judgment or self-criticism.

Self-compassion is a choice you choose to make even when you don't feel compassionate. This can be very challenging for many people. Anxiety sufferers are good at feeling shame and being self-critical. How often do you beat yourself up for having a negative thought, avoiding, or doing a compulsion? Having emetophobia was not your choice. It's time to accept yourself.

When you make a mistake, notice it without self-criticism. Imagine how you might respond to a child or a friend if they made a mistake or were displeased with themselves. Gently stroke your arms and notice what that feels like. Give yourself permission to feel what you feel and notice it without judgment. *I'm noticing I'm feeling anxious and that's ok.* Gently rub your arm and say out loud, *even though I have anxiety I love and accept myself.* This might bring up certain emotions and if it does, notice them mindfully without judgment. *I'm noticing I'm feeling sad. I'm noticing a tear roll down my cheek.* Try this exercise now. As you gently stroke your arms, say to yourself several times with your eyes closed, *even though I have anxiety, I love and accept myself.* Practicing mindfulness while doing simple activities will prepare you for challenging activities and exposures.

Guided Meditation

A guided meditation is a relaxation exercise. It is easier than actual meditation because you are guided by another person's calming voice. There are several types of relaxation exercises and all you have to do is listen and follow along. On the ***Stress Free*** download from QuietMindSolutions.com, three different calming voices narrate six relaxation exercises including Guided Imagery, Autogenic Relaxation, and Progressive Muscle Relaxation. Each combines soothing music with sounds of nature, and vary in length from seven to fifteen minutes. The tracks will relax your mind and body, and with practice, help you become the relaxed person you desire to be.

Before you listen, make sure your bladder is empty and your cell phone is off. Then sit in a comfy chair, take off your shoes, and wear headphones to block out distracting noises.

Your mindset, the type of guided meditation, your physical environment, and the voice that guides you, will be key factors in your success. While some people prefer a male voice, others prefer a female. A voice you find irritating, another person may love. This is also true for the type of exercise. *Stress Free* has six to choose from, giving you the opportunity to see what works best for you.

Most important is your mindset. Let relaxation build at its own pace. Don't try to force it. Be patient. Let it build gradually and if you don't feel relaxed, there's always tomorrow. Listening to one relaxation exercise each day will have a cumulative effect over time.

In addition to daily practice, listen to a relaxation exercise when you feel anxious. The key is to focus on listening and not on reducing your anxiety. **Don't try to make yourself relax.** Your anxiety will usually diminish if you DO NOT focus on trying to lower it. Just listen and follow along. Your mind will wander. That's normal. When it does, notice that it wandered away and then bring it back to what you are hearing.

While some people find guided meditations relaxing, others have difficulty. If you are in the latter group, listening daily without expectations is key. Over time your mind and body will figure it out and you will find these exercises relaxing.

Listen to one guided meditation each day to help you become the calm person you desire to be.

Slow Down

The common denominator of 3 by 3 Relaxation Breathing, Mindfulness, and Guided Meditation, is the slow pace each modality requires. Many anxiety sufferers engage in life at a rapid pace, moving quickly, multitasking, and walking fast. To reduce your overall stress level, it's important to train your body to slow down. Do you tend to walk, work, or move fast? If so, do an experiment and try walking 30 seconds **very slowly** to experience what that feels like. Try this now.

How did it feel? Uncomfortable? Many of my brisk walking patients feel uncomfortable walking slowly. If you move through life like an Olympic sprinter, retraining your body to move slowly will be vital to your success. You will not be able to fully reduce your overall anxiety level, unless you learn to move at a leisurely pace. This will take practice.

Patients have told me that it takes a month of daily practice for walking slowly to feel comfortable but once this is achieved, it reduces their overall anxiety level. Walking slowly will not be easy to remember so you will need to set reminders on your phone and place sticky notes on your walls and car. Practice one time a day and purposefully walk slow whenever you have the opportunity. If you are in a rush, move quickly; otherwise, take your time. Be mindful as you walk. Notice without judgment how you feel and notice everything around you.

STEPS TO FREEDOM

Walk slowly: Practice one time a day and any time you are walking.

3 by 3 Relaxation Breathing: Practice five to ten times a day.

Mindfulness Exercises: Do one a day. Suggestions: Tap various objects with a pencil. Plant a flower. Sit or walk outside.

Guided Meditation: Listen to one a day. Check out *Stress Free* on iTunes, Amazon or QuietMindSolutions.com. It's a great download. I should know. I created it.

Victory Journal: Record successes on a daily basis. You should have several successes every day. Since a success is any step forward, listening to a guided meditation, practicing mindfulness, walking slowly, and doing 3 by 3 Breathing are all successes. Write the date and list your victories:

May 12

Today I practiced breathing about 6x. I also practiced mindfulness while petting my dog and I listened to a guided meditation. I also noticed when my monster was telling me I might barf. I told him to F-off.

Chapter 16
Time to Soar: How to Do Exposures

You must go into your anxiety to get out. When I explained this to a pilot with OCD, he grasped this concept as he recalled learning how to fly. One day, as he flew above the clouds, his instructor praised his flying and then told him that he was now ready to fly in turbulence. As a new pilot he was terrified: *Turbulence! No! Not today.* ***NO!*** He did not want to fly in turbulence, but to be a pilot, this is exactly what he needed to do. His instructor had him fly into turbulence on purpose. This was the only way to overcome his fear and master the skill. When we fly on commercial jets, pilots avoid turbulence as much as possible, but pilot trainees fly in it as much as they can. As a trainee, my patient purposefully flew in parts of the sky that tended to be windy, flying towards the wind, and through it. Initially this was terrifying, but with practice he got used to it, and now he loves it! With enough repetition **what was once scary is now enjoyable.** (Don't worry, he doesn't fly commercial jets—yet!)

When you flee from an anxiety-provoking situation, you are training your brain to believe that the situation is dangerous. When you stay in an anxiety-provoking situation, you are training your brain to believe that it is not dangerous and you can handle it. Over time your brain chemistry changes, your brain is rewired, and what once elicited fear is no longer difficult. You achieve this goal by increasing your tolerance to anxiety.

People training to become firefighters go through something similar. How do you learn how to put out fires? The instructor lights a fire and then you put it out. He then lights a bigger fire and you extinguish that one. Then a different kind of fire is lit (an electrical fire, for example) and you put that out. To master the skill of extinguishing fires, fires must be lit first. This is exactly what you will be doing: purposefully creating anxiety for the sole purpose of practicing your responses and training your mind and body to not let it have power over you.

Whether it is lighting a fire, flying into turbulence, or inviting the hit like Ali, anxious thoughts, situations, and symptoms are **opportunities**. Whether you intentionally create anxiety or it happens spontaneously, these moments are your opportunities to strengthen your tolerance muscles by withstanding discomfort and uncertainty. Like I discussed in Chapter 1, you must look at your anxiety from a different perspective.

When your monster hits you with anxiety and you respond, ***Thanks for this opportunity to practice. This is exactly what I need right now,*** you have shifted your perspective enough to begin the process of moving through it. Reacting with, *Oh my God! I feel sick. I don't think I can do this*, intensifies the anxiety. You have to change your point of view and outsmart your opponent. The more you practice, the better you become at responding to anxious thoughts and feelings.

Purposefully create anxiety to strengthen your tolerance muscles.

Putting Out the Fire Exposure

This is a good exercise if you have practiced *3 by 3 Relaxation Breathing* and find it calming. Read these instructions twice and then give it a shot.

1) Put on your game face and say out loud, *Bring on the anxiety. I can handle it.*
2) Close your eyes and create anxiety by picturing something disturbing, like someone vomiting or you vomiting. Visualize it until you feel anxious.
3) When you begin to feel anxious, open your eyes and say out loud, *Thanks for this opportunity to practice. This is exactly what I need.*
4) Close your eyes and do *3 by 3 Relaxation Breathing* to bring your anxiety down.

The purpose of this exercise is to demonstrate how you can raise your anxiety with your mind and bring it down with your breath. Give it a try. Start with step one and go for it. *Bring on the anxiety! I can handle it!*

How did it go? Imagine that. You can create anxiety and bring it down. Doing this on a daily basis will help build confidence that you can manage your anxiety. This is not something you will **want** to do, but it is something that you **need** to do.

Thanks for this opportunity to practice.
This is exactly what I need right now.

Flying into Turbulence Exposure

Unlike the previous exercise, in this exercise you will be flying through your anxiety, rather than trying to extinguish it. Similar to my pilot who was not trying to stop the turbulence, **you will not be trying to stop your anxiety.** In this exposure you will be metaphorically driving down the road of discomfort and uncertainty by purposefully creating anxiety and learning that you can handle it. This exposure could be terrifying for some while others will find it easy.

You will be writing down and saying out loud certain words and phrases. Remember, exposures are challenges, experiments, and opportunities. What you write and read might be challenging. It's supposed to be. They are also experiments to discover if what you expect will happen actually occurs. Will you get nauseous? Will you vomit? And finally, exposures are also opportunities to build tolerance to discomfort and conquer your fears.

If you never face a fear, you never give your brain a chance to disconfirm the threat. As a result, your brain learns that what you are avoiding is actually dangerous, which causes your amygdala to send out danger signals every time you experience something similar.

Below is a list of triggering words and phrases. **Write** each word and phrase several times and then read them **out loud**. If you believe this exposure will not trigger anxiety, then do the exposure **while eating**. First, declare out loud, *Bring on the anxiety! I can handle it!* Go for it:

Vomit: ____

Puke: ____

Barf: ____

I'm excited to puke: ______________________________

I will vomit: ______________________________

When we feel threatened, our instinct is to protect ourselves. The problem occurs when people always seek to protect themselves in the face of discomfort and uncertainty. When you make that decision, you push away all threats and when discomfort returns, you push it away again. In his book "Stopping the Noise in Your Head," Dr. Reid Wilson writes, *When we act on our intentions to avoid the difficulties we need to face, we manufacture more fear, more symptoms, stronger symptoms, and greater urge to avoid. Eventually we end up in a never-ending cycle of feeling threatened and then trying to get rid of that feeling.*

Elevate your willingness to embrace doubt and distress while feeling afraid.

STEPS TO FREEDOM

Fire extinguishing exposure: Close your eyes and imagine something that will elicit anxiety and then use 3 by 3 Relaxation Breathing to bring your anxiety down. Do this three times in a row each day.

Flying into turbulence exposure: Continue to say the triggering words and phrases every day until they do not elicit much discomfort. Add your own triggering words and phrases. Once you can do this comfortably, walk outside your home and say the triggering words and phrases again. The purpose is to create discomfort and uncertainty and teach yourself you can handle it. Walk down the block say it again: *I might vomit.* Do this every day, as often as you can. Once this exposure does not elicit anxiety, increase the intensity. Every time you eat a snack or a meal say, *It's okay to puke. The fear of vomit is overrated.* Check out the Vomit Thesaurus at The Vomitorium:

Chapter 17
Cartoons, Magic, and Eating

Exposure Therapy is a specific form of Cognitive Behavioral Therapy and is the gold standard for treatment of many forms of anxiety. With exposure therapy you will rewire your anxious brain by exposing yourself to feared situations while learning to tolerate your anxious feelings. Practicing exposure therapy will help to *create new brain circuitry resulting in an absence of fear when faced with previously frightening stimuli* (Goldin et al., 2013). In other words, as you do Exposure Therapy and CBT on a daily basis, the neurocircuitry in your brain changes and you become less fearful.

When you expose yourself to a fearful stimuli, it's important to ride the wave of anxiety and tolerate the feelings until they decrease. If you flee from an anxiety-producing situation before your anxiety has reduced, you are teaching your brain that the situation is in fact dangerous. This will increase the likelihood that you feel anxious the next time you encounter the same situation. Escaping prevents you from developing the ability to handle anxiety and teaches you that the best way to respond to discomfort is to flee.

We can train our brain and change neurocircuitry with our behavior. Escaping an anxious situation teaches our brain that what we are fleeing from is dangerous and we can't handle it. Staying the course teaches our brain that it's not dangerous and we can survive. Be prepared to feel discomfort and stay with it until your anxiety reduces by at least 50%.

An exposure that produces no distress does nothing to help you overcome anxiety while an exposure that elicits too much distress might be overwhelming and discourage you from doing it again. With that said, there is value in doing very easy and very difficult exposures. An easy challenge that creates minimal anxiety is helpful in the beginning because it allows you to practice exposures correctly without pressure. Just as martial arts students punch and kick air, you will be practicing proper technique without your opponent in the room. Alternatively, the confidence people feel when they withstand a level-9 exposure is powerful. After surviving a high intensity exposure, moderate level ones often feel easier. As a general rule, attempt exposures that create a moderate level of distress, somewhere between a 4 and a 7.

I have created a hierarchy of exposures, based on my years of working with emetophobes, starting with the least distressing and moving up gradually. You have already faced the first exposure by saying *vomit, throw-up,* and *barf* out loud. Escalate the intensity of this exposure by saying triggering words and phrases outside your home and while eating until doing so no longer creates distress. The next set of exposures involves looking at pictures of cartoon characters puking. Like all exposures in this book, this will be easy for some and challenging for others. If you do not anticipate any distress, do the exposures regardless so you can rehearse the process – facing exposures with the proper mindset and response.

Challenging exposures are never something you **want** to do but they are what you **need** to do. You have no choice. Remember why are doing this. What is your motivation? Like a mourner going to a loved one's funeral, it's something you need to do. You need to do exposures to overcome your fear and live the life you desire and deserve. Like the young pilot flying in turbulence, the goal is to learn how to manage anxiety, not stop it. You will be purposefully driving your bus down the road of discomfort and uncertainty.

- On a scale of 1 to 10 what level of distress do you expect to have while you look at puking cartoon? _____

- What do you fear will happen when you look? _______________

  ____

Here are the steps:

1) Before you do the exposure, put on your game face and say out loud: ***Bring on the lies and the discomfort! I can handle it!***
2) Use your QR code reader to view a sketch of a cartoon character puking.
3) As you look at the cartoon, maintain your game face and say out loud in a **calm, assertive voice tone:**
   This is exactly what I need right now. I can handle it.

Try this now beginning with step one. Declare out loud: ***Bring on the lies and the discomfort! I can handle it!***

This is exactly what I need right now. I can handle it.

Congratulations! You went down the road of discomfort and uncertainty and you tolerated it. You're winning. Flying into turbulence is no fun, at first. It is not meant to be. This treatment won't make you feel better but it will help you be better.

What was your level of your distress on a scale of 1 to 10 when looking at the cartoon? Was it as bad as you thought it would be? Did what you fear would happen actually occur?

Frequency and duration are key components to all exposure work. You must do the exposure repeatedly and long enough to feel your distress subside. Look at the sketch for **one minute** while doing *3 by 3 Breathing*. Invite the anxiety – *Bring it on. I can handle it.* And as you breathe, think: *keep it coming - I got this.* Go for it:

Were you able to tolerate looking at the sketch for one minute? If not, try again. Don't give up. Whether it's learning how to play piano, roller blade, or speak a new language, frequent practice is vital to success. **The more you practice, the more quickly you overcome emetophobia and live the life you desire.** With that said it's time to repeat the exposure, this time looking at the same illustration for **two minutes**. If this exposure does not illicit any distress, look at it for two minutes while eating.

Bring on the lies and the discomfort! I can handle it!

Go for it:

Intensity, frequency, and duration are essential to all exposures. Make beating emetophobia a priority. Do exposures daily, multiple times a day, and eventually what was once disgusting and uncomfortable becomes easy. If an exposure in this book does not trigger any anxiety or disgust, practice doing the exposure properly and move on. Otherwise, repeat it until it elicits minimal anxiety and distress.

Like a magician, your opponent is very tricky. I should know – I used to do magic. If I could get my audience to focus closely in one direction, I could do something tricky without them knowing. Magicians call this misdirection. Your opponent does something similar. He gets you to focus on something unimportant (your worry or symptoms) instead of focusing on where your attention should be (your mindset, strategy, motivation, and the task at hand.) If anxiety can trick you into focusing on thoughts of becoming nauseous, the exposure will become more challenging.

Like an audience member watching a magic act, if you focus in the direction where the magician wants you to look, you will be fooled. Don't be fooled by your opponent when doing exposures. If you worry about the possibility of becoming nauseous, your current symptoms, or the difficulty of an upcoming exposure, your anxiety will increase making it more difficult to complete the exposure at hand. Don't focus where anxiety wants you to look. Focus on your strategy, tools, and motivation -- not on your symptoms or thoughts.

Stepping Forward with Doubt, Uncertainty, and Passion

Many of the exposures in this book will be challenging and you won't be certain you can handle them. Your anxiety monster will not allow you to be confident but you must step forward regardless, live your life, and do the exposures despite feeling doubt. There will always be doubt when taking the uncertain road. That's how you know you are headed in the correct direction.

Absolute certainty is an illusion. Last week I took a flight to Atlanta. Neither I, nor anyone else, could be absolutely certain the plane would land safely but I was *certain enough.* I did not seek reassurance by asking the pilot for his license or forcing him to take a breathalyzer test to make sure he was sober. I was certain enough and I wanted to visit my son. Sometimes you will be certain enough and other times you will expect disaster. The more exposures you do where the expected disaster does not occur, the more you will understand the deceit of your opponent.

When sports commentators announce a game, they often talk about the team that wins is the team that wants it more. This is always true for the underdog: the inferior team. They win because they want it more. How much do you want your freedom? Ignore your opponent's taunts, boasts, and lies, and focus on what you need to do. You must face your fear while ignoring the prediction that this is going to end badly.

If you are having trouble doing an exposure, it's possibly due to your negative beliefs. Strongly held beliefs will create resistance and slow your progress. Doing exposures daily will tear down your negative belief system and help you see that you can handle it.

If you are feeling uncomfortable and uncertain, you're doing it right.

Facing fears is exhausting and you will need to take breaks. If you do not want to tolerate discomfort and uncertainty, drive your bus down an easier road. You don't need to do exposures all day. Do them periodically. After an intense exposure you will need to relax. Try taking many small steps into anxiety's territory, every day, with small breaks in between and then eventually string together as many steps as you can. The goal is to always choose roads of discomfort and uncertainty. Whether it's video games, soccer, dancing, painting, math, or languages, the more time and effort you put into these endeavors, the faster you improve.

Avoidance of Eating

All emetophobes have various fears surrounding the consumption of food. As you have learned, the fear of vomiting or the fear of becoming nauseous results in avoidance and safety behaviors. Not only do these behaviors maintain the phobia, avoidance will intensify anxiety to extreme levels of terror. It's a vicious and dangerous cycle which often begins with a bodily sensation, often a normal sensation all people experience on a routine basis: bloating, loose stools, gas, heartburn, sensations of hunger, gurgle sounds in the stomach, menstrual cramps, etc.

With each sensation, your mind/monster fabricates great works of fiction. One of my patients periodically experienced heartburn and gas and these symptoms always triggered a fear that she would vomit. This of course never occurred but it did cause her to stop eating. In turn, this led to hunger pains which were misinterpreted as stomach upset— a sign she may vomit. This led to further food restriction. After all, if vomiting is imminent, it's better for the stomach to be empty. Or is it?

When the body does not consume food, it becomes compromised. It begins with decreased energy and gets worse from there. Within days the body begins to feed on itself, consuming carbs, fats, and then the protein parts of tissue. Metabolism slows, iron levels reduce, kidney functioning becomes impaired, and the immune system weakens. The heart, lungs, muscles, ovaries, and testes begin to shrink. Body temperature drops and becomes dysregulated, causing one to feel chilled. Your blood sugar levels rise causing damage to organs, nerves, and blood vessels. It becomes difficult to concentrate and with a lack of energy, people isolate in their bed.

As emetophobes isolate, they focus on their symptoms of starvation, misinterpret those symptoms, and engage for hours with the lies in their imagination. As their body deteriorates from lack of food, it is also being impacted by their adrenal glands pumping adrenaline and cortisol into their body, resulting in symptoms of anxiety and terror.

This vicious cycle must end!
*The **only** way to break the cycle is to **eat** despite your monster's lies.*
This begins with exposures.

Food Exposures

Begin by identifying your avoidant and safety behaviors concerning food. This might include not eating until dinner, eating tiny amounts of food, only consuming safe foods, or not eating before anything important. Step by step, one by one, confront these behaviors with exposures. Start small and do them daily. Begin with foods you once enjoyed. Take one bite. A couple hours later, take two more.

One of my patients had a diet comprised of only six foods and she rarely ate until after work and after she socialized with friends, which sometimes did not occur until 8 p.m. Her exposure work began with small steps. Despite her anxiety and reluctance, she agreed to eat one apple slice for breakfast and one piece of broccoli for lunch. She was afraid this small amount of food would cause anxiety, nausea, and vomiting. It turned out it did not and by the third day she was eating an entire apple for breakfast and several pieces of broccoli for lunch. Once she began to eat more, she felt better and less anxious.

Since all emetophobes have different avoidant and safety behaviors surrounding the consumption of food, it will be up to you to identify yours and tackle them one by one. These exposures are vital to your success and must be done on a daily basis. Your anxiety monster's goal is to make you miserable and if he can get you to avoid eating, he will succeed in trapping you in the Land of Misery and prevent you from finding freedom.

STEPS TO FREEDOM

Eating Exposures: Regardless of how you feel or what you fear, push yourself to consume more food and different foods throughout the day. Eliminate safety behaviors step by step. Begin by creating a list of food exposures and rank them from least difficult to most difficult, starting with foods you once enjoyed.

Cartoon Photo Exposures: It's time to look at more vomiting cartoons. You can access these photos in two ways:

1) Go to *QuietMindSolutions.com/Emetophobia.* Click on Photo Exposures and then Cartoon Exposures.

2) Use the CR Code Reader App or the camera on your phone to view the photos below.

Remember to do these steps for all exposures:

1) Invite anxiety before looking at each photo: ***Bring on the lies and the discomfort! I can handle it!***
2) As you look at the cartoon maintain your game face, do *3 by 3 Breathing,* or say out loud in a calm, assertive voice: ***This is exactly the feeling I need right now. I can handle it.***

Look at the cartoons repeatedly until they no longer distress you.

Running to the toilet | Little girl puking | Puking man

Leaning on toilet | Barfing on husband

Chapter 18
Changing Your Brain with Grit and Victories

The brain contains roughly 86 billion neurons, each of which is connected to and communicate with other neurons. Imagine billions of telephone wires connected to one another and crisscrossing throughout your brain. A few decades ago, it was thought that the brain was fixed beyond puberty and the only changes that took place were negative (memory loss, processing speed, etc.) but neuroscientists have since come to understand that our brain changes throughout our life in positive ways. The ability for the brain to reorganize itself by forming new neural connections is called neuroplasticity. But how does this happen?

Lara Boyd, PhD, Researcher, Faculty of Medicine at the University of British Columbia in Canada, spoke in a TEDx talk at her university about how the brain changes with different kinds of learning. *The best driver of neuroplastic change in your brain is your behavior. The problem is that the dose of practice that's required to learn new skills is very large.* She went on to say, *there is no neuroplasticity drug you can take. Nothing is more effective than practice at helping you learn and the bottom line is you have to do the work. Your brain is tremendously plastic and it's being shaped structurally and functionally by everything you do but also by everything that you don't do.*

To change the physical structure of the brain takes practice over time and is related to long-term memory. A person who practices typing on a keyboard for one hour can improve in that single session but will notice some regression when they return the next day. Dr. Boyd explains, *In the short-term your brain was able to increase the chemical signaling between your neurons but for some reason those changes did not induce the structural change that is necessary to support long-term memory.* What supports long-term memory and structural changes in the brain is **regular practice over time.**

After many months of typing practice, the neurocircuits of the brain change and a person can type somewhat accurately without thinking. The fingers seem to magically know where to go. But it's not magic. The new neuronal pathways that have been created in the brain with hours of practice are the reason a person can type quickly without looking at the keys. If a person stopped typing for three years and then tried to type, they would perform well because the neuronal connections still exist. However, if several years go by without practice, the neuronal pathways in the brain become weaker and so does the ability to type.

If the keys on the keyboard were rearranged, a person would have to relearn the new keyboard step by step, hour by hour, and with enough practice their brain would rewire itself and typing would eventually become effortless.

Repeated experiences can strengthen neuronal bonds. The more neurons fire together, the faster and stronger they wire together, producing larger and stronger neuronal networks. This means when you focus your attention on one thing, you grow it, and it becomes bigger and stronger, and over time, you begin to see the world through that particular neuronal network/lens. With all of the attention you have given to the fear of vomit, you have inadvertently strengthened this neuro-network, intensifying the phobia. Here's the good news:

Just as you have learned to be afraid of vomit, you can unlearn it. Because of neuroplasticity, you can rewire your brain not to be afraid.

Liam Mason, a clinical psychologist at King's College in London, used brain scans to identify changes in the brain after a six-month course of CBT. What he and his colleagues identified was the strengthening of the connections between two regions of the brain. The improvements occurred between the amygdala, the part of the brain that controls fear and emotion, and the frontal lobes, which are involved in thinking and reasoning. In his study published January 2017 in the journal, Translational Psychiatry, Mason stated, *What we are really excited about is that these stronger connections appear to be linked to long-term improvement in people's symptoms and recovery, even as much as eight years later.*

Patricia Ribeiro Porto and her research team conducted a systematic review of research investigating neurobiological changes related to CBT in anxiety disorders through neuroimaging techniques. Their study was published in the Journal of Neuropsychiatry and Clinical Neurosciences in 2009. Researchers used brain scans to examine how CBT modified neural circuits involved in regulating negative emotions. Researchers used fMRI and PET scans to investigate the neurobiological changes experienced in individuals treated for OCD, PTSD, specific phobia, panic disorder, and social phobia.

The researchers concluded that the studies *demonstrate that CBT is able to modify the dysfunctional neural activity related to anxiety disorders in the patients who responded to treatment.... Cognitive Behavioral Therapy modified the neural circuits involved in the regulation of negative emotions and fear extinction in judged treatment responders... neuroimaging studies revealed that CBT was able to change dysfunctions of the nervous system.*

As long as you are doing CBT properly and with enough frequency, you can change your brain. But the bottom line is you have to do the work.

Angela Duckworth, PhD, a psychologist at the University of Pennsylvania, conducted research on what makes people successful. She and her research team studied adults and children in various settings and set out to answer the question of who is successful and why. They studied the cadets at West Point Military Academy, the students at the National Spelling Bee, students in the Chicago public schools, new teachers working in tough neighborhoods, and salespeople in challenging sales positions.

In a Ted Talk in 2013 she explained her findings: *One characteristic emerged as a significant predictor of success. It wasn't social intelligence. It wasn't good looks or physical health, and it wasn't IQ. It was grit. Grit is passion and perseverance for very long-term goals. Grit is having stamina. Grit is sticking with your future, day in and day out, not just for the week, not just for the month but for years and working really hard to make that future a reality.*

She summed up her research in the Journal of Personality and Social Psychology: *Grit demonstrated incremental predictive validity of success measures over and beyond IQ and conscientiousness. Collectively, these findings suggest that the achievement of difficult goals entails not only talent but also the sustained and focused application of talent over time.* Needless to say, **grit is what you will need to rewire your brain and beat emetophobia!**

How many gritty little *Steps To Freedom* have you taken on a daily basis? If you had taken a functional MRI of your brain before starting this journey and then again after two years of working hard, every day, you would be able to see the changes in your brain. Your brain chemistry is actually changing and will continue to transform as you take more steps towards conquering emetophobia. But you don't need an fMRI to see your progress. As you drive your bus through the maze of life, occasionally look in your rear view mirror and see how far you have come. You can accomplish this by periodically rereading your Victory Journal.

Daily victories over your anxiety monster are the only way to rewire your brain and free yourself from anxiety. Writing those successes down is important for several reasons. A Victory Journal is a physical reminder of what you need to do each day **and** it reinforces what you learn. It allows you to focus on your growth and the positive aspects of your recovery, as well as remind you of how far you have come when you are experiencing one of those difficult days filled with frustration and hopelessness.

A victory is any step forward, big or small. A victory is any effort you make, even when you're feeling anxious, nauseous, and don't feel any immediate results. Writing your successes in a Victory Journal allows you to be creative and your entries do not need to be long. Here is an example of what it might look like:

Feb. *7*

I ate a bagel for breakfast. It was uncomfortable and my monster told me I would vomit but I told him "Fake news. I got this." I kept eating. I didn't get sick like I thought. It was really was fake news.

I looked at photos of cartoon characters puking. I worried I was going to vomit but I didn't. It wasn't that bad. After 10 minutes the pictures didn't bother me at all. I have to do exposures every day.

Felt better this morning because I ate breakfast.

I practiced 3 by 3 Breathing about six times today and did it once when I was anxious in the market. It calmed me. I was able to keep shopping.
I listened to one relaxation exercise from Stress Free. My mind wandered but it really relaxed me. I need to do this every day.

Feb. 8

I looked at the lower level photo exposures on the Quiet Mind website. I used the strategy and invited anxiety. I was very anxious but I welcomed it. I kept telling myself, "I'm excited to look at puke! Keep it coming!"

I practiced 3 by 3 breathing about 7 times today. Feels nice to take breaks.

There was one photo on the site I was avoiding because my anxiety monster told me I was going to be sick if I looked at it. I told him, "It's a beautiful day to do hard things." And of course he was wrong again. I didn't like it but I did not puke. He always lies. I will not let him win!!!!

I practiced mindfulness while I was moving my laundry from the washing machine into the dryer. When my wet shirt accidentally fell on the floor, I noticed it without judgment or frustration. Noticing things without judgment is pretty cool.

I reread the chapter on the brain. Knowing that I can change my brain with hard work is really awesome. Gotta have grit.

If you do a challenging exposure and do not feel much anxiety or nausea, this is a victory and should be recorded. Keep in mind, however, an absence of nausea or anxiety is not the type of achievement you are pursuing. The majority of time you **will** experience anxiety and nausea and your **response** is the victory that you will record. It's how you respond to the anxiety that matters:

Feb. 9

I went to a restaurant with my mom. I was very anxious. I could not eat food from the menu but I did bring a granola bar and ate it there, which is better than usual. Used my tools and strategy. I also ate a roll with butter. I was anxious the entire time but I did not vomit and it was definitely a victory. Periodically I thought to myself, "This is exactly the feeling I need right now. I can handle it." I did 3 by 3 breathing and practiced mindfulness one time. Tomorrow I will make myself go to another restaurant and this time I will eat more!

While eating I looked at photo exposures. I felt very uncomfortable but whatever. I can take it. I stayed with it even though I was anxious.

Once an exposure is no longer challenging and does not cause doubt, there's no need to record it as a success unless you have learned something from the experience. Keeping a Victory Journal will give you a sense of accomplishment, validate your growth, reinforce what you learn, and motivate you to create more victories. And remember...

If you do an exposure correctly and don't experience a reduction in discomfort or anxiety, it is still a victory!

To rewire your brain, you must do exposures every day. If by the end of the day you haven't recorded any, show some grit and do a planned exposure. Your anxiety monster will attempt to trick you into doing it later and if you listen, **later** often becomes **never**. Most of the time you will not feel up to doing exposures. Grit is what you will need when your mind is occupied with doubt and your body is churning with anxiety.

As exposures become easier, turn up the intensity and duration. Do it longer. Do it **without** safety behaviors. Put two exposures together: 1) Look at a photo of someone barfing 2) while you eat. Research has discovered that combining exposures is one of the best ways to reprogram your brain not to be afraid (Gillihan, Williams, Malcoun, Yadin, and Foa, 2012). After you put two together add a third: make yourself dizzy then look at barfing photos while eating.

While attempting to invent the light bulb, Thomas Edison failed thousands of times before succeeding. His grit led him to create several wonderful quotes:

I haven't failed -- I've just found 10,000 that won't work.

Many of life's failures are people who did not realize how close they were to success when they gave up.

Genius is one percent inspiration and ninety-nine percent perspiration.

STEPS TO FREEDOM

Eating exposures: Continue to eat in uncomfortable and uncertain situations and times of day. Step by step, let go of safety behaviors. Eating is vital to your success. Begin by taking a few bites of foods you enjoyed previously but stopped eating out of fear.

Victory Journal: Purposefully create multiple successes each day and record them in your journal. List spontaneous exposures as well as realizations.

Tally Counter: If you do not like to write or find it tedious, another option is counting your victories with a tally counter app. Download a tally counter app to your phone and as you go through your day give yourself a point with each victory. At the end of the day, write down the number of points you scored against your anxiety monster. Try to beat the score of the previous day.

Mindfulness: Do one activity mindfully each day. Be mindful as you move a heavy object, pet a dog or cat, or while you garden. Notice what you are hearing, seeing, touching. Notice what it feels like in different parts of your body. Notice your breathing. Notice it all without judgment. "My mind is noticing…"

Lower Level Photo Exposures: Go to ***QuietMindSolutions.com/Emetophobia*** or access the photos on your phone via the QR codes below. The Lower Level Photo Exposures are photos of real people in various stages of nausea and vomiting. **Vomit is not displayed in any of the photos.** Feel free to play your theme song before and during the exposure. Remember to invite anxiety before looking at each photo: ***Bring on the uncertainty, lies, and discomfort! I can handle it!***

As you look at the photos, maintain your game face and breathe or repeat out loud in a **calm, assertive voice:**

This is exactly the feeling I need right now. I can handle it.

Girl with hand on stomach

Woman holding in gag

Woman looking inside a barf bag

View of nausea from inside toilet

Holding mouth over toilet

Hand on stomach by toilet

Man with head in toilet

Man with head in toilet

Chapter 19
The Fear and Benefits of Medication

Medication and supplements for acid reflux, heartburn, nausea, IBS, and anxiety will play a vital role in your recovery but emetophobes are usually fearful to try because of the belief it could make them vomit. There is also a tendency to overuse anti-nausea medication (and other medications) as a preventative.

Remember, you are playing a mental game against a tricky opponent. **Before trying a new medicine or increasing the dose of your current medicine, anxiety will attempt to bait you into a conversation.** As you sit at the fork in the road, he will repeat horrific scenarios of vomiting and show you images of puking endlessly. He won't stop until he convinces you. Your imagination will ask you thought-provoking questions: What if the medication makes you nauseous? What if increasing the dose makes you vomit? What if you become addicted? What if stopping anti-nausea medication makes you sick? Consider these questions:

Is it possible that I'm depriving myself of a remedy?
What if medication eases my suffering?
What if it's not possible to conquer emetophobia and panic disorder

without medicine? What if medication does not make me vomit and actually helps me? What if I don't need anti-nausea medication?

Psychotropic Medication

Anti-anxiety medications (benzodiazepines) reduce anxiety quickly but have the potential to be addictive if used irresponsibly. They are commonly used as needed: when experiencing a panic attack or to reduce anxiety when flying. Many patients with panic disorder seldom take the benzodiazepine they are prescribed but keep it with them at all times. Just knowing they have it available enables them to face their fears more easily and provides a sense of security and comfort. Some psychiatrists prescribe a small dose once or twice a day to help patients cope, particularly if antidepressants fail to reduce anxiety.

Antidepressants are prescribed for depression or anxiety. They are taken on a daily basis and after four weeks many notice their overall level of anxiety has reduced and their symptoms of panic are not as intense. Patients begin to feel more secure as facing fears becomes easier. Although antidepressants may not work for everyone, most anxiety sufferers find success when they utilize cognitive behavioral therapy and an antidepressant simultaneously. Some people worry that it will change their personality. Street drugs do this but antidepressants do not.

It's important to understand that CBT alone is sometimes not enough and a prescription for an antidepressant becomes **essential** if you experience any of the following:

A. Your anxiety is so high your food intake is at an unhealthy level and you are underweight.
B. You are unable to do exposures properly and on a daily basis.
C. You are doing everything in this book properly and sufficiently for many months but you are not improving.

If you are experiencing any of the above, you are suffering needlessly and have regressed to a point where medication is imperative. Although you might be terrified due to the potential vomiting side effect, for legal reasons, all possible side effects are listed. Do not confuse possibility with probability. Just because a side effect is possible does not mean it's likely.

In all my years working with thousands of patients, I have never had a patient vomit from any medication. They have reported other side effects, but not vomiting.

Some people do not experience any side effects from antidepressants while others have minor ones they can tolerate. It's common to experience side effects for one to two weeks and once the body acclimates, the side effects disappear. This will require you to be patient and persistent. Start off on a small dose and work with your doctor to increase the dose as needed.

If you experience side effects that are persistent and intolerable, consult your doctor. Once you stop taking the antidepressant, the side effects will cease. Fortunately, there are many different antidepressants to try. You might hit the jackpot with the first medication but some patients suffer through trials of various ones until they find the right combination (sometimes two are needed). This can be an arduous process but worth it in the end.

Unfortunately, some people are not able tolerate any antidepressant and must rely solely on CBT. If this is you, do not give up hope. With a lot of hard work, dedication, and persistence, you can find the Land of Freedom. It just might take a bit longer.

Antidepressants are not addictive but once people feel the medication is helping, there is a reluctance to try to come off. Think of antidepressants as training wheels on a bike and Cognitive Behavioral Therapy and Exposure Therapy as pedaling. To learn how to ride a bike, children need training wheels and a lot of practice. If a child tries to ride without training wheels they fall and injure themselves, become afraid, and give up. They need the security of the training wheels (medication) to practice pedaling (therapy). If a child sits on a bike with training wheels (medication) but never pedals (therapy), they also won't learn to ride. To learn they need both the training wheels and pedaling just as most emetophobes need medication and CBT.

Ideally medication (the training wheels) will help reduce your symptoms and give you enough security so you can do the exposure work (pedaling) more effectively. Once you have minimal symptoms for eight to twelve months, you can slowly take off the training wheels (the medication) and continue to ride (live your life). As you reduce the medication slowly over several months, make sure you are doing exposures and the other self-help tools in this book on a regular basis.

Some people have tried a few antidepressants and have found them unhelpful. If you are not doing CBT at the same time, the medication will only have minimal impact. It's also possible the dose was not high enough or you were not on the correct medication. It's worth speaking with a psychiatrist and trying again.

I asked one of my former emetophobia patients about her medication experience:

I was very reluctant to try medicine. I felt I was strong enough on my own and I was also terrified it would make me sick. In fact, I was convinced antidepressants would make me throw up especially after I researched side effects online. This was a big mistake. As time went on it was very clear I need more help. I was suffering terribly. I took a big leap of faith and reached out to a psychiatrist and honestly, I'm so thankful I did.

When I first started there were some side effects. In reality, it was just my anxiety about the medication that was creating what I thought were side effects. But I stayed with it and after a few weeks I started to see a drastic change. That medication turned out to be a godsend. It gave me an appetite and I started sleeping regularly. And it did not make me throw up.

Getting me to the right dose and medication was a journey. It was a long process because I delayed doing what was recommended because of my fears of what might happen. Eventually I was prescribed a second antidepressant because the first one wasn't enough. I had to try different doses of that one. Now I'm on a combination of two antidepressants which thankfully work really well together.

For me the antidepressants make things easier. I was finally able to utilize Ken's tools and strategies when doing exposures. I could literally feel my brain changing because I was able to do the exposures correctly. I have taken huge leaps forward where as before I was taken smalls steps forward and several back. The medication has helped dramatically.

Gastrointestinal and Acid Reflux Medications

In addition to psychotropic medication, other prescription and over-the-counter medications will be an important part of your recovery. If you search online you will find many medications and supplements that help alleviate acid reflux, indigestion, heartburn, stomach discomfort, and IBS. I recommend speaking to a gastrointestinal doctor for their recommendations.

I've worked with many patients who suffer from various gastrointestinal diagnoses, all of which flare-up with stress. If you have emetophobia, those flare-ups usually trigger fears of vomiting which increase anxiety and impact behavior. The most common behavior is avoidance, particularly of eating. When people stop eating, it makes their gastrointestinal symptoms worse which causes more anxiety and food restriction, and ultimately malnutrition and weight loss. Sufferers also pay a huge psychological price in the form of hopelessness and depression.

This vicious downward spiral is easily avoidable. Weeks of suffering with anxiety, gastrointestinal distress, heartburn, hopelessness, and hunger could be prevented by taking medication when symptoms first appear. You can avoid weeks of suffering by ignoring your monster's lies and by taking the medication immediately upon experiencing symptoms.

Using Medication As A Safety Behavior

The overuse of anti-nausea medication is a safety behavior used to prevent nausea and anxiety. Do not take it in anticipation of becoming nauseous. Use the tools and strategies in this book to accept the discomfort and uncertainty. Take small gritty steps and free yourself from dependency by slowly reducing the frequency of use.

Don't Be Fooled by your Anxiety Monster

Emetophobes will usually experience nausea (or gastrointestinal distress) when trying **any** medication and then assume it's a side effect. Remember, nausea and stomach issues are symptoms of anxiety. It's likely that your emetophobia is creating so much fear, the nausea you are feeling is not a side effect but rather, a symptom. If you make this critical error and stop the medication, you will perpetuate your suffering and cause needless regression. Instead, commit to following through and take your medication daily without deliberation. Otherwise you will contemplate taking it every day, which will put you in the back of the bus, conversing with your opponent, resulting in more anxiety.

The nausea you feel after taking a medication is most likely due to anxiety. To beat emetophobia, you must choose the road of uncertainty and discomfort.

Remember, your anxiety monster's goal is to keep you miserable. Because he knows medication might help, he will lie to make sure you never try. He will repeatedly ask, *What if it makes you sick?* As long as your mind requires certainty, you will never take a risk. Consider this question: *What if the medicine doesn't make you sick and it actually helps you?* That's a more productive question.

Tolerate the uncertainty and start off with a very small dose. If you become nauseous or have an upset stomach, this is likely due to your anxiety.

If you have not tried anti-nausea and anti-vomit medications, they can play a role in helping you take brave steps. If this is what you need to get on a cruise ship or airplane, go for it. You are living your life and that's what is most important. Be aware, however, these medications can be psychologically addictive when used on a daily basis. If you are dependent, slowly decrease your dependency by reducing the dose and changing the times you take the medicine. For example, if you take an anti-nausea medication thirty minutes before every meal, begin taking it 15 minutes prior to eating. After a week, take it as you start your meal and then eventually after eating. Gradually extend the time until you realize you don't need it.

STEPS TO FREEDOM

Photo Exposures: Continue to expose yourself on a daily basis to all Lower Level Photo and Cartoon Exposures at *QuietMindSolutions.com/Emetophobia* or through your QR Code Reader App. Move on to the next chapter once all of the Lower Level and Cartoon photo exposures cause minimal distress or anxiety.

Eating Exposures: Continue to eat in uncomfortable and uncertain situations. Try new foods. Increase your speed. Eat more than usual.

Mindfulness Exposure: Practice mindfulness with something that is unpleasant or uncomfortable. Identify a food or beverage that you usually avoid but not something you find disgusting. Something you can tolerate. Perhaps a raisin, avocado, beer, mushroom, or mayonnaise. I worked with a patient who liked bananas and peanut butter but did not like them together. Identify two foods you like but would never put together (a carrot dipped in whip cream). Although you might be resistant to taking a bite and fearful you might puke, this is a great opportunity to practice tolerating something that is uncomfortable and uncertain. Your monster is predicting you will barf. Will you? This exercise will help teach you how to stay in the present and accept the discomfort and uncertainty, instead of fleeing. You're driving the bus so you decide the size of the bite. Without judgment, notice what it tastes and feels like. *I notice it tastes bitter. I notice the texture is rubbery.* And when anxiety tells you, *Gross. Spit it out. You're gonna puke,* respond, ***I'm noticing my anxiety wants me to spit it out and I'm noticing my determination to swallow it.*** Put on your *game face* and try this unpleasant food exposure/mindfulness exercise.

Chapter 20
Combating Resistance

How has the homework been going (3 by 3 Breathing, Victory Journal, Exposures, Mindfulness, Relaxation Exercises)? This is what I ask my patients. I assume they do the homework because they want to get better but I also assume they don't. Life can be busy with many demands but the most notorious explanations are anxiety and hopelessness, the twin pillars of resistance.

If you are not putting in adequate time and effort on a daily basis, try to identify the nature of your resistance. Perhaps there is a belief that it's pointless to do the work because it won't help. Various attempts over the years with little results certainly leaves anxiety sufferers believing that it's impossible to get better. The work in this book is also difficult. It's easier and more enjoyable to engage in the various forms of entertainment on your laptop or television than to do the exercises in this manual. If being a hard worker is not a character trait you possess, taking steps forward will be challenging. But even if you do have a strong work ethic and you do believe you can get better, resistance to doing exposures is always present due to a fear of becoming nauseous, vomiting, or having a panic attack.

Try to identify other specific worries. I treated a patient who was worried that if she overcame emetophobia, she would be less fearful of throwing up. You would think that this is exactly the point of treatment but the monster in her imagination was cunning. My patient thought that if she stopped worrying about vomiting, she would stop trying to prevent it, which meant it would be more likely to happen. The deceit of her anxiety monster did not end there. It also warned that her personality might change once she no longer suffered with anxiety. Not knowing who she would become if she conquered emetophobia was terrifying. The more she was lured to the back of the bus to consider these issues, the more anxious she became, which prevented her from doing what was necessary to win her freedom. With the help of therapy and medication, she eventually learned that getting better and letting her guard down did not result in vomiting or a change in her personality.

Your anxiety monster's strategy is to convince you to spend most of your energy worrying about vomiting and trying to prevent it, instead of making efforts to overcome this phobia: *If you do this exposure you will get anxious and nauseous. Do you feel sick? How are you going to make sure you don't puke today? The more exposures you do, the less control you'll have. It's not a good day to do exposures. Your day has been hard enough. It's raining. You didn't sleep. It's that time of the month. Do the exposure tomorrow. You don't feel well.* If you only do exposures on days you feel good, you will never achieve the freedom you desire.

Doing exposures won't make you **feel** better
but they will make you **be** better.

By doing the exposures in this book, you will reach a point where vomiting and vomit are no longer vile or terrifying and the focus of your life will be on living instead of worrying. You are in the beginning stage of retraining your brain.

Be patient and persistent. Rewiring the brain takes time and effort.

Look at this process as similar to other endeavors that take time and work, like learning a new language. It can take years to train the brain to speak fluently, especially if you are learning in a classroom. The quickest way to learn a language is to live amongst the people that speak it and to force yourself to listen and talk. The more you expose yourself to the language, the faster you pick it up. If you do exposures (and the other work in this book) for ten minutes a day, you will not progress as quickly as someone who is working two hours a day.

Find Your Motivation and Focus on It

Remind yourself why it's important to push hard. Read your Statement of Determination and envision the outcome you desire. Focus on that outcome. **Make this process mandatory.** It is not a choice. It is something you MUST do. You must beat anxiety and reclaim your life. Be determined. This is the time. This is **your** time! Making this a mandatory endeavor is the choice that you've chosen to make because this is what is important to you. It is now your number-one priority. You will turn your life around one step at a time. Nothing can stop you. You will fight for your life and prevail. **Ridding yourself of emetophobia and panic is your only option.** And when you finally do, you can live the joyful, stress-free life you desire.

…. It was Halloween night. My seven-year-old son peered across the street at the scary house and monsters with loud chain saws. *I don't want to get candy there.* I empathized with his fear and reassured him that we would skip that house. Trick-or-treating on Louise Ave. was always a blast. The street drew a huge crowd as many of the houses got into the spirit of the holiday. We walked to the end of the long block and crossed the street. As we made our way back up the hill, my son repeated several times, *I'm not going to the house with the chainsaws.* I told him that they give out huge candy bars and if he changed his mind, I would hold his hand. He was not having it.

The mob outside the front yard buzzed with excitement as a stream of kids and teens made their way through the haunted front yard. Suddenly my son grabbed my arms, wrapped them around his body, and was ready to face his fear with a plan. He took a deep breath and stepped into the haunted front yard. As I walked behind him, holding him tight, he yelled at the first monster, *I'm not afraid of you!* Each time a monster growled at him he growled back or responded with something funny, *You're ugly and so is your mom! Don't mess with me punk. You smell. Take a shower.* Without any prompting from me, he went on offense. He did not let the scary creatures or the disgusting, bloody body parts on the lawn deter him from getting the giant chocolate bar at the end. As we walked through the yard, he become tougher and braver and by the time we got back to the sidewalk, he radiated with pride, excitement, and a huge smile. He earned that big candy bar. He never would have realized he could do it, without trying.

Now that's how to play the game!
That's how you beat your anxiety monster!

Break Down Exposures

If an exposure feels too frightening or difficult, instead of giving up, find a way to make it happen. Break the exposure down into smaller steps. If you can't look at a disgusting photo for thirty seconds, look at it for five. Then work hard to push it to thirty and beyond. If eating a meal and driving across town causes too much anticipatory anxiety, begin with what you can do. Take one bite and walk to your mailbox. The next day take two bites and walk ten steps further. Do something and repeat that something until you can take the next step forward.

To get **out** of your anxiety, you must first go **in**….

Use All the Tools in this Book

To get out of the haunted front yard, my son first had to go in. Intuitively, at that moment, he used **tools** he was not even aware of. He had motivation and a goal (the huge candy bar). He took a deep breath and broke down the exposure into a manageable step (he grabbed and wrapped my arms around him instead of entering alone). He walked into the monster's territory with doubt and an offensive mindset, responding to each monster with toughness and humor. And he kept moving forward with a determination to complete the task.

Learning and using the **tools** in this book are vital to your success. Tools make all jobs easier but if you don't have experience with a specific tool, it's challenging initially. Say for instance, you've never used a hammer. If you were given a hammer and a nail and asked to hang a picture on a wall, you would have three options: 1) Try your best to hammer the nail into the wall. 2) Not do the job. 3) Try to put the nail into the wall without using the hammer. Tools work when used properly and with enough practice. Avoiding or not using tools, makes life hard and painful. Whether it's hanging a picture or conquering emetophobia, use the tools I am providing. If you don't, do not expect to free yourself from anxiety. Like building a house, using one tool is not sufficient. You will need to use all of them to build your new life.

Keep in mind there is a learning curve to using tools. My son who walked through the haunted front yard as a child, went off to college this year and got a work-study job in the set design department creating massive theatrical sets with heavy machinery, unfamiliar tools, and precise measuring. This was difficult and scary. After a few weeks he called and said he wanted to find a different job because he couldn't do it. I asked him if he thought he would get better with more time and practice. *No! Absolutely not.* His mind was in a fearful, futile place and he did not believe the job would get easier. Yet, he showed up each shift and with enough practice, his skill level improved and by the middle of the year he was more comfortable using the tools. With enough practice, the tools in this book will also become comfortable.

As I stated previously, if you are so anxious you cannot show up to do exposures or use the tools correctly or sufficiently, then make an appointment with a psychiatrist to discuss how medication can relieve your suffering. Medication is a valuable tool and if it's going to help to stop mental and physical anguish, then it is worth a try.

Your Family and Friends Can Help but it's Up to You

Family members and friends can encourage you to do the work but do not put them in the position of being a nagging parent. You must hold yourself accountable. If a spouse is forced to pester you to eat, that will take its toll on the marriage. It's up to **you** to push yourself. Loved ones can play the role of cheerleader, support, and reminder. They can go with you to places you are too afraid to go alone and they can remind you of strategies and tools you forget. Texting a loved one when you complete an exposure is a great way to celebrate the victory, generate momentum, and demonstrate your effort. It's important that your loved ones know you are working hard.

It's also important for them to understand that you are the one in charge of your recovery. You are driving the bus. You decide what exposures to do, how often, and the duration. When anxiety sufferers feel pressure from others, they develop mistrust and fear of the person applying pressure. This usually results in more avoidance. You must work together as a team, with the emetophobe as the team captain. My son and I walked through the haunted front yard together, but he was the one who decided to face his fear. He was in charge. I was his support.

Beating Anxiety to the Punch

With anticipation of exposures comes high level of anticipatory anxiety and symptoms. The longer you put off doing an exposure, the longer the anticipation, and the more severe the symptoms. This is why it's advantageous to do exposures sooner rather than later. The more you procrastinate, the more opportunities your opponent has to engage you in a conversation and convince you not to do it. This applies to anything you put off, including getting out of bed.

Some of my emetophobe patients feel the most anxiety in the morning while others feel it build in the late afternoon. Once a pattern develops, it's easy to dread these times of day. To overcome the anxiety associated with morning or evening anxiety, behavioral change is necessary to break the pattern and this includes beating anxiety to the punch.

Those who suffer with morning anxiety usually linger in bed for what they think is a logical reason: *If I stay in bed longer, I can put off facing my anxiety-filled day.* Have you ever noticed that the longer you stay in bed, the more anxiety builds? This is because you are not alone. Your monster is in bed with you, whispering scary questions and threats in your ear.

Usually people with morning anxiety do a lot of thinking as they lay in bed half asleep. When you are in this state of consciousness, you are more susceptible to believing the lies in your imagination. Beliefs become exaggerated, amplified, and feel more real when you are not fully awake (similar to how dreams feel real). It's also difficult to use tools properly when you are semi asleep.

The best remedy is to beat anxiety to the punch and get out of bed immediately before anxiety escalates. Your monster will try to entice you to stay in bed. *You're so tired. It's warm here. You don't want to get out of bed. It's going to be another terrible day. Stay with me just a little longer.* **Ignore the deception and get out of bed as soon as you wake up.**

Start your day before anxiety begins to build. Most sufferers of emetophobia and panic disorder delay leaving the house. If you usually feel anxious in the morning, you must change your morning routine and do the opposite of what anxiety demands. Get out of bed immediately, make your bed, and take a short walk in the neighborhood (rain or shine). You will be pleasantly surprised how good this makes you feel. Mindfully walk through your neighborhood, observing everything you see, listening for all sounds, touching surfaces you don't normally touch, and smelling flowers and plants you usually pass without noticing. Bring a small snack and enjoy it along the way. Engage all five of your senses and disengage from the lies of your imagination. Your monster will tell you not to do this and come up with all sorts of scary predictions. Refuse to believe the lies. Remember, following his advice is what got you in this situation.

Once you return home from your mindful walk, you'll feel the pride of accomplishing three tasks: making your bed, taking a walk, and eating. Keep the momentum going and continue on with your day. Do not go back to bed or sit on the couch. Instead, eat breakfast. Take your medication. Do an exposure. Exercise. Shower. Start working. Do whatever anxiety tells you not to do. Although you will feel anxious initially, taking charge of your morning (and your monster) will give you energy and a sense of accomplishment.

If you experience anxiety primarily in the later afternoon or evening, the same strategy applies. You must beat your anxiety to the punch and change your routine. A current emetophobe patient shared how her evening anxiety has subsided since following this strategy. Instead of bracing for anxiety each afternoon by staying inside and playing it safe, she now eats something small and leaves her house (walks, drives, reads in a café). Although she was nervous to change her routine, she found it very liberating. After forcing yourself daily into a new routine, within a few months it will feel natural and anxiety will no longer be associated with a time of day.

STEPS TO FREEDOM

Eating Exposures: Continue to eliminate your avoidant and safe behaviors about food and eating. Purposefully expose yourself to the same fear multiple times a day until it no longer makes you afraid. Start small and build from there.

Write a Letter to Yourself: The purpose of the letter is to motivate you. First review Chapter 11, then write the letter and mail it to your home. That's right – snail mail. In the letter, write about the reasons you need to work hard even if you don't believe you will succeed. The tone should be supportive, encouraging, and understanding but also firm, insisting that you push hard every day. Identify how you might procrastinate using various excuses. Write about what emetophobia has taken from you, what you value, and the life you desire. Remind yourself of other hard things you've accomplished. Finally, write about standing up to the bully and refusing to believe his lies. Write the letter in any way you desire with your personality and creativity. Along with the letter, you can include photos of the people who are rooting for you, places you want to travel, and goals you want to accomplish. Mail it to yourself and then read it out loud when you receive it. To automate motivation, read it daily.

Chapter 21
Walking Into Anxiety's Territory

Mantras have been utilized around the world for thousands of years. They serve to remind us of what is important, inspire us to take action, and affirm the way we want to live our life. *I will not exaggerate problems and I will not underestimate my abilities* is an example of a mantra. This mantra serves to offset the myriad of amplified worries and the belief of incapability. For a mantra to be affective, it must be believable and be recounted many times a day. Reading a mantra five times a day will have minimal impact. This is not enough to outweigh the deluge of negative thoughts you have had for years.

First identify a problem and then create a mantra. A common problem is avoiding exposures due to worries: *This is gonna go badly. What if you vomit? You're gonna panic. You can't handle it. Do it later.* If you take your opponent's words seriously, you will either cautiously proceed with dread looking for a way out or back away entirely. Since doing exposures is key to your success, you will need a mantra to motivate you to face your fears. Here are a few examples:

I'm excited to be anxious because I'm excited to be free.

It's a beautiful day to do hard things.
Challenging exposure will rewire my brain and give me freedom.

Repeat your mantra out loud at least 10 to 20 times a day to automate the message and to counteract the years of lies. Post the mantra in several places in your home and car and make it the screensaver on your phone. Write it, read it, and say it out loud all day long.

Many of my patients notice that exposures are seldom as horrific as they imagine. One patient created the mantra, *it's never as bad as I think*, to remind himself that his anticipatory anxiety is worse than the exposure itself. He repeated it throughout the day which helped him when he faced a fear. Another patient, who worried she would vomit if she relaxed, created this mantra: *it's okay to relax. I'm safe.* It took a few months for her mind and body to fully accept this statement. Here's a few more mantras to choose from:

Embrace uncertainty, rewire my brain, and live a happy life.
It's just anxiety. Keep moving forward.
The goal is to live my life -- not to be comfortable.
Vomiting is not that bad. I'll survive.
Do the opposite of what anxiety demands.
One gritty step at a time. Keep going.
Reject the lies, rewire my brain, end the fear.

In my practice in Los Angeles I have the pleasure of working with people who suffer with all sorts of symptoms including patients who experience racing heart, chest pressure, and irregular heartbeat. Instead of the fear of vomiting, these patients fear having a heart attack. One such college student who had countless EKGs, echocardiograms, and other medical tests (all of which turned out negative) slowly realized that what he had been believing for so long was a huge lie. When his heart beat fast he was not having a heart attack. It was just adrenaline.

The first step in changing his belief was to create a mantra. *My thoughts are lies. Don't give them power.* Recounting this mantra throughout the day, helped him each time his heart raced. This was the first step, but to fully grasp that his thoughts were false, he had to back up his mantra with action, by calling his monster's bluff. When his heart raced, he declared out loud, *Race faster. Give me a heart attack. Kill me now. I dare you.* Initially he was terrified to say this while his heart was racing, but to prove to himself that his thoughts were powerless, he took a leap of faith. When he did not suffer the consequence he feared (a heart attack), he felt empowered, and his thoughts diminished in power over time. He did not stop there, however. He pushed himself further.

Just as physical trainers push their clients to tolerate more weight, more reps, and increased duration, you will be pushing yourself to tolerate higher levels of discomfort and uncertainty. My patient pushed himself too. When his heart raced, he declared, *give me a heart attack* and then purposefully made it race more by doing push-ups or sit-ups. Prior to treatment he would sit down, breathe, and try to slow his heart beat, which reinforced the false belief. Using a paradoxical strategy completely extinguished his fear of heart attacks as well as his racing heart and chest pressure. Creating the mantra, *my thoughts are lies. Don't give them power*, was the first step.

Taking Action and Prove Your Thoughts Have No Power

Once you begin using a mantra, in this case, *my thoughts are lies. Don't give them power*, you must back it up by taking action. Take a leap of faith, stand up to the bully, and prove that thoughts are powerless by performing the following experiment: Read each thought below one at a time and then rate your level of discomfort on a scale of 1 to 10. You will then wait and see if any of them come true. Read the following **out loud**:

Today I will trip, fall, and severely injure myself. _____
There will be a major earthquake in the next five minutes. _____
I hope someone I love is hit by a car today. _____
I will learn that a friend was diagnosed with cancer. _____
I want to get held up at gunpoint today. _____
I want to throw up. Make it happen right now. _____
In the next five minutes I will vomit. _____
Give me a panic attack right now. I want to panic. _____

Will reciting these statements out loud make them happen? This is an experiment. You will learn the outcome soon enough. Most anxiety sufferers give their thoughts too much power and consequently fear them. With each anxious thought taken seriously, adrenaline secretes, resulting in more symptoms of anxiety. Let's break that cycle by turning this experiment into an exposure. By repeatedly expressing uncomfortable thoughts out loud, you can desensitize to those thoughts and diminish their power. Read out loud repeatedly any of the above statements you rated higher than a four. Continue reading until it reduces by fifty percent. Go for it!

Once you are able to say scary statements out loud without triggering anxiety, take the next step and repeat them out loud when you experience a symptom. For example, when you feel nauseous, boldly state, *I want to vomit. Make it happen. I dare you*. When your heart races, declare out loud, *I want to panic. Give me a panic attack. I dare you.* And then turn away and focus on something else. Since we cannot control our physical symptoms, I am teaching you to invite those symptoms to build tolerance, learn that you can handle it, and rewire your anxious brain. Walk into anxiety's territory with your game face and, if possible, a sense of calm by using *Three by Three Relaxation Breathing*.

When facing a fear, it's common to brace for the hit by tensing up and holding your breath. Before doing an exposure, do one set of *Three by Three Relaxation Breathing* and **slowly** think the phrase, *Wet… Noodle.* As you inhale think *Weeeeeeet* and as you exhale think *Noooooooodle.* Allow your body to become a wet noodle as you breathe. Then open your eyes, put on your game face, and complete the exposure without bracing for the hit.

Do not breathe in an attempt to stop your anxiety. Breathe to contain it. As I have noted, consider breathing to be like an umbrella in the rain; use it to help you get through your symptoms. If you are able to reduce those symptoms with a few breaths prior to facing an exposure, great, but sometimes this is not possible. If you can't, that's okay. Instead, go completely on offense: *Bring it on asshole! I can handle it!*

Double Dare Exposure

Let's combine two exposures into one and integrate *Three by Three Relaxation Breathing.* Take three breaths using the phrase wet… noodle. Then look at the Low Level photo below (with your QR code reader) and declare out loud, ***I want to throw up. Make it happen right now.*** Even if you don't believe these words, say them anyway. Repeat them as you look at the photo for 30 seconds. Put on your game face, take a few breaths,

How did it go? Did you vomit? Was it as bad as you thought it would be? Have you noticed that some exposures are not as horrific as you expect? Periodically they are, and that's when you stay with it and keep going. When intensity is high, duration and frequency is key. Push through to the other side.

become a wet noodle, and go for it!

Trifecta Exposure

In this exposure you will face three fears at once:

1) Look at the same Low Level Photo.
2) Say out loud, *I want to vomit. Make it happen right now.*
3) Do this exposure outside your home.

Initially start close to your home and then walk further away, eventually driving to various locations (park, elevator, mall). Try this exposure now, doing one set of *Three by Three Relaxation Breathing* first.

____

It's time to put on your game face and read the next Trifecta exposure. When you read it, don't wince. Maintain your game face even if it scares you. First take a breath: *weeeet - nooooodle.*

1) Look at different Low Level Photo.
2) Say out loud, *I want to puke. Make it happen right now.*
3) While eating a snack.

Anxiety will claim that if you do this exposure you will puke or won't be able to handle it. Refuse to believe this or any other lie. It's just anticipatory anxiety; your opponent trying to prevent you from choosing the winning road and finding the *Land of Freedom*. He knows with every step into his territory you get closer to happiness.

Stand up to the bully and declare out loud, ***if this is what I have to do, I'll handle it.*** Before doing the exposure try to become a wet noodle with *Three by Three Relaxation Breathing*. Then, as you eat, look at the photo and think, *I want to vomit. Make it happen.* If you feel anxious, think to yourself, ***this is exactly the feeling I need. I'm excited because I'm rewiring my brain and winning my freedom.***

Try this exposure now with a small snack: a few crackers, trail mix, a piece of fruit, or whatever you want. Breathe, invite anxiety, and then do the exposure:

Go for it:

How did it go? Was it as bad as you imagined? You are purposefully driving your bus down roads of discomfort and uncertainty for the sole purpose of beating your anxiety monster and overcoming emetophobia. You won't **want** to do exposures but you NEED to do them to achieve the life you desire.

As with all the exposures in this book, if the exposure is easy and does not elicit anxiety or fear, do it once and keep reading. Otherwise, repeat the exposure daily until your level of discomfort and anxiety reduces fifty percent. Then move on to the next level/exposure, in this case, full meals with higher level photos and videos.

Manage Expectations: Perfection, Disaster, Preventing Anxiety

Some exposures will be tougher than others and there will be times you feel like you failed. This is part of the process. Do not put pressure on yourself to do exposures perfectly. Let go of those high expectations. Focus on the task immediately in front of you and become the resilient and persistent person you desire. Instead of expecting to meet your own high standards, expect imperfection, learn from each imperfect experience, and try again. Similar to learning any new skill, there is a learning curve to each new exposure, and you won't perform well at first. Like learning how to hit a golf or tennis ball, accept that it will be awkward and uncomfortable. It's supposed to be. Whether you *think* you succeeded or not, each step out of your comfort zone is a victory as well as an opportunity to learn and improve.

It's also difficult to perform well if you expect disaster -- believing you're going to projectile vomit and humiliate yourself. If you face a challenging exposure expecting catastrophe and planning your escape, you will tighten up, lose focus, and perform poorly (or retreat).

Finally, you won't perform well if your focus is on stopping anxiety. Several years ago, I climbed a 60-foot-high rock wall, the highest climbing wall I'd ever seen. Although I was harnessed in securely, I rarely engage in these sorts of adventures and I felt a bit anxious as I made my way towards the top. My focus was precise – placement of my hands and feet and reaching the pinnacle. I did not try to stop my anxiety. If my attention was on trying to halt my quivering and wobbly legs, I never would have made it. I needed to be 100% focused on the task and the steps, and not on stopping my symptoms or allowing my thoughts to have power.

When doing exposures do not expect perfection, disaster, or an absence of anxiety. Instead focus on 1) your strategy, tools, and the task at hand (responding with a winning mindset) and 2) pushing through to the outcome you desire (finishing the exposure without rushing through). Instead of asking yourself, what if I throw up? Ask yourself, *what if I retrain my brain and win my freedom?*

STEPS TO FREEDOM

Double Dare and then Trifecta Exposure: Do the exposures in this chapter multiple times a day. You can access all cartoon and Low Level photos at *QuietMindSolutions.com/Emetophobia.* Look at all Low Level and Cartoon Photos while eating snacks and meals. The more frequently you do this exposure, the closer you inch towards freedom, so force yourself to do this step multiple times a day. Listen to your theme song before the exposure to get you in the spirit of the competition. Feel free to move on to the next chapter as you work on all of the Double Dare and Trifecta Exposures.

3 by 3 Relaxation Breathing: Continue practicing breathing five to ten times a day and breathe when you begin to feel anxious (don't wait until your anxiety is high). Also, before facing an exposure, remember to take one to three breaths.

Mantra: Create a mantra. Post it in different locations of your home and make it your screen saver. Repeat it out loud twenty times a day.

I will not overestimate risks and I will not underestimate my abilities

Chapter 22
My Vomit Stories

Put on your game face and take a breath. Don't wince. *Bring it on!*

Every child has vomited for some reason. I recall being so nauseous on an elementary school whale watching trip I barfed on the boat. As a child, I also puked in the hallway outside my pediatrician's office. We all learn from our experiences and if traumatic, those experiences can shape our thoughts and behaviors for years to come. Fortunately, my early nausea and puking experiences were unpleasant but not traumatic, and I learned from them.

I quickly realized as a child that I get motion sickness. My whale watching fiasco did not generalize to other situations. I did not begin to worry about all boats or all motion. I boated on a lake and rafted on a wild river with no problem but roller coasters did make me nauseous. I lived my life and learned my limits. As a teenager at Disneyland I nervously waited in line with my friends to ride Big Thunder Mountain, the Matterhorn, and Space Mountain. Fortunately, none of the rides resulted in any nausea. I avoided Magic Mountain because I knew those roller coasters there were too intense.

As a young adult I snorkeled off a small boat in the middle of the ocean. I wanted to try because I heard that the coral reefs and the fish were spectacular. This might have been true, but I was too busy feeling nauseous to notice. I barfed a few times on the boat and remained nauseous for an hour after arriving back on shore. But at least I was living my life and learning my limits.

In my late thirties, in Maui, I wanted to try parasailing but this required me to be in a boat on the ocean. A risky move but I went for it. Once on the boat the driver announced it was too windy and they had to drive twenty minutes to calmer skies. This concerned me but I hoped for the best. I loved the speed of the boat bumping along the surface of the water as the cool mist hit my face. Loved it! But once the boat stopped, my stomach felt the motion of the ocean. Yikes! *Get me off this thing!* I volunteered to be the first to go parasailing before any nausea set in.

Up I went, a tandem ride with my niece. As the boat pulled us high in the air, I was surprised how peaceful and calm it felt: a bit like the hot air balloon I flew in New Mexico. As I admired the Maui coast, I even thought it was a little boring. Then, after three minutes in the air, nausea struck suddenly and out of the blue. I was shocked. I couldn't believe it. I felt awful and within a minute I was puking from 800 feet in the air. The Pacific Ocean was my toilet bowl.

The story is funny to me now but it wasn't while up in the sky and later lying nauseous on the boat, pale and limp, with my head in a bucket. Bobbing up and down, unable to stop the motion or the nausea, I heard the crew talking, *The boat won't start. There's something wrong with the engine*. I lifted my head out of the bucket. *You can't be serious.* All I wanted was to get back to shore but there was nothing I could do but survive. I puked two more times as they tried to fix the boat. Once back on shore I laid on a lounge chair for two hours until the nausea went away. The worst part of the experience was **not** the vomiting. The worst part, by far, was the extreme nausea. The vomiting for me was secondary. This has always been the case.

That experience in Hawaii reinforced my knowledge that I cannot ride small boats on the ocean. But what about a cruise ship? This was risky because I would be on the ship for several days. I started with a three-day Mexican cruise and did not feel one ounce of nausea. I then did a seven-night Alaskan cruise. It was awesome. I also enjoyed a week-long Caribbean cruise. So much fun. In each situation I was living my life with uncertainty and without motion sickness medication.

I knew I couldn't ride intense roller coasters but could I do a simulated ride? I loved the *Star Wars* movies as a teen and I wanted to try Star Tours at Disneyland. I figured if I felt nauseous, I could close my eyes. The ride was fantastic and I had no nausea. Several years later I tried the Simpsons simulated ride at Universal Studios. This one was more intense. I felt a wave come over me so I closed my eyes. It didn't help at all! I still felt like I was on a roller coaster. There was nothing I could do. I didn't barf but I felt nauseous for the next two hours.

When I was about forty, I was at California Adventure (a Disney park in Los Angeles) and contemplated going on California Screaming, a roller coaster with a loop, something I had never done before. I decided to go for it. I loved it! Except for the last thirty seconds which felt like thirty minutes. I did not hurl but I felt nauseous for the next two hours. At least I was living my life and learning my limits.

I learned that I cannot do roller coasters or simulated rides and I was okay with that. Flying in airplanes was different. I was not going to let my motion sickness stop me from visiting the places I wanted to see and I was willing to vomit to get there. The goal is to live your life, not to be certain. Fortunately, I rarely feel motion sickness on planes but it can happen. I live with uncertainty each time I fly. I take a motion sickness pill and I make sure a barf bag is handy in the seat pocket.

My wife and I took a red-eye back from our honeymoon. I took a sleeping pill and slept the entire way. When I woke up ten minutes before landing my wife said it was the worst flight she's ever taken. Turbulence the entire time. Thank God I slept through it. I didn't feel it at all. What luck. My father-in-law picked us up and about ten minutes into the car ride I began to feel nauseous. How is that possible? Within two minutes I was barfing on the side of the road.

That experience did not stop me from flying. I've been to many states and countries. Last year I spoke at the annual conference of the *Anxiety and Depression Association of America* in Washington, D.C., on the topic of Emetophobia. As we began our descent into D.C., the plane began to experience severe turbulence. Landing could not come soon enough. Why was it taking so long? Why was the pilot not landing the plane? As we circled the windy sky, my nausea circled my stomach and up through my throat. Like the boat with a broken engine, there was nothing I could do. I remember thinking to myself, *In two days I'm going to be giving a talk on the fear of vomiting and in about two minutes I'm going to vomit.* I grabbed the barf bag and opened it up, ready to load it with the sandwich I just ate. Although the sandwich tasted pretty good for airplane food, I regretted eating it. I wondered, *If I puke, could I get my money back?* I was hoping the guy next to me did not have emetophobia. And then about three minutes before we landed, I tossed my cookies. Actually, it was a chicken wrap. I felt better after and it gave me a great intro for my talk --

and a fun story for this book.

Not all of my vomiting has been caused by motion. When I worked in an office years ago, I suddenly felt sick. I went to the restroom, puked, felt better, and returned to my desk to continue working. I have no idea why I threw up. Perhaps it was food poisoning or a 24-hour flu.

Everyone has vomit stories. Emetophobes, however, usually don't have many, and the ones they do have are usually very traumatic, a topic I will address in the next chapter.

STEPS TO FREEDOM

Talk About Puke: Ask people to share their vomit stories and listen with your game face. Bring it up in the context of conversations. If someone is talking about an upcoming flight or a cruise, ask if they get motion sickness and if they do, ask follow-up questions: *Have you ever thrown up?* If people at work are talking about flu season, ask if they have ever vomited because of the flu. If a friend mentions he ate something bad, ask if he's ever gotten food poisoning. Ask family and friends to share their vomit stories. Put on your game face, listen, and ask questions.

Listen to vomit stories: Watch videos of people talk about their vomiting experiences. **You will not see or hear vomit.** Watch each video until they no longer elicit distress. Then watch them outside your home while eating a snack. *Bring it!* **Check out these vomit stories** via this QR code or go to quietmindsolutions.com/emetophobia. Click on video exposures and then vomit stories.

After listening to all the vomit stories, push aside your anticipatory anxiety and check out the QR code below. **It's a fabulous** video with an important message at the end so be determined to accept uncertainty and stay the course. It can also be found on the website under *Videos with a Message.*

Seek out uncertainty and focus on where you have control: Your response -- how you handle the unexpected: ***This is exactly what I need to be free. Bring on the uncertainty! I can handle it!***

Sam Fuentes: "Our mission is simple"

Chapter 23
Vomiting Trauma: How to Heal Your Past

Before I discuss the topic of trauma, I'll address the Sam Fuentes video. If you haven't seen it, watch it! There is an important message to be learned. If you have watched it, continue viewing it every day.

In this chapter I will address traumatic experiences related to vomit, not other types of trauma. If you have a history of abuse, sexual assault, or other traumatic events, and you believe it's related to your emetophobia, seek out treatment with a trauma specialist who can help you process those experiences.

A traumatic vomiting event is common for an emetophobe. It often happens when the person is a child or a teen and usually triggers the disorder. Perhaps you suffered with food poisoning or a bad flu. Perhaps you witnessed someone else vomiting violently. A puking experience can be traumatic if it includes any of the following:

- Continuous vomiting, one episode after another
- Barfing on yourself
- Vomiting in public and feeling humiliated
- Having a panic attack while vomiting

- Being yelled at for throwing up
- Painful, loud puking
- Witnessing a loved one vomiting

Since emetophobes seldom vomit, that horrific childhood/teen experience might be your only one. The memory of that trauma might be very clear or a bit fuzzy. What is usually remembered is the horrific emotions of the experience, which are often laced with feelings of anxiety, fear, disgust, helplessness, and embarrassment. When those emotions are amplified and the event replayed in one's mind year after year, vomiting is no longer just vomiting. Vomiting has become the most horrific experience possible. But is it?

Anything becomes horrific when accompanied by disgust, helplessness, embarrassment, or anxiety. If a little boy's first experience with a clown is filled with terror, he might develop coulrophobia. As he desperately avoids clowns, the fear amplifies in his mind. On the occasion he crosses paths with a painted-faced creature with orange hair and floppy shoes, he experiences a **rush of anxiety**, which reinforces the fear. As an adult he understands logically that clowns aren't scary, but he avoids them because he doesn't like the symptoms of anxiety that appear simultaneously.

Clowns are horrific to people who have coulrophobia because of the intense fear they experience when in the presence of a clown, not because clowns are horrific. Most people find them amusing. Is it possible that the reason vomiting is so horrific is because of the intense fear that comes along with it? Is it possible that the reason you have intense fear now is because you experienced anxiety, humiliation, helplessness, or disgust, when you puked years ago?

A current patient believes his emetophobia stems from hearing his father vomit day after day for months. As a child of seven, he did not understand that his father's vomiting was caused by his cancer treatments. When his father died, he associated vomiting with death. As an adult, he understands rationally that he will not die if he throws up, but emotionally he believes he will.

If you experienced a vomiting trauma and continue to have intrusive memories or images of the event, the trauma will need to be addressed. Without processing the event, you will have difficulty fully overcoming your emetophobia.

In this chapter I have included an exercise to help you move on from any previous vomiting traumas.

MEMORY RE-SCRIPTING

There are two parts to this exercise. First, write your traumatic vomiting story in the **present** tense including as many **details** as possible. Don't hold back. Make it as intense as you remember and write it in the present tense, **as if it were happening to you now.** Once complete, read your memory **out loud.** This will be difficult and you might feel various emotions, but push through it.

Part two involves creating a **new ending** to your memory: your present-day self talking to your traumatized-self. Write about how your present-day self, comforts and reassures your traumatized-self. Be creative and include dialogue between your two selves and any others who were involved. Make sure your present-day self is encouraging, supportive, and gives the advice your traumatized-self needs to hear. Take your time writing. Put effort into this assignment. Once you have your ending the way you want it, read the entire memory, with the **new** ending, **out loud.** Continue reading both versions out loud **every day.** This re-scripting exercise will reduce the intensity of the memory and help you move on from the trauma.

STEPS TO FREEDOM

Memory Re-scripting: Write the trauma in the present tense. Read it out loud and give yourself permission to experience any emotions that surface. Don't run from them. Then change the ending and write how your present-day self comforts your traumatized-self. Read both stories out loud at least one time a day. If doing Image Re-scripting on your own for several weeks does not reduce the intensity of the trauma, you might need to seek out a therapist to help you process the traumatic events. EMDR is a powerful therapeutic technique specifically used for trauma. If you cannot find a therapist in your area that does EMDR, check out *The Anxiety Solution Series* at *QuietMindSolutions.com.* In this audio program is a self-help tool I created that is very similar to EMDR, called Image Reprocessing. Like EMDR, it will help you reprocess your trauma.

Chapter 24
The Buffalo, Adam Sandler, and Your Secret Identity

The following excerpt from my book, *Break Free from Anxiety*, was written by Bella Carter, a former anxiety sufferer. She is a writing teacher, a personal coach and the author of *Raw: My Journey from Anxiety to Joy.*

I lost my identity. I was filled with regret and tortured myself with endless questions that heightened my anxiety: What if there's something wrong with my heart? What if I'm going crazy? What if people think I'm insane? Will this ever stop? Why is this happening? What's wrong with me?

I was asking the wrong questions. I redesigned my "What if" questions: What if this is my path? What if my path isn't supposed to follow a straight line? What if every obstacle we face is an essential part of our journey, a teacher or lesson disguised as a problem? What if when we think we're being thrown off-course we're really being redirected? What if fear is a big, fat liar? What if fear is a voice in my head that I can choose to ignore? What if I can accept my discomfort and live my life the way I want? What if that's the goal: to live my life?

These were more productive questions. I learned to form a new relationship with anxiety. It wasn't easy. My resolve to quit abusing myself with venomous inner chatter set me on the path to healing. I tried to take a step back and observe what was happening as if I were an impartial witness. I approached my healing like a buffalo, rather than a cow. According to Native American folklore, when a storm approaches, buffalo turned toward the storm and ran into it, which helped them get through it faster. Cows, on the other hand, ran away from the storm. This meant the storm was at their backs, chasing them, until it finally caught them, which made the ordeal last longer.

I loved this Native American tale because it fits perfectly with anxiety sufferers. When sensing danger there is an instinctive impulse to flee. Whether it's a storm or anxiety, being chased engenders fear as you run for your life! Like the cow, you are eventually caught and enveloped. Buffalo, on the other hand, run towards the storm with force. They charge at it, which generates courage and power. And because they run towards and through the storm, it passes more quickly.

Performing exposures tentatively creates more anxiety. Facing exposures like a buffalo in a storm, a pilot in turbulence, or my son in a haunted yard will mitigate the anxiety. Put on your game face, demand to be uncomfortable and uncertain, and charge forward. You **will** feel anxiety. Expect it. It means you're doing it right and have chosen the winning road. When you initially walk into anxiety's territory, you're going to feel anxious but after doing it repeatedly with the correct mindset, you realize that you can handle it, your confidence grows, and your anxiety diminishes.

One of my patients was so inspired by the story, he tattooed a buffalo on his arm. Wow! That's a powerful reminder of how to face fears.

Commit to exposures and see them through: By charging at your fear like a buffalo, you are committing yourself to pushing through the exposure. You are charging forth with a determined attitude. There is no escape or turning back. You have closed the door on ambivalence and your anxiety monster. If the door is closed and locked, your opponent will have trouble getting in. If the door is cracked slightly with ambivalence, it won't take much for anxiety to push it open.

I treated a patient with an intense fear of wide-open spaces, heights, and places outside his comfort zone. He was working hard in therapy and making nice progress when he decided that his next exposure would be Griffith Park Observatory, a beautiful building located on a mountain overlooking the city of Los Angeles. He felt confident as he and his girlfriend drove up the hill, but to his surprise, **anxiety and fear struck hard**, and at the last moment he turned off on a side street and went back down. He felt disappointed with himself. He saw it as a failure. It wasn't because he learned from the experience. He needed to be prepared for anxiety to strike and he had to be ready with a response. He decided he would say, *Keep it coming. I can handle it,* with an attitude, while playing his theme song.

A week later he tried again, more prepared and more determined. This time he passed the turn off and headed towards the top with confidence. Suddenly he was in **bumper-to-bumper traffic! This was unexpected. *Yikes.* There was no turning back or escaping.** He crept along and the feeling of being trapped caused his anxiety to skyrocket. Although he was not prepared for traffic, he was prepared for discomfort and uncertainty. **Because he could not escape, he focused solely on the tools and strategy instead of focusing on fleeing.** This was his only option. By the time he reached the top, his anxiety was mild. He had to sit with the anxiety and give it time to diminish. When anxiety sufferers flee and don't hang in there long enough, they never experience a reduction in symptoms.

The traffic turned out to be a solution disguised as a problem. If there is a possibility of fleeing, anxiety sufferers focus their energy on trying to escape. Once you consider the option of fleeing, you are ambivalent and not fully committed. Ambivalence always increases anxiety. Why? Because as you deliberate the option of escaping, what you are actually doing is engaging with anxiety in the back of the bus. The longer the conversation, the more adrenaline is being secreted. Not only that, but if your focus and energy are on escaping and not on your tools or strategy, you will lose every time. Conquering a powerful opponent requires your **full** attention, energy, and commitment.

Before doing any exposure, tell your monster you will be pushing through and not running away. Close the door on ambivalence. Do not seek escape. Put all of your energy on staying on offense and allowing time for your anxiety to subside (which can take five minutes but at times up to an hour or longer). Like the buffalo running towards the storm, do it with ferocity, making sure your intensity is at least equal to that of anxiety. Otherwise, you might get blown away. What might help in these situations? A secret identity.

Your Secret Identity

You are in an epic battle with a tricky and devious opponent. You have a strategy, tools, and theme song but something is missing.... Clark Kent was a socially anxious reporter with a secret identity – Superman. Bruce Wayne was a mild-mannered millionaire with his own secret identity -- Batman. As an emetophobe you could use a secret identity too: a character you can bring forth in dire situations. One of my patient's secret identity was *Cat Woman* and she released her inner *Cat Woman* when she needed to take charge of a situation. One of my other emetophobic patients created an alter-ego he called *Iron Stomach Man.*

I am currently working with an OCD patient who was a barrel racer as a teen. As she sat on her horse, ready to fly out of the gate, she thought of herself as a *bad ass*. And she was. To push through her present-day fears and compulsions, she summoned her *inner badass* and took charge. Another adult, female patient was a softball pitcher in high school. With each batter that walked up to the plate, she put on her game face and thought to herself, *I'm gonna strike your ass out.* Bringing forth this forgotten identity and attitude, as she faced her anxiety monster, was extremely helpful.

Think about an alter ego that you can summon when needed. A clever creation or former self that has been buried by fear. That part of you still exists and it needs to be brought to the surface. Give it a name: *Barf Man, Captain Kick-Your-Ass, Daredevil, The Incredible Hurl, Brave Boy, Captain Fearless, Bad Ass, Striker.*

Watch this clip of Adam Sandler in the movie *Happy Gilmore.* His character goes to a batting cage to toughen up for next year's hockey season. Listen to his self-talk, not only what he says but how he says it. Your tone of voice communicates more than the words you use. *Bring it on* said quietly means something completely different than *BRING IT ON* with volume. Responding to anxiety with passion will help you believe your words. Otherwise you won't have confidence in what you are saying.

I'm about to reveal your next set of exposures..... The storm is coming. Are you going to run away and let it chase you or are you going to charge forward? Before you read the following exposure put on your game face and summon a secret identity, perhaps a time in your life when you were tough. Don't grimace. *Bring it on. I can handle it.*

Look at a photo of a boy with puke on his shirt for 10 seconds.

Be determined to beat anxiety. Use the same mentality as Adam Sandler. Do it quickly before anxiety convinces you otherwise. Say it with conviction: ***Bring it on! I can handle it.***

Breathe and repeat:
This is exactly the feeling I need right now. Keep it coming. I can handle it.

If this or any exposure does not cause you distress, practice the process regardless (put on your game face, invite the anxiety and respond out loud). Rehearsing the process with easier exposures will help when they become more difficult. If it was easy, look at the photo again while eating.

The NBA Star

As a Los Angeles Clipper, DeAndre Jordan, a top NBA center, was frequently fouled intentionally during games by the other team, sending him to the free throw line. Why? Because as a career 45% free throw shooter, he would likely miss, and the other team would regain possession of the ball. To give perspective, the NBA league average hovers around 75%. Despite regular practice and adjustments to his shot, his free throw shooting never improved.

In 2016 Jordan admitted to his teammate, JJ Redick, that his struggles were *more mental than anything. You can get reps up in the gym as much as you want, hours and hours of practice,* Jordan said on The Vertical Podcast with JJ Redick, *but when it comes to the game…it's so different. The pressure is on.* He admitted to being frustrated and nervous when he shot free throws. *I used to think, "Don't fucking airball. Anything but airball. I don't want to be on Shaqtin' a Fool"* (a show that highlights NBA bloopers). It's clear that Jordan's mindset was defensive with the focus on missing the rim and feeling humiliated. With his anxiety threatening humiliation, no wonder he shot 45%.

In the 2018 season, after ten years in the NBA, Jordan's free throw shooting suddenly improved to 75%. It was remarkable. Kevin O'Connor wrote about Jordan's improvement in The Ringer and interviewed sports psychologist, Don Kalkstein, *We don't want the thought process to be, "I have to make the shot." We want the process to be, "I'm going to catch and shoot."* Don tells athletes to focus on the process of shooting, which eliminates the pressure. In other words, focus on what you need to do and not what anxiety is threatening might happen.

Jordan used to remain quiet after he was fouled and while standing at the free throw line. Now he talks to his teammates, asking questions and pointing out opposing players. By doing this he's staying out of his head and avoiding conversations with his anxiety monster. Jordan told USA TODAY Sport, *I'm trying not to think about it as much (as before).* Jordan made other changes too. O'Connor wrote, *Immediately, after Jordan is fouled, he seeks out the ball. He'll chase it down, or touches it while the referee is holding it.... Today he moves towards the ball; in the past, he moved away from it.* This is the equivalent of the buffalo running towards the storm.

STEPS TO FREEDOM

Identify a Secret Identity: Come up with an alter ego you can summon when things get intense. Create a secret identity or recall a time in your life when you were tough. Then channel that identity when facing exposures.

Start an Emetophobia Wall of Fame: As I mentioned, people learn languages most efficiently when they immerse themselves in the language by living it every day. It's time to immerse yourself! Print out the vomit cartoons and other photos and tape these disgusting pictures to your wall. Like an athlete displaying his medals and trophies, put your conquests on display. Consider this to be your ***Emetophobia Wall of Fame.*** Each time you look at the pictures, taunt your opponent, *You're no match for*

___________________________.
(secret identity)

Medium Level Photo Exposures: Time to move on to more intense photos. Employ the same strategy you have been using to face these disgusting pics. Bring on the discomfort like Adam Sandler and stare at the photos mindfully. Look at every photo until you can stomach each for two minutes with minimal discomfort. Then go outside your home (down the street, mall, café) and look at the photos. Lastly, look at the photos while eating. Look at the photos, eat mindfully, and practice not reacting. You can achieve this by noticing your internal and external experience without judgment:

My mind is noticing the vomit on his shirt.
My mind is noticing I'm feeling nauseous while I eat this sandwich.
I'm noticing what the food tastes like as I look at this photo.
I'm noticing the wind on my face as I stare at this picture.

Baby spitting up

Cat Puking

Toilet with vomit inside

Head over toilet with puke

Chapter 25
Positive Emotions and Natural Abilities

If you can calm yourself with *3 by 3 Relaxation Breathing* before facing a challenging exposure, great, but this is often not possible. Repeated efforts can result in frustration and more anxiety as you desperately try to relax yourself. There are other options if you are unable to reduce your physical symptoms. Instead of trying to reduce your anxiety, override it by accessing a competing emotion, preferably one that is in line with your personality.

Dr. Barbara Fredrickson at the University of North Carolina has researched the topic of positive emotions. Her findings suggest that if a person can pull up a positive emotion in the face of a negative one, this will dismantle the physical preparation to run. The idea is that you purposefully generate a positive emotion that is counter to anxiety. You then decisively step forward, out of your comfort zone, cognizant of your goals (freedom from emetophobia and panic). Stepping forward with intention and a competing emotion can transform your experience.

Anger and Attitude

I've discussed in previous chapters that facing exposures with an attitude of toughness or anger can propel you through fear more easily. As you have learned, adrenaline is nicknamed the *fight-or-flight* hormone because in an emergency it gives us what we need to take action. The choice is be defensive and flee or go on offense and fight. If you're going to fight, being tough and angry is advantageous and if this is an innate part of your character, then use this emotion. The physiology of anger is similar to anxiety – racing heart, muscle tension, high blood pressure, shaking, and rapid breathing. Reappraising your symptoms of anxiety as anger and directing it at the anxiety monster can help you override your symptoms. Never direct anger towards yourself, no matter how frustrated you feel. Frustration, disappointment, and self-loathing will prolong your recovery. You're going to lose many battles with anxiety. Instead of being angry at yourself, congratulate your opponent and move on.

Do not get angry at yourself.
Direct your anger towards beating your opponent.

Even if you seldom lose your temper, try to recall a time in your life when you did. Think about this now. Identify a memory. Who did you get angry with and why? How did you experience and express your anger?

Anger is a normal, human emotion, and sometimes it's appropriate to express it outwardly. Your anxiety monster is a liar, a bully, and has ruined your life. It deserves your anger. It's time to stand up to him. Although anger may not be a part of your character, a few previous explosive episodes mean you are capable of it and it's worth trying. Access a past memory of being tough to manufacture anger in the present. Put on your game face, clench your fists, and raise your voice. You will be shocked at how helpful it is to face anxiety with an attitude. The tougher the better. Pound your fist. *Don't fuck with me! I'm not taking your crap!* Unleash your inner-beast any time you face an exposure or feel anxiety rising. *Bring on the disgust! I can handle it, bitch!* Then growl ferociously with your game face. It may sound silly (and it is) but it will give you what you need to push through, instead of flee.

If manufacturing the emotion of anger is not possible, consider being assertive, with a firm tone, not an angry one. As long as your voice rises to the dominant position, this will be effective. **Your** voice needs to be in charge. *I will not let you win! I'm in charge!*

Some people view anger (or anything that resembles it) as negative or harmful. Perhaps you've had traumatic experiences with angry people. If anger has an undesirable connotation, perhaps other emotions will fit your personality better. ***Love, excitement, and amusement*** can also help you through uncertain and uncomfortable situations.

Amusement

Using the competing emotion of amusement might be more in line with your personality. If anxiety is the result of amplified, distorted thinking, then it's important that we not take our thoughts seriously. There are several amusing ways to transform the seriousness of a thought and mitigate the intensity of the emotion.

When your opponent tries to scare you with questions and threats, you can diminish the power of the anxiety by repeating the fear out loud with an accent (British, Southern, New York, French, Indian, etc.). Imagine how the Queen of England might say this sentence: *I'm noticing my anxiety monster messing with me by telling me I'm going to puke.* One of my patients told me that when she hears herself verbalize her worries out loud in a British accent, the thoughts sound silly. She then exclaims out loud, *That's rubbish! Tata darling.*

This is an extremely effective intervention even if you have no ability to speak with an accent. Don't worry about the quality. That doesn't matter. You will only be using this intervention when alone. Try saying the following worry out loud in any accent you choose: *My monster is messing with me by telling me I'm going to have a panic attack. Piss off!* The more you try to get into the accent, the better. By focusing on how silly the worry sounds, you are less focused on the content, so do your best to put yourself into character. Try verbalizing the same worry twice using two different accents.

This tool is effective for two reasons: Thoughts feel factual in your head but when you verbalize them out loud, they don't feel as true. When you say them out loud with an accent, they sound silly, which is exactly what you want. Use this intervention every time you are alone with a worry.

Another amusing way to respond to worries is with lines from movies. Say them out loud or think how the actor expressed it in the movie:

"Frankly my dear, I don't give a damn." -- *Gone with the Wind*
"Mama always said life is like a box of Chocolates." -- *Forrest Gump*
"I'll get you my pretty and your little dog too." -- *The Wizard of Oz*
"You feel that...heat? That's from my undercarriage." -- *Bridesmaids*
"Prepared to be fucked by the long dick of the law." -- *Superbad*
"Just keep swimming." -- *Finding Nemo*
"You sit on a throne of lies." -- *Elf*
"I'm gonna finish him like a cheesecake!" -- *Pitch Perfect*

Anxiety sufferers have wonderful imaginations. You might as well use it to your advantage. Use your imagination and picture your anxiety monster standing before you. Is it gigantic like a gorilla or small like a mouse? Close your eyes and picture it standing in front of you.

This time visualize your opponent with your eyes open -- dancing! You are the choreographer. You decide the style of dance. It may sound silly but try it anyway. Go for it!

If your monster is huge, use the power of your imagination to shrink it. Point your finger at it and shrink it down to the size of a bug. Go for it!

Remember, adrenaline is for taking action (fighting or fleeing). By physically moving your body and asserting your will, you are taking action. Now that you've shrunk your anxiety, step on it! Physically stomp your foot. Or flick him away with your finger and watch him fly across the room. As you take action, picture it in your mind. Give this a try now.

Feel silly? Good. That's exactly the point. Using the positive emotion of amusement in the face of anxiety will help you face your fear instead of run. Your opponent puts 100% effort into scaring you, shouting lies so loud that your body reacts with nausea and you follow his orders. **To beat him, you must match his intensity, conviction, and passion.** In this case, with amusement.

In a moment you will grab your opponent, take it into a bathroom, throw it into the toilet, and flush it down. As the water circles around the bowl and as you picture your monster struggling to stay afloat, sing the chorus *Na na na na, hey hey, good-bye* by Steam (check it out on YouTube). If you feel silly or amused, you did it right. Imagine your monster as clearly as you can and take action with amusement. Before reading on, flush him down the toilet. Go for it!

You might feel awkward being silly but this will diminish with frequency and effort. There are many amusing ways to dispose of your anxiety monster. Use your environment and your imagination. If you're in the kitchen and suddenly have an anxious thought, put him in the microwave and radiate his ass. If you're in a car, throw him out the window. I worked with a young boy who imagined shooting his monster with a paintball gun. Any time your monster tries to trick you, dispose of him in any amusing way you desire. Be creative when you are alone. If you are in public or with family or friends, be subtle. Squeeze your opponent in your hand while singing in your head "Another One Bites the Dust" by Queen. Before doing an exposure, swat him like a bug and sing the chorus of Survivor's "Eye of the Tiger." Try this now with any exposure you have successfully overcome. Go for it!

The goal is to not take your thoughts seriously thereby not engaging.

If you don't take them seriously, your brain doesn't signal your adrenal gland and your anxiety will be minimal. Another amusing way to accomplish this goal is through an app called *AutoRap* by Smule. After downloading this app, write a simple three-line song. For instance:

What if you vomit?
You're really sick this time.
Don't eat it!

Open up the app and select one of the free song choices. Press the "Talk" button, record your three-line song, and then listen to your creation. This app is a lot of fun. Change your song choice and write new lyrics:

You're gonna puke!
Fuck off monster.
I want to puke!

Let loose and have fun. Try it now.

Excitement

Imagine two teenagers seated in the front row of a roller coaster. As they inch towards the top of the hill, one has her arms stretched over her head while the other clutches the metal bar in front of her like magnets. As they fly down the tracks, the first girl yells with excitement while the other yells in fear. Same situation, two different responses. Those responses are based on the meaning they give to the experience. If you can change the meaning of something you fear and use a competing emotion to mitigate the anxiety, you can push through the experience more easily.

Sometimes my dog is so excited to receive a treat or go for a walk he physically shakes. Shaking is also a physiological response to anxiety. There is a slight overlap between these two emotions that we can utilize to help us when we are anxious. In the December 2013 issue of the *Journal of Experimental Psychology,* Dr. Alison Brooks of Harvard Business School shared her research findings in her piece entitled, "Get Excited: Reappraising Pre-Performance Anxiety as Excitement." She summed up her findings:

> *Individuals often feel anxious in anticipation of tasks such as speaking in public or meeting with a boss. I find that an overwhelming majority of people believe trying to calm down is the best way to cope with pre-performance anxiety. However, across several studies involving karaoke singing, public speaking, and math performance, I investigate*

an alternative strategy: reappraising anxiety as excitement. Compared with those who attempt to calm down, individuals who reappraise their anxious arousal as excitement feel more excited and perform better. Individuals can reappraise anxiety as excitement using minimal strategies such as self-talk (e.g., saying "I am excited" out loud) or simple messages (e.g., "get excited"), which lead them to feel more excited, adopt an opportunity mind-set (as opposed to a threat mind-set), and improve their subsequent performance.

Participants in her study who repeatedly said out loud, "I am excited" before doing an anxiety provoking act performed better than those who said, "I am calm" or nothing at all. Participants who stated, "I am anxious" performed the weakest. It's remarkable that changing one word can be so helpful. Dr. Brooks concluded that reappraising anxiety as excitement did not decrease anxiety but it did help people perform better. Frequency of one's self-talk is also important:

The more often individuals reappraise their pre-performance anxiety as excitement, the more likely they may be to trigger upward motivational spirals, and the happier and more successful they may become. Instead of trying to "Keep Calm and Carry On," perhaps the path to success begins by simply saying "I am excited."

Generate excitement with your mind and body. Pump your fist as you imagine success and declare with passion, *Bring it on baby! I'm* ***excited*** *to kick your ass! I'm* ***excited*** *to watch these disgusting videos. I'm excited to eat in the restaurant. I'm excited to be anxious. I'm excited to be nauseous! I'm excited to feel disgusted.*

Imagine for a moment you are walking through a park with a friend and you see vomit on the ground. Instead of reacting like you normally would, declare, *I'm so excited to be grossed out. Give me a high-five.* Slap hands and move on. *Love it!*

When utilizing a competing emotion, you are not reducing your emotion with reason. The purpose is to help you face your fears, tolerate them, and keep moving forward by activating a positive emotion that expresses a different meaning. *I'm excited to feel nauseous.* The purpose is not to exchange fear for excitement; rather, it is to help you unlock the impact that anxiety has over your mind and body with an enthusiastic aspiration to be anxious and disgusted. And here's the key: **mean what you say.** *I'm excited to feel nauseous!* Why would you be excited to feel nauseous? Because when you learn to tolerate nausea, you are another step closer to freedom. And that's something to be excited about! *I'm* *excited to take hard steps because I'm excited to be free!*

When people persevere over a difficult challenge, they feel a sense of triumph. Think of a time in your life when you felt this way. The emotion of triumph is a fantastic feeling but the only way to get that feeling is by doing something hard. Therefore, get excited about doing hard things: *I'm excited to eat at a restaurant! I'm excited to watch vomit videos! I'm excited to eat a meal and go for a drive.* If you are excited to feel a sense of achievement and freedom, then get excited about performing challenges that will give you those feelings. *I'm excited to feel anxious when I ride in a subway because I'm excited to be free!*

Your anxiety monster will not make it easy. As you declare with passion, *I'm excited to feel anxious*, your opponent will retort, *Oh no you don't.* These thoughts will instantly activate anxiety and an urge to flee. Feel the resistance. Feel the doubt. Then quickly push through it as you repeat, *I'm excited to feel sick! I'm excited to feel anxious. I'm excited to beat anxiety.* You won't believe it at **first** but do it anyway. The key to believability and success is matching your opponent's intensity. Declare out loud with volume and passion: ***I'm excited to be anxious because I'm excited to be free!*** Try this now!

Excitement and anxiety are similar in that they both produce an arousal level before an event. Reid Wilson writes in *Stopping the Noise in Your Head,* "If feeling excited helps people perform, then they don't have to calm down in order to perform better… If you must relax in order to perform better, you will have to change your whole psychology and physiology to a non-aroused state… Wouldn't it be easier if you had to change only your attitude about being aroused?"

One of the exposures you will eventually have to conquer is watching videos of people puking. Will it make you anxious? Absolutely. Will you feel disgusted? Positively. Will you vomit? Doubtful. But you might feel nauseous and you might worry about vomiting. View this exposure as a step towards freedom, not a potential catastrophe. By doing the exposure repeatedly, day after day, you will acclimate to vomit videos and they will no longer trigger disgust, fear, or anxiety symptoms. Since that's something to be excited about, get excited about feeling disgusted and nauseous. *I'm excited to feel disgusted.* Then, while watching the vile videos listen to the Pointer Sisters, "I'm So Excited."

Get excited because just on the other side of disgust is freedom.

Whether you are facing planned or spontaneous exposure, use a competing emotion. Every time you feel nauseous, stomach distress, or worried, you have an opportunity to rewire your brain to be the calm person you desire to be. Get excited about these opportunities.

Since the best way out is through, visualize past the fear to a **successful outcome.** Focus on the positive result and the pride you will feel. See past the fear to what you desire: Arriving at your destination after the plane has landed and hugging your loved ones. As you see through the fear to the other side, pump your fist. Smile. *YES! I got this*. Then flick away your monster and sing Journey's "Don't Stop Believing."

Like learning any new skill, using positive emotions will feel awkward at first and you will doubt its effectiveness. As you incorporate excitement and amusement into your exposure work, you will see improvement and ultimately feel the power of this strategy. Try combining excitement and amusement with an exposure you have successfully overcome. Go for it!

Happiness

Manufacturing a smile and a bit of laughter might be what you need to face and push through anxiety-filled situations. It will feel forced and contrived but there just might be something to that old adage, *Grin and bear it*, and the research supports it!

Tara L. Kraft and Sarah D. Pressman at the University of Kansas found that smiling participants, regardless of whether they were aware of smiling, had lower heart rates during stress recovery than the neutral group did. They concluded that there were physiological and psychological benefits from maintaining positive facial expressions during stress.

Coles, Larsen, and Lench at the University of Tennessee, Knoxville and Texas A&M analyzed nearly 50 years of data, testing whether facial expressions can lead people to feel the emotions related to those expressions. Using a statistical technique called meta-analysis, Coles and his team combined data from 138 studies testing more than 11,000 participants from all around the world. According to the results of the meta-analysis, facial expressions have a small impact on feelings. For example, smiling makes people feel happier, scowling makes them feel angrier, and frowning makes them feel sadder.

Dr. Isha Gubta, a neurologist from IGEA Brain and Spine stated that a smile spurs a chemical reaction in the brain, which releases the hormones dopamine and serotonin; the former increases happiness and the latter reduces stress.

Before facing a planned or spontaneous exposure, manufacture a smile and a chuckle to yourself, *I'm happy to do hard things because I'm excited to be free!*

Love

Some people find the competing emotion of ***love*** fits their personality the best. Expressing love and behaving in a loving way can mitigate anxiety when the love is directed towards one's self, a loved one, God, or even your anxiety monster. Instead of viewing anxiety as an adversary that must be conquered, the goal is to make peace with anxiety. With this goal in mind, your response to anxious thoughts and feelings will be loving and compassionate. When facing a fear, worry, or in the midst of panic, ***think of the object of your love, pet your arm, and declare in a nurturing voice tone:***

Even though I am scared, I love and accept myself.
My love will conquer this fear.
Thanks for sharing. Have a nice day.
I will be okay.
I will push through this fear with love.
My love for __________ is more important than my fear.
I am taking care of myself because I am important.
I am choosing myself over my fear.
I am softening my anxiety with love.
I am pushing through this fear because of my love for________
Sending love and hugs to my anxiety.
I see you. I love you. We will make it through.
Let go, let God. Love conquers all.
God has given me the strength to handle this.
My passion and love for God will help me through.
I'm choosing faith over fear because I love God.
Anxiety will not stop my love of life, myself, and what I value.
I love you. I'm okay. (blow anxiety a kiss)

Bring forth your natural strengths, abilities, passions

Some of us have been blessed with natural abilities and others have developed skills in certain areas. What are your strengths? What are your passions? What's something you do pretty well? You don't have to be the best at it but you might love it. Or perhaps you possess a positive character trait. Whatever ability, passion, character trait, or positive strength you possess, incorporate it into your recovery. Superman *was faster than a speeding bullet. More powerful than a locomotive. And able to leap tall buildings in a single bound.* He used his strengths to conquer the bad guys. To conquer emetophobia and panic disorder, you must utilize your strengths as well.

If it is in your nature to take care of others, bring that characteristic to the surface and direct it towards yourself as you face your fears. If you have a protective instinct and stand up for other people, utilize this instinct and stand up for yourself. If you are innately nurturing, use a soft voice-tone as you nurture yourself through worry. If you tend to be more submissive, beg your anxiety monster to give you more distress and nausea. To remind yourself of your strength, find a photo or picture that represents it, post it somewhere visible, then practice using it.

Perhaps you are a competitive person with athletic proficiency or a gamer who has mastered various video games. Use your competitive instincts, determination, power, and wits, to beat your anxiety monster as you recall memories of triumph on the field, court, or screen. Stepping up to do an exposure is the same as stepping up to the plate with your game face, ready to hit the ball hard. Use the same mentality.

If you have a flair for the dramatic and a powerful imagination, use those innate abilities to dispose of your opponent in creative and theatrical ways. When doing exposures, use your skill as an actor to act as though you got this, even when you are not sure.

If you love music or singing, bring this into your recovery to make your drive to the Land of Freedom more pleasant. People who stutter when they talk do not stutter when they sing. Music has a way of touching the soul and engendering energy which is why gym enthusiasts listen to music when they work out. Focus your attention on music and the feeling it generates, to help you face your fears. If you have not done so already, identify your theme song. Do you love to write or do art? If so, write a story or create a picture of triumph as you sit in a new café, miles from your home, enjoying food you have never tried.

As a boy I was very shy. To help with my insecurities, my mother enrolled me in magic lessons. Soon I was showing tricks to my family and later as a teenager I performed shows for children's birthday parties. The magic helped me get out of my comfort zone and talk to people. In my case, it was a new hobby that helped me to overcome my anxiety. In your case, nothing new is required. Just return to something you love. Unfortunately, when emetophobia and panic hits hard, people stop their passions. If you enjoy yoga, art, dance, fitness, etc., return to those hobbies and do them several days a week. Join a class and do what you love to do. Then drive to a class further from your comfort zone, meet new people, and go out to lunch.

Are you a person of faith? If so, choose faith over fear. Step forward into uncertainty and distress, let go of your worrisome thoughts, and TRUST that God will help you through. Rather than devoting yourself to what you fear, a false prophet in sheep's clothing, you will **devote yourself to God.** With blind trust, your devotion needs to be in the dominant position. Like a thrill seeker jumping off a bridge having complete faith that the bungee will not break, you will be jumping into exposures knowing it will be all right with God at your side. To enhance your connection to God, spend time at church, synagogue, or your house of worship.

Whatever natural ability you possess and whichever positive emotion you choose, use your voice, body, and facial expression to bring forth those abilities and emotions, so they flow through your entire being, maximizing the possibility of success, as you push through discomfort and uncertainty. It's not just the words you use but how you say those words. Express them with your body and face to match your opponent's intensity whenever he tries to scare or engage you. Before doing an exposure, formulate a plan and visualize implementing it using your natural ability and a positive emotion.

STEPS TO FREEDOM

Positive Emotions and Natural Abilities: Utilize a positive emotion and a natural ability to face planned exposures and any spontaneous exposures that take you by surprise. Utilize songs and music to generate excitement, power, and motivation, and *AutoRap* to help you not take your thoughts so seriously.

Vomit Video Cartoons: Some will find these videos gross and anxiety provoking and others will laugh and have no trouble. Get excited to watch them as you invite the discomfort and ask for more. Watch **all** the video cartoons at *QuietMindSolutions.com/Emetophobia.* Click on Videos Exposure and then Vomit Cartoons. The *Family Guy* video is the most triggering.

Vomit Video
Cartoons

Chapter 26
Creating a Hierarchy of Exposures

Now is your opportunity to practice using the competing emotions of love, excitement, amusement, or toughness with nine new exposures, in whichever order you choose. **You will create a hierarchy from the easiest to the most difficult and tackle one at a time, focusing only on the exposure at hand.** First breathe and become a wet noodle. Put on your *game face* (don't wince). Say *Bring it on!* After you read each exposure declare out loud, *I'm excited to be FREE!*

- Look at High Level Photo Exposures (quietmindsolutions.com/emetophobia)
- Watch Low Level Video Exposures (quietmindsolutions.com/emetophobia)
- Spin in a chair and make yourself dizzy
- Make realistic vomiting sounds into a trashcan
- With water in your mouth, pretend to barf in a sink
- Pour pea soup into your toilet and look at it as closely as you can
- Eat (snacks or meals) outside of your home

- Eat something you are afraid to eat
- Put on an item of clothing you are afraid to wear

These exposures might be scary to imagine and each will create elevated levels of discomfort, uncertainty, and anticipatory anxiety. But perhaps they won't be as horrific as you imagine. Perhaps it's just your opponent scaring you. You are driving the bus so you are in control.

You get to decide the order of the exposures and whether or not to break them up into smaller pieces. Follow these steps:

Step 1) Rank the exposures from least difficult to most.

Step 2) Select a competing emotion: love, excitement, amusement, or toughness. Write what you will say to your opponent to **invite** him to play and/or what you will say to yourself as you take a breath before facing the exposure:

____

____

____

____

Step 3) Identify how you will incorporate a competing emotion into a **response**: what you will say and do when you feel anxious, nauseous, or have anxious thoughts:

____

____

____

____

As they say, there's no time like the present. Go on offense and begin with the least difficult exposure **right now! Don't hesitate. Go for it!**

Did you vomit like your opponent threatened? If your anxiety was high, you are on the right road. It's not about how you feel. It's about how you respond to those feelings. If you felt discomfort and tolerated those feelings with a winning response, you're winning! If it wasn't as bad as you thought it would be, that's great too. Either way you win.

Repeat the same exposure four more times in a row with short breaks in between if you desire. **You can handle it.** Go for it!

Read your motivational letter and repeat the exposure four more times **increasing the intensity if necessary.** For instance, if you pretended to barf in the sink but it did not sound realistic, increase the realism. If you spun in a chair three times, do it four times. The goal is to increase your tolerance. Go for it!

Congratulations! You're winning because you are doing the opposite of what anxiety demands! Perform another round of four later on in the day, increasing the intensity of the exposure, as needed.

Do Exposures Correctly and Prepare Correctly

Doing exposures is important to your success but how you do them is vital. I know patients who do exposures every day but **never** improve. Like baking a cake or hitting a baseball, unless you do it properly it's not going to turn out well.

Doing planned and spontaneous exposures correctly begins with your thought process **before** the exposure. It is common for anxiety sufferers to prepare for exposures by trying to figure out what they would do should the worst occur -- if they experience a panic attack, feel nauseous, or vomit. As I mentioned, planning and preparing for a panic attack or a vomiting emergency might seem like a good idea but all this does is make you more anxious as you engage with anxiety by anticipating the worst. This usually culminates in avoidance or facing the feared situation in a heightened state.

There is no need to figure out anything by having a discussion with your anxiety monster in the back of the bus. There is nothing to prepare for except for the strategies outlined in this book: having an offensive mindset, being committed to pushing through anxiety to the predetermined goal, breathing, not engaging, and responding to anxious thoughts and symptoms using a competing emotion. **Do not imagine worst case scenarios under the guise of figuring out a plan.**

If you have a fear of driving out of your comfort zone and you do it every day, one would think you would eventually conquer the fear. This is not necessarily the case. If you are clutching the steering wheel, driving slowly, praying you don't have a panic attack, and looking for an exit while holding your breath, all you are doing is strengthening your fear. This fearful mindset will always override any courageous acts. As you face your fears, you must shift your attitude. If you don't, you will remain stuck despite your best efforts. The game you're playing with your anxiety monster is mental, and requires you to be cunning and tough. Do planned and spontaneous exposures with an attitude.

When you do exposures, don't try to stop anxiety or nausea. Do the opposite. Ask for more. Reid Wilson, PhD, writes in Stopping the Noise in Your Head, *You don't need to get rid of that feeling. As soon as you take the stance that you have to get rid of that feeling, you have put Anxiety back in the dominant position. If your doubt or distress gets stronger, then want it to be stronger. If your doubt or distress sticks around, then want it to stick around. Your job is to handle the present moment… We must, first and foremost, learn to step on the cracks rather than stepping around, over, and in between them. As you move towards activities you've been backing away from, be willing not to know for certain how things are going to turn out.*

When anxiety hits, it's easy to forget what you've learned. Write down what you need to remember and then practice repeatedly to rewire your brain and automate your response.

STEPS TO FREEDOM

Hierarchy Exposures: Work on each exposure until you complete all nine in your hierarchy. Do the exposure five times in a row, twice a day until you can tolerate (spinning, gagging, looking, eating, and listening). Once you can perform each exposure with minimal discomfort, increase the intensity by reducing safety behaviors, performing the exposure longer, eating more, and dining in unfamiliar places further from home. Then combine exposures: Listen to a vomit video as you spin in a chair and then puke water into a sink as realistically as possible. Remember, to summon your secret identity and play your theme song to get you in the right frame of mind.

MINDFULNESS: Do the exposures mindfully. As you are spinning around, notice what it feels like without judgment. As you stare at the soup in the toilet, notice what it looks and smells like without judgment. Notice what the outside of the toilet feels like. Notice your discomfort and stay with it.

CONTINUE READING: As you work through all nine exposures in your hierarchy, move on to the next chapter.

Chapter 27
Shift Your Focus to Living Your Life

> I was driving down a highway when splat! A giant bird turd landed on my windshield. Even though it was gross, I kept looking at it, hoping the wind would blow it off. Focusing on the toilet art made it difficult to drive safely, but when I changed my attention and looked beyond it, at the road and landscape before me, I was fine. I barely noticed it. The problem was, I had a strong need to focus on the disgusting splatter and an intense desire get rid of it! So, I flipped on the windshield wipers and the soapy water. I'm not sure what kind of bird decided to use my car for target practice, but no amount of wiping removed it. In fact, the wipers smeared the turd across my windshield, obstructing my vision!

When people suffer with emetophobia, they focus intently on their symptoms and thoughts, with urgent desperation to stop them. Unfortunately, focusing on symptoms and trying to make them stop worsens the problem. At this point, you have shifted your **perspective** from looking at your anxiety as a struggle within yourself, to viewing the problem as a mental game against a tricky opponent. You then shifted your **mindset**. Instead of playing the game defensively you switched to an offensive mentality, forcefully moving into anxiety's territory with a competing emotion.

Now you must shift your **focus** -- away from anxiety to living your life.

Winning any competition requires focus on what's important. The bird turd on my windshield was **not** important. What was paramount was driving safely, which required me to look past the turd and focus on the road.

Until now your focus has been on making sure you are certain and comfortable. Everything you do has been with these goals in mind. Focusing on comfort and certainty means staying home when everyone else is going out. It means making choices based on what you fear, not on what you value. **It is time to shift your focus to living your life.** Like a photographer with a zoom lens, as you focus on living, the monster in the foreground becomes blurred. His lies, threats, and orders are present but are muted as you live your life.

The goal is to live your life, not to be comfortable or certain.

Living your life means going to a restaurant even though your opponent claims there is a possibility of vomiting. Living your life means going to a party, movie, or concert with friends or family even though you are uncertain about the outcome. Declare out loud: *I'm excited to do uncertain things because I'm excited to live my life.*

Avoiding life is depressing. Living life can be scary but also rewarding. When you focus on living your life, you recapture what you have lost and much more. Live your life based on what you value (family, friends, career); not what you fear. Every day is a new opportunity and as you focus on living, what was once frightening, becomes mildly stressful and eventually easy and enjoyable.

Your anxiety demands you stay alert: *At any moment something could go wrong and you won't be able to handle it. Be vigilant!* Emetophobes look out for possible vomit situations because they believe they are likely to occur, the experience will be horrific, and they won't be able to handle it. Then they brace for the impact. Anxiety grows when you focus your attention to all possible threats. People **without** emetophobia are oblivious to the threats you perceive. Instead of focusing on their bodily sensations, other people's behavior, food, etc., they focus on living their life.

Mary decides to plant a vegetable garden. To learn how, she goes online to research the steps. She spends hours reading articles and watching videos on You Tube. She makes detailed notes on how to build it, the best location to maximize growth, and the best time of year to plant. The next day she heads out to purchase supplies, visiting several different stores and asking a lot of questions. She takes notes and spends time making sure she purchases the correct tools.

Over the next week she spends hours creating her garden: From pulling weeds and enriching the soil, to digging holes, planting the seeds, and finally, securing the garden to prevent rodents from invading. Over the next several months, she waters on schedule, eliminates insects, pulls weeds, and guards against rodents. Week by week she watches her garden grow until the vegetables are fully grown and it's time to harvest.

When you tend to a garden and give it attention and focus, it grows. The same is true for worry. If you tend to your worries, they grow! Give them a lot of attention and focus, they grow huge – like weeds. What happens to a garden if you don't pay it any attention? It never grows. And this is true for your worries as well. This is why shifting your focus away from worries to living your life is so important. When you stop tending to your thoughts with safety behaviors and instead focus on living, those worries die.

Focus on what you want to grow – your life, not your symptoms or thoughts.

Many years ago I learned to rollerblade at a popular roller skating rink. Every Wednesday morning from 10 to 12 about twenty adults showed up for free skate with light individual instruction. I had never skied or skateboarded or did any activity that required balance, so skating was going to be a challenge. Basketball, tennis, track, and soccer were my games. Needless to say, learning to skate was uncomfortable and uncertain. I was risking falling, hurting myself, and embarrassing myself. I was awkward, stiff, and tense. I was not comfortable. So there I was at age 32, trying my best to balance on eight wheels as Gwen Stefani blared "Hey Baby."

A woman my age started learning around the same time. We each wore a helmet but as the weeks rolled on, she added more and more protection. Knee pads, wrist guards, elbow pads, extra layers of clothing, and a butt pad that seemed to grow every couple of weeks. Her focus was on not falling. Whereas I fell periodically, she never did. She carefully and slowly walked/rolled around the rink, looking down at her skates, arms out, bracing for the fall, while trying her best not to. My focus was learning how to skate. After six months I was skating comfortably doing various moves while she was skating the exact same way – bracing for the fall. Falling wasn't fun for me but it also wasn't horrible. I just picked myself back up and kept going. She, on the other hand, never became comfortable skating even though she skated just as much as I did. Why? Because her mindset was defensive and her focus was on being comfortable, certain, and not falling.

After I learned to rollerblade, I took my son to a group lesson and the first thing the instructor had them do was fall. They practiced falling to get used to it, to learn they can handle it, and to not be afraid. Metaphorically speaking, falling is part of life. If you are hypervigilant in your efforts to never fall or constantly bracing for the fall, you can't enjoy your life. As long as you are protecting yourself from vomit, thoughts of vomit, nausea, or discomfort, you won't be happy and you will never beat emetophobia. Don't just be willing to fall, do what the kids did in the class: fall on purpose. In other words, expose yourself to what you fear. As you embrace the discomfort, your amygdala will eventually learn not to signal your adrenal glands to secrete adrenaline, and soon enough you won't be so afraid.

The mental game against anxiety requires you to go on offense which necessitates an offensive mindset. You will not move forward if you are only playing defense by trying to protect yourself.

To enjoy life, do not brace for the fall; rather, lean into it and accept it.

When skilled poker players sense opposing players are bluffing, they call their bluff. That's what you will be doing with your anxiety monster. When you feel nauseous and anxiety claims you will vomit, call his bluff. *Make me puke. I dare you.* Anxiety expects that you will beg him to stop. Encourage your monster to give you more. *Give me more nausea. This is not enough. I can handle it.* As I've said before, this strategy is counterintuitive. This is not a natural way to react, but to beat anxiety you must respond in a way anxiety does not expect. It will be easier to adopt this new strategy if you let go of your old one. The paradoxical approach I'm offering will take practice and faith. There's a learning curve so be patient and persistent.

Anxiety will tell you that you can't do it and you will never succeed.

Refuse to allow this thought to dominate you. Your opponent will be particularly loud when you experience setbacks. Refuse to believe him. You **will** succeed if this is the choice you have chosen to make. Make the decision to beat anxiety at all costs. *This is hard but I* **will** *win with GRIT!* And then do every single exercise in this book even if you have doubt.

STEPS TO FREEDOM

Focus on Living Your Life: Make a list of hobbies, sports, and social activities you have ceased doing and restart one by one. This includes making lunch and dinner plans with friends, getting a haircut, going to a nail salon, exercising at the gym, going to the movies, taking an Uber, and getting a massage.

Letter to your Opponent: Write a letter to your anxiety monster reminding him of your victories and how you are going to win. Feel free to boast and trash talk. He deserves it. Write a letter about recapturing your life and finding freedom and happiness. Write about how you are forming a new relationship with anxiety by making peace with it and regaining control. Address it and mail it to yourself. Once you receive it, read it out loud periodically.

Hierarchy Exposures: Step by step, work on one exposure at a time, until you complete all nine in your hierarchy. Do the exposure five times in a row, twice a day until you can tolerate it (spinning, gagging, looking, eating, and listening). Learn to tolerate the discomfort. *Give me more. I can handle it.* Record your victories!

3 by 3 Relaxation Breathing: Continue to practice five to ten times a day, before and during exposures, and any time you feel anxious.

Continue Reading: As you work through all nine exposures in your hierarchy, continue reading.

Chapter 28
Spontaneous Exposures: A Move-by-Move Game

Imagine a fish in a lake searching for food. He spots a juicy worm and instinctively consumes it. Suddenly he's filled with anxiety, HOOKED, caught in a struggle for his life. This is what happens when you take your opponent's bait. When anxiety asks you a question, makes a threat, or shouts a demand, if you react instinctively and take the bait, you become hooked, and your anxiety spirals.

Just as fishermen change their bait when fish aren't biting, your monster will change his, by asking different questions and dropping various threats. In other words, your worries will not stop, at least not until you change your behavior. When does a fisherman stop dropping his line? When the fish stop biting. Eventually, he gives up and goes home. Your anxious thoughts will not stop until you stop taking the bait and stop doing what your opponent demands. In other words, **to stop your worries, you must stop your anxious behaviors first.** It does not go in reverse.

It is difficult not to engage in a constant battle between the urge to avoid and the push to do what is uncertain and uncomfortable. By externalizing anxiety and personifying it, you remove the inner struggle and replace it as a clear battle between you and an opponent whose sole objective is to make your life miserable.

As you focus on living, your anxiety monster will attempt to draw your focus back to your worries and symptoms. As you drive your bus through the maze of life, you and your opponent will make moves back and forth. To win this mental game, you must outsmart him, move into his territory with an offensive mindset, be focused on living your life, and be determined not to engage or take his threats seriously.

Spontaneous exposures will present themselves each day. View these exposures as opportunities to improve your skills, rewire your brain, and further your place in the game. You will not be trying to stop your worries or symptoms. Rather, you will raise your voice to the dominant position, so you become the executive.

A Move-by-Move Game

You are playing a move-by-move game with your opponent. Here's how a courageous and successful day might play out, as you make your way through the maze of life:

- As you begin to wake up in the morning, your opponent immediately asks a question: *How are you feeling?*

- Because he always asks the same questions, you are ready with your response: ***I'm not taking the bait. Not answering the question.***

- Anxiety knows that if he can keep you in bed in a semi-asleep state and engage you in a conversation, he can cause your adrenal gland to secret adrenaline: *Don't get out of bed yet. You're so tired. Do you think it's going to be another bad day? Is your stomach is upset? What's your plan to make sure you don't vomit today?*

- He's so predictable. Similar to playing chess, you anticipate your opponent's moves and are prepared. ***Not taking the bait. Not answering the questions.*** You then do the opposite of what he wants and IMMEDIATELY get out of bed before anxiety takes hold. ***You can't fool me. Bring it on. I can handle it. I'm going to rewire my brain.*** You focus on living your life. You get dressed and take a short walk, and as you do, you mindfully observe your environment.

- You return home feeling good but then notice some slight indigestion and your opponent asks, *Why do you have indigestion? Do you think it's from last night's dinner?*

- You're not fooled by the questions. ***Not taking the bait. Not answering the questions.*** You know taking your indigestion medication helps you feel better but your opponent warns, *What if it makes you puke?*

- You take the indigestion medication before he has a chance to convince you otherwise. ***You're a liar. I'm doing the opposite of what you tell me.***

- Your anxiety monster gives you an order: *Don't eat anything this morning. You already don't feel great and you have plans. If you eat something and get nauseous, you'll have to cancel.*

- You make your move: ***I'm doing the opposite of what you tell me. This is a beautiful day to do hard things. I'm excited to rewire my brain.*** Then you eat breakfast and consume a little more than usual, just to show your opponent who is in charge.

- He doubles down: *What are you, crazy? You might have the flu! Don't risk it. What if it makes you nauseous?*

- You verbalize your worries out loud in an English accent: ***My anxiety monster is messing with me by telling me I will feel nauseous if I eat more. That's RUBBISH!*** The fear does not feel as real when you verbalize it out loud in an accent. You swiftly grab your opponent off the kitchen counter, throw him down the garbage disposal, and turn it on. ***See you later, alligator.*** As you continue eating your breakfast you sing to yourself, "Don't Stop Believing" by Journey.

- As you complete your morning routine and prepare to leave your home, anxiety asks a series of questions: *Maybe you shouldn't go out? What if you get sick when you're with your friend? Did you eat too much? Should you cancel your plans? What if you have a panic attack? Will you ever be normal? Why are you like this? What do people think of you? Should you wait for your food to digest before you leave? Should you cancel?*

- You do not go to the back of the bus by answering any of his meaningless questions. With each question you respond the same: ***I'm not answering your questions. I'll handle it.*** Instead of contemplating retreating, you go on offense. You do a planned exposure you have already conquered. While eating breakfast you watch the Sam Fuentes video for inspiration and the Family Guy video for humor. To minimize anticipatory anxiety, you do it quickly, before your monster has a chance to convince you otherwise. Your opponent is stunned by your tenacity: *What the hell is happening? I'm losing my touch.*

- You take a shower and get dressed. You feel anxious about meeting your friend. You go to the bathroom and have loose stools.

- Your anxiety shouts, *This is a sign that you're sick!* You immediately feel a rush of anxiety. *You're going to vomit!*

- You face your fear head on with an offensive mindset. ***Bring it on. Make me puke. I dare you.*** You put water into your mouth and pretend to puke in the trashcan. You feel empowered and the fear subsides.

- You leave the house to meet your friend. You experience a shot of adrenaline as you drive out of your comfort zone: racing heart, light-headed, jitters, hot and cold flashes, sweating, and nausea.

- Your respond with your game face rather than react. ***This is exactly the feeling I need right now. Give me more nausea. I can handle it.*** You stuff your monster in the glove box and slam it shut. You focus on living your life by turning on your music and singing with passion. You are determined to meet your friend for lunch because reclaiming your life is what is most important.

- Your opponent is upset that you are not paying attention to him. You continue on with your day despite your worry about having the flu or experiencing a panic attack. You focus on living your life, not on your symptoms or doubt. You refuse to allow anxiety to have power over you.

- You keep repeating in your mind calmly, ***The goal is to live my life, not to be comfortable or certain.*** You sing along to your favorite tunes and think, ***I'm doing fine. Even though I'm anxious I'm ok.*** As you drive you do 3 by 3 Relaxation Breathing to help contain the anxiety. You decide to listen to a podcast and as you become engrossed in the topic you forget about your symptoms.

- You arrive at your first destination (the cleaners) and your nausea is still present. Anxiety shouts: *You're still nauseous. Nothing is working. You must really be sick this time. You're definitely going to vomit! Cancel your plans and go home.*

- You verbalize the worry out loud this time in a southern accent: ***My anxiety monster is messing with me by telling me to cancel my plans because I might puke. Kiss my grits.*** You hit the lies hard like my son on Halloween: ***You're a phony. Is that all you got?*** You grab anxiety from the glove box and shove him in your pocket. ***Come on baby. We got plans. I'm excited to do hard things.*** And like the buffalo, you charge forward into the storm, exiting your car without hesitation. You take him with you to prove to anxiety that you will not be intimidated and you can handle it. (Also because he's going to come anyway.) ***I'm excited to be anxious because I'm excited to be free.***

- As you continue on with your day, your monster tries to bother you but you easily dismiss him. You notice that anxiety has subsided and you're feeling good. You scroll through Facebook on your phone and see a post about the stomach flu. Adrenaline instantly shoots through your body but you respond quickly, ***I feel you. I love you. Welcome back. Stay as long as you like.*** And you continue on with your day.

- When he orders you to do something, you do the opposite. When he threatens you with the possibility of vomiting, you tell him he's a liar. You look for and take uncomfortable and uncertain roads. Though you feel anxious, worried, and nauseous you are winning! You are retraining your brain to view these situations as **not** dangerous.

- You accept the symptoms, reject the lies, and keep moving forward. You remind yourself why you are doing this: Because your life has been a living hell and this is what you need to do to free yourself from emetophobia and be happy. You remind yourself that your fear and worry will dissipate only when you stop avoiding, stop your safety behaviors, and stop your compulsions. Going into anxiety's territory with an offensive mindset is the only way for the fear to go away.

- After taking care of a few errands, you drive to a restaurant where you are meeting a friend. The chess match continues:

- *Why are you still nauseous? It's not going away. What if you're sick?*

- You gently stroke your arm, ***My love will conquer this fear.***

- *It's been a long day. You've done enough. Cancel your lunch plans and go home. Your friend will understand. What if you have a panic attack?*

- You gently stroke your arm. ***My love will conquer this fear.***

- *What if you vomit in the restaurant?*

- ***My love will conquer this fear.*** You avoid dwelling (going to the back of the bus) by repeating the same response. You smack the passenger seat with your hand and shout, ***My love will conquer this fear!*** Your monster is surprised by the blow. He sees that you're not backing down and you're not believing his lies. Now **he's** getting anxious. *Holy crap. What the hell is happening?*

- You arrive at the restaurant. ***Let's go. You're coming with me.*** You put anxiety and doubt in one pocket and courage and determination in the other and exit the car immediately before he has a chance to change your mind.

- You meet your friend with a big smile and a hug even though you feel anxious and nauseous. After you sit down you apologize for canceling so many times and disclose what has been going on. ***I'm embarrassed to share this with you but I want to explain why I've been acting the way I have been. I consider you a good friend and even if you can't fully understand, I know you will be supportive and won't judge me. Please keep this between us. I suffer with panic attacks and emetophobia.*** You go on to explain the disorder and how difficult it is to be in a restaurant. Your friend is supportive and kind. By the time you are done telling her about emetophobia you have noticed that your nausea has gone away. And as soon as you notice, it comes back.

- Your monster makes an attempt to get you into the back of the bus with questions. *Why does your nausea keep coming back? Will this ever go away? Does your friend think you're a freak?*

- ***I'm not answering your questions.*** (Since you are with your friend, you think your response.) You spot a dish on the menu that sounds delicious but you have not eaten it in years.

- *Don't order it. It might make you sick and if you puke in the restaurant, it will be so embarrassing. DON'T DO IT!*

- ***Fuck off!***

- *You're still nauseous. What if you really have the flu? DON'T DO IT!*

- From under the table you flick your opponent off your knee and think, ***Fuck off! I don't believe you anymore. I'm excited to eat.***

- The waitress arrives at your table and asks what she can get you. To the shock of your anxiety monster, you defy his orders and tell the waitress the exact food item he told you not to get. Your opponent begins to freak out: *I'm losing my powers. How is this happening? I'm so depressed.*

- Similar to a large crowd at a sporting event when the home team is getting slaughtered, your monster becomes quiet. Rambunctious fans fall silent the further their team falls behind.

- Your food arrives and your opponent sees this as a new opportunity. *Are you sure you want to do this? What if you puke?*

- **I'm not answering your questions.**

- You start to feel anxious again and think, ***Welcome back. Stay as long as you like. This is exactly the feeling I need right now.***

- *People get food poisoning from this. What if they didn't cook it long enough?*

- ***I'm not answering your questions.***

- *What if the chef is sick and didn't wash his hands?*

- ***I'm not answering your questions.*** And you take your first bite quickly. Anxiety surges but you get involved in the conversation with your friend instead of the dialogue with anxiety.

- Your anxiety subsides but it is still present. You excuse yourself and go to the restroom to take a break and calm yourself. You do 3 by 3 Breathing and renew you determination. ***I'm not leaving. Even though I have emetophobia I accept and love myself. I can do hard things. I'm not leaving. I'm pushing through because I love my friend and I'm finally living my life.***

- You return to the table, reminding yourself to ***Push through. I can do this. I'm not going to vomit. It's just adrenaline.***

- As the meal continues, you are aware of your monster's presence but you don't let him stop you. When you take small bites, you don't judge yourself for it, and you don't worry about what your friend thinks. Your anxiety subsides as you become engrossed in the conversation.

- You complete the meal and are ready for the check. The restaurant has become crowded and your waitress is nowhere to be seen.

- *Holy crap! This is going to take forever.*

- ***This is my opportunity to practice. Bring it on. I can handle it. I'm excited to do hard things because I'm excited to be free.***

- Your waitress comes to the table and asks if she can get you something else. Instead of asking for the check, you order dessert and tell her to take her time.

- *Are you crazy? What if you have a panic attack?*

- ***I'm excited to do hard things because I'm excited to be free and live my life.***

- When you arrive back home you feel exhausted but triumphant. Nothing anxiety predicted came true. It never does. You greet your mailman with a smile and he tells you about his recent vacation. He shares a story about how wonderful it was except for when he puked on the plane.

- *Oh my God. Change the subject. Go inside!*

- You choose to lean into the anxiety, accept the discomfort, and listen to his story with a smile. ***Thanks for this opportunity to practice. Bring it on.*** You tolerate the discomfort and instead of escaping, you ask him questions about his experience. ***Do you usually get motion sickness? Do you worry about vomiting when you're on a plane?*** He tells you another vomit story and you listen with interest.

- You enter your home and journal about all of your successes. Pushing through anxiety is draining but very rewarding. You feel fantastic! You're finally living your life.

As you live your life, spontaneous exposures like the mailman and lunch crowds will present themselves. **See them as opportunities to practice, rewire your brain, and further yourself in the game.** Spontaneous exposures are no longer situations to avoid; rather, they are opportunities for you to improve your skills. When they present themselves, respond, ***Thanks for this opportunity to practice. Bring it on!***

Some days will go better than others but if you are patient and persistent you will notice that the more you focus on living your life, the more quickly your anxiety and worries subside. There will be a natural inclination to evaluate if you are winning, i.e., getting better. The definition of getting better is more than a reduction of symptoms. It includes responding with an offensive mindset and doing things you previously avoided.

Having emetophobia is upsetting and frustrating and it's normal to feel angry for being unable to do everyday tasks that others do easily. It also can be depressing to feel behind in life. Feeling depressed and angry at your situation will make it difficult to move forward. We must accept where we are in life, while simultaneously taking steps forward.

It's fabulous when symptoms subside and worries diminish but don't be fooled. Anxiety is tenacious and won't give up easily. He will reappear, and when he does, he expects you to be disappointed, frustrated, and hopeless. Don't be. Welcome him back like an old friend you haven't seen in a while. Although it's normal to feel frustrated and hopeless when anxiety returns, giving into these emotions will only make your anxiety last longer.

I'm reminding you to think of emotions as crashing waves. When anxiety resurfaces it's like a wave crashing on you. It feels terrible but if you accept it, you'll only be hit by one wave. If you don't, you'll be clobbered by a series of emotional waves, one after another: disappointment, frustration, anger, self-loathing, hopelessness, and depression. Accepting the wave of anxiety will prevent you from drowning in an emotional tsunami.

Setbacks are part of the process. Accept them.
You cannot be set back unless you have taken steps forward.

STEPS TO FREEDOM

Focus on Living your Life: Engage in activities you once enjoyed. Be patient and persistent. Do them every day and give yourself time for the joy to return. Make plans with friends, take a class, and start a new hobby – one step at a time.

Hierarchy Exposures: Step by step, continue to work on exposures multiple times a day and build your tolerance to discomfort. *Give me more. I can handle it. I'm excited to rewire my brain by doing hard things.* Record your victories!

3 by 3 Relaxation Breathing: Continue to practice five to ten times a day, before and during exposures, and any time you feel anxious.

Read Motivational Letter: Automate motivation by remembering why you are doing this and what your new life will be like.

Chapter 29
More Planned Exposures: Creating Your Hierarchy of Success

Sixteen-year-old baseball player Manny is pretty good at fielding but struggles with hitting the ball. To become a better baseball player, Manny needs to focus on his weaknesses. He asks his pitcher to throw him curveballs and fastballs. You have a similar task. Every morning, step up to the plate and invite your anxiety monster to throw you something challenging, something you don't expect. Then focus on living your life, ready to respond to the pitch. When you invite your anxiety monster to trick you, you are taking ownership of your life. When you invite discomfort and uncertainty, you are now controlling the bus and your path to victory.

Like a baseball player, be ready to smash whatever lie is thrown. Be prepared to hit your anxious thoughts **hard**. As I discussed previously, it's a basic law of physics. If you want to change the direction of an object you must hit it with force. Changing the direction of a worry requires power. **Focus on where you have influence (your behavior and thoughts) and accept what you cannot control (your physical symptoms).**

Use a competing emotion. Although it sounds silly (and it is), flush your monster down the toilet, radiate him in the microwave, or flick him off your shoulder.

Do it with force, to reverse anxiety's course.

What is important in this mental game against anxiety is the same as in any game: your preparation, your determination to win, your effort, your strategy, and your acceptance of what you can't change. It's about playing hard and doing your best even when you don't think you'll be successful. It's about not backing down from an opponent that appears bigger and stronger and using your wits to outsmart him while simultaneously not falling for his tricks.

Like Manny striving to become a better batter by inviting curveballs, you will continue to step up to the plate and invite discomfort and uncertainty. Acting as though you can handle a challenge when your confidence is low will require a leap of faith. Your opponent claims that you must be confident before you move into his territory. This is a trick. If you wait until you feel confident, it will take you a long time to conquer emetophobia. Your task is to take steps forward despite your doubt, surpass your monster's intensity, and rise up to be the executive voice. *I'm not certain about this but I will handle it. Bring it on asshole! I'm in charge now.* You do not need to take large steps. Only frequent ones.

Continue working off your exposure list and once that is complete, proceed with more challenging lists in chapters to come. Order the exposures from least to most difficult. If you anticipate a particular exposure will produce too much anxiety, feel free to break it down into smaller steps. For instance, if eating a meal in a sit-down restaurant is too big of a step, reduce the exposure to something more manageable. Perhaps eat an appetizer at a fast-food restaurant where you pay first. If pretending to vomit into a sink with water in your mouth is too intense, break it down into pieces and then put it all together. A) Practice making barfing noises with increased realism. B) Practice spitting water into a sink. C) Then put it together and make barfing noise as you spit water into a sink.

Once you conquer two exposures, combine them. For instance, if you have conquered the fear of riding in the back of a taxi and you no longer feel anxious watching vomit videos, combine these two exposures into one: Watch vomit videos while sitting in the back of a taxi. Then add a third: Watch vomit videos while sitting in the back of a taxi and eating.

As I've stated several times, exposures are not what you WANT to do but they are what you NEED to do, despite your resistance. Kimberly

Morrow and Elizabeth Dupont wrote in their book *CBT for Anxiety*, "Resistance is normal. It is our instinct to listen to our amygdala and to avoid discomfort and danger." To help lower your resistance and take action, read your motivational letter and your letter to your monster at least twice a week.

Doing exposures is exhausting and it's normal to take breaks. It's also common to stop doing exposures when you begin to feel better. Think of exposures as steps through the maze. Once you stop taking steps forward, your progress also stops. If you feel discouraged about your lack of progress, try to identify the problem. Perhaps you are not doing enough exposures each day or you are not doing them correctly. Maybe medication is the answer. It's common to experience no improvement for a few weeks, despite daily effort, then suddenly take a giant step forward.

What follows is list of exposures for emetophobia. (There is a separate list of exposures for Panic Disorder in Chapter 32). The exposures here are not listed in any particular order. You decide that. Repeat them several times a day and increase the duration and intensity. Record your successes in your Victory Journal as you continue reading this book. **All the videos are located at QuietMindSolutions.com/emetophobia** and you can find plenty more vomit videos on YouTube.

Exposures for Emetophobia

- Put your head into the toilet and pretend to vomit with water in your mouth. Make it sound realistic
- Have your partner or parent surprise you by doing something unexpected (tape a vomit photo inside a cabinet, pour soup in toilet, pretend to vomit in toilet)
- Print out barfing photos and tape them to a wall
- Watch vomiting scenes from movies
- Watch Medium Level Vomit Videos
- Watch High Level Vomit Videos
- Watch someone else pretend to puke soup into a toilet
- Leave the house immediately after eating a meal
- Eat a meal in a familiar restaurant
- Eat a meal in an unfamiliar restaurant
- Eat a meal in a restaurant where you pay first
- Eat a meal in a restaurant where you pay the check after the meal
- Eat unfamiliar food at a restaurant
- Wash hands only before eating, with one pump of soap
- Place food (cheese, turkey, apple slices, etc.) on the kitchen counter for one minute and then eat it

- Do not clean your phone, plates, cups, or utensils before using them
- Host a potluck dinner and eat other people's creations
- Do not check expiration dates more than once
- Drink or eat one day past the expiration date
- Leave refrigerated food out for two hours and then eat it
- Walk through a hospital
- Sit in a doctor's office
- Wash dirty dishes with your hands
- Sit in a bar and drink a glass of alcohol
- Go places without safety supplies (gum, water, cell, etc.)
- Eliminate a safety behavior (asking for reassurance, taking anti-nausea medication)
- Write "I'm excited to vomit today." Put it in your pocket
- Ask your partner or parent to tell you every day that they feel sick
- Change your routine (wake up earlier, leave the house, do things in a different order)

Focus only on the exposure you are working on. Thinking about an upcoming exposure will make doing the current one more difficult and cause more anxiety. Your monster will try to convince you to delay doing easier exposures in anticipation of tougher ones. Don't fall for his tricks. Simply focus on the task at hand – that's all. Your opponent will claim that you won't be able to do any of them. We know he's a big liar. Think about all you have accomplished thus far and didn't think possible. When needed, break exposures into small steps and increase the duration and intensity.

STEPS TO FREEDOM

Exposures: Review the list of exposures and highlight the ones that will be the least difficult. Tackle these first, one at a time, in the order that you see fit. Each time you prevail, cross the exposure off the list, add it to your *Wall of Fame*, and record your successes in your Victory Journal. Begin right now by identifying an easy exposure and facing it head on. Then continue on to the next chapter as you work through your exposure list.

How to work through an exposure hierachry.

Chapter 30
The Vomit Stories in Your Mind

Emetophobes rarely vomit but they have many stories in their mind: horrific stories of disgust, humiliation, vomit, and panic. Unlike traumas, these stories have never taken place yet they can be just as traumatic if repeated enough times in the mind. Remember, **all** anxiety is based on lies: tricks of the imagination where thoughts and images are amplified, distorted, and exaggerated.

Imagine ten people at a party standing on a large balcony of a tall building. It's a beautiful view and all the guests are having a wonderful time except for three anxious people. One feels lightheaded because his mind is telling him he might fall off the balcony. Another guest is worried that the cute dog roaming around the apartment might bite her. And the third imagines that the other guests think she is ugly and weird because her palms were sweaty when being introduced to people. If you happened to be at this party, you might be anxious due to a variety of worries, including drunk people puking, food that might make you sick, or having a panic attack on the elevator ride down. All the other guests enjoy themselves because their minds are focused on having fun and not on what might happen. By the end of the evening no one was bitten by the dog, fell off the balcony, or got sick. And the guy who was afraid of heights asked the woman with the sweaty palms for her number.

The mind is powerful. It can make us focus our attention on places where no one else is looking and make us believe things that are false. Take for instance a tall woman who suffers with anorexia. She is 90 pounds and believes she is fat. She is not seeing reality. As an anxiety sufferer, you must demand reality. You must confront the stories in your imagination and change your emotional reaction to your imagery. You can do this by facing your fear -- by writing a detailed description of your worst fear and then reading it out loud repeatedly. Sound awful? It might be, but only temporarily. This writing exposure will diminish your anxiety, reduce your worry, and increase your tolerance.

When writing the story about your worst fear coming true, don't hold back on details or the depth of the terror. Take your story to the bitter end. The purpose is to scare yourself. If you feel anxiety while writing, you're doing a great job.

Before writing your horror story, write on the top of the page, ***Bring** on the lies, nausea, and discomfort. **I** can handle it. I'm **excited** to win my freedom by doing hard things.*

Then write your horror story **in the present tense.**

At the end of the story write, *This is **exactly** the feeling I need right now. Keep it coming. This is a bunch of **bullshit**. **I** can handle it!*

You will then read the entire page **out loud**. Reading it out loud is key. The goal is to create anxiety (turbulence) and experience handling it (not trying to stop the turbulence). The first time you read it, your anxiety might be very high and you could perceive this as a failure. It's not! Facing your fear is a victory. You're victorious because you're choosing discomfort by going down the winning path and tolerating it! After reading your story four or five times in a row, your anxiety will settle.

Go on offense by **inviting** anxiety **with intensity** and **responding** at the end of the story **with passion**. Slap your leg with your hand as you invite anxiety before reading the story and then again as you respond after reading it. I **bolded** the words you should emphasize with a slap. If your anxiety is very high after you read it, feel free to do a few minutes of *3 by 3 Relaxation Breathing* in between readings. Record the story on your phone and then listen to it with headphones. This will desensitize you further to your fears.

Before writing your **own** horror story, read the one below. Remember, emphasize the words in bold with a slap on your leg and read it all **out loud.**

You: "***Bring*** *on the lies, nausea, and discomfort.* ***I*** *can handle it. I'm* ***excited*** *to win my freedom by doing hard things."*

Sample horror story: *I'm feeling anxious sitting in the restaurant. What if I'm sick? Why did I come? Everyone is having a good time and I can't stop thinking about vomiting. I don't think I should have eaten that bread. Why did I eat it? What if someone in the kitchen has the flu and touched it? What if I catch it? Oh my God! That guy over there looks drunk. If he orders one more drink I'm leaving. What's that smell? Is that someone's perfume? It's making me nauseous. I ask my friend if it's hot in here. She says no and asks me if I'm ok. I'm not but I tell her I am. I'm feeling lightheaded. My nausea is getting worse. I think I caught the stomach flu from that little boy I met yesterday. I really don't feel well at all. I excuse myself and go to the bathroom. It's occupied and there's two people in front of me. I'm in hell. I can't take it. I am so sick. This is definitely the flu. I feel like I'm going to vomit. I gotta get out of here. I run back into the restaurant to tell my friends that I'm leaving but before I reach our table I puke all over the floor. Everyone turns around and gasps. I am violently ill. I can't stop vomiting. It's loud and disgusting. Chunks of smelly, brownish-green puke are everywhere – the floor, chairs, tables. People are screaming and running out of the restaurant. My friend is disgusted and screams at me. I run back to the bathroom but it's locked. I throw up all over myself. People are yelling at me to get out but I can't move. I fall down to the floor and barf again."*

You: *"This is* ***exactly*** *the feeling I need right now.* ***Keep*** *it coming. This is a bunch of* ***bullshit. I*** *can handle it!"*

If you're experiencing anxiety you're WINNING. That's the goal. As my friend Reid Wilson says, *This is short-term pain for longer-term gain.* If you need to take a few *3 by 3 Breaths* go ahead. Then read it out loud again. Go for it!

Read the story two more times in a row, once with an accent (English, American, French, etc.). Go for it!

Write multiple horror stories based on your specific fears. If you fear experiencing a panic attack in an elevator, write a story about being trapped and panicking. If you have been avoiding a specific exposure, write a horror story about it. For instance, if you are too scared to pretend to vomit in a toilet, write a story about what you imagine will happen when you do the exposure -- the worst thing imaginable. Read it out loud four times a day (one time with an accent) for a few days in a row. This will help you to acclimate to the fear and face the exposure.

STEPS TO FREEDOM

Horror story: After you write your story in the **present tense,** do the following one step at a time:

1. Read it out loud four times in a row, once with an accent. Do this daily until your anxiety settles then move to #2.
2. Read it **outside your home** four times in a row. Repeat daily, then move to #3.
3. Record and listen to it **while eating a snack.** Repeat daily, then move to #4.
4. Listen to it **outside your home while eating a snack**.
5. Listen to it with headphones **in an uncomfortable place.** (restaurant, back of a bus, underground parking)

Chapter 31
Obsessions and Compulsions

An obsession is an unwanted preoccupation, repeated image, or thought that causes anxiety. It goes without saying that emetophobes are preoccupied with vomit but not all emetophobes have compulsions. Compulsions are behaviors or rituals that neutralize the intensity of the anxiety or stop the obsession. Washing your hands for several minutes every time you think your hands have been exposed to germs is a compulsion. Cleaning your cell phone ten times a day is also a compulsion as is constantly researching the rate of digestion for specific foods, repeatedly checking expiration dates, and compulsively checking the refrigerator door to make sure it is closed so food will not spoil. Compulsions can also be mental. Praying to God repeatedly to protect you from vomit is an example of a mental compulsion.

Compulsions will relieve your uncertainty and discomfort and help you feel better but that *better* feeling does not last long. Your anxiety monster is quick to make another threat or ask another question. *Are you sure your hands are clean? If you don't wash them again you might get sick*. Soon you must wash your hands again to make the obsession stop.

It is common for obsessions to come in the form of disturbing images, either traumatic memories or unwanted pictures fabricated by the mind.

A former patient experienced intrusive images of herself vomiting. She had to engage in an elaborate hand moving ritual to stop the upsetting images and prevent herself from throwing up. Otherwise, she believed she would vomit. Engaging in the hand moving ritual was stressful but once she completed the compulsion, her anxiety subsided -- temporarily.

Compulsions can become ritualized. For instance, washing your hands in a certain way or for a certain length of time. If you don't perform the ritual exactly the way your obsession demands, you have to repeat it until it's done perfectly. Many emetophobes have ritualized ways of eating. They will only eat certain foods, at certain times of the day, and in a specific manner, otherwise they will vomit. At least this is what their anxiety monster threatens.

Some compulsions are repeated until it *feels* "just right." Only when it feels right can you stop the ritual and move on. For instance, if a person has intrusive and unwanted thoughts about vomiting, the phrase *I will not vomit* must be repeated compulsively until it is said correctly or it feels just right. This could last a minute or hours. The sufferer feels compelled to repeat the statement or risk vomiting. This is an example of a mental compulsion.

Other types of compulsions have no logical connection with the fear. I worked with a patient who had to flip a light switch off and on a certain number of times or blink repeatedly to prevent something bad from happening. Throughout the day she would experience periodic thoughts or feelings of doom which would prompt her to engage in these compulsions. Part of her understood that this did not make logical sense but she was compelled to do it, to be certain, and alleviate her fear. Unfortunately, logic does not change feelings when you have obsessions. Therefore, treatment has to make emotional sense, which requires a change in behavior.

The only way to stop your obsessions (thoughts) is to first stop your compulsions (behaviors). Compulsions feed and strengthen the obsession. Every time you do a compulsion, you are making your anxiety monster stronger (strengthening your worries). Once you stop your compulsions, the obsessions can slowly dissipate. It cannot be done in the reverse order. Let me repeat: the only way to stop your anxious thoughts is to first stop your compulsions, avoidance, and safety behaviors. You do this by going on offense with an offensive mindset.

If you avoid touching door handles and use hand sanitizer compulsively, go on offense and purposefully touch as many door handles as you can. I have my patients demand distress and uncertainty as we walk together down the hallway of my office building touching door handles one after another. We chat and periodically respond to the anxiety monster: *This is exactly the feeling I need right now. Keep it coming. I can handle it.* Each time anxiety threatens disaster, patients respond back, *That's a bunch of crap.* Sometimes they verbalize their fear out loud in an accent (in this case southern) *I'm noticing my monster trying to fool me by claiming the germs on these door handle are going to make me sick. – Kiss my grits!*

Going on offense with your game face and exposing yourself to what you fear is only half the battle. Exposure and Response Prevention (ERP) requires you to prevent the response you would normally have following an exposure. After the exposure (touching twenty door handles) we prevent the response (compulsive hand washing). Instead, patients touch their cell phone, the steering wheel in their car, and if they are brave, hold a piece of chocolate with their fingers and eat it. After the response prevention piece has been completed, they practice washing their hands in less than twenty seconds, using one pump of soap.

Of course, all of this makes sufferers feel terribly uncomfortable which is exactly the feeling they should be seeking. That's how they know they did it right. After completing the exposure, instead of dwelling on the distress and fearful thoughts, they go live their life and focus their attention elsewhere. After a certain period of time the distress will dissipate. This might take five minutes but for some it could be hours.

If you do ERP in this manner several times a day, you will notice over a period of weeks that the urge to do the compulsion weakens in intensity, frequency, and duration. As the compulsions weaken, the obsessions dissipate and eventually become periodic thoughts which can be easily dismissed.

Your amygdala will not fire off once it learns that touching door handles is not dangerous. Your adrenal glands will not secrete adrenaline once your brain learns that washing your hands in less than twenty seconds will not lead to vomiting. Once this happens you will not have to worry about touching objects or washing your hands for a certain length of time and your obsessions will subside naturally.

Identify your compulsions and conquer them one by one, step by step. Go on offense!

If you compulsively use a wipe to clean your phone, stand up to the bully and refuse to do what he orders. Go on offense, do the opposite, and purposefully touch your phone to something you consider to be unclean. This will increase your anxiety as you worry about the consequences of this action. Maintain an offensive mindset, refuse to believe the lies in your imagination, and like the buffalo, push through the storm despite your opponent's threats. Then make a phone call, put it in your pocket, and move on with your life. As you focus your attention on living your life, the distress will subside. Repeat this several times a day and your brain will learn that not cleaning your phone is safe and will not cause you to vomit. This is the only way to change your beliefs.

Before facing an exposure, mentally prepare for the challenge. Tell yourself, *This is a beautiful day to do hard things. I'm excited to change my beliefs. Bring it on!* And then do the exposure quickly before your monster has a chance to convince you otherwise. **Starting quickly is key.** As John Wooden would say, *Be quick but don't hurry.*

Whether compulsions are physical or mental, having obsessions and compulsions is time consuming. If you must engage in a physical or mental ritual, to prevent thoughts of vomiting, your monster will attempt to engage you for as long as possible. This includes engaging you in a mental debate in which you must reassure yourself repeatedly that you will be fine. Only when you win the debate or reassure yourself enough do you feel better. Strategizing to keep yourself safe, trying to figure out why you are nauseous, over-preparing, and over-analyzing are other ways obsessions can grab your attention for long periods of time. These attempts at attaining certainty in an effort to reduce anxiety only strengthen anxiety and create more fear.

Reassuring yourself or seeking reassurance from others is a compulsion Sally Winston and Martin Seif write about in their book, *Needing to Know for Sure: A CBT-Based Guide to Overcoming Compulsive Checking and Reassurance Seeking*. They write, *Certainty is a feeling, not a fact. And certainty is neither possible nor necessary.* They explain how compulsive reassurance seeking is not about finding facts; it's about trying to reduce anxiety. The problem is, it doesn't. It actually increases anxiety because you can't get the 100% certainty you desire and because you are engaging with your anxiety.

I'm currently working with a seventeen-year-old boy with emetophobia who asks his parents several times before bed if he will vomit. Unless they reassure him that he will not throw up, he feels anxious. The reassurance reduces his anxiety temporarily but does not heal it. For healing to occur, his parents must stop accommodating him. I advised them to respond, *it sounds like your monster is messing with you*, every time their son asks for reassurance. This initially escalated his anxiety when he went to bed. He began to mentally reassure himself but soon realized this was not necessary and eventually learned to fall asleep without seeking reassurance of any kind from anyone, including himself.

It's okay to remind yourself why you're unlikely to puke if you eat at a new restaurant or why you are unlikely to see a person vomit on a plane but remember your opponent's second strategic move – to get you to the back of the bus. Be ready for anxiety to try to engage you with *but what if it does happen?* If you answer the question, you will be sucked into a prolonged conversation. It's best to accept the uncertainty: *I'm certain enough and that's good enough.* Or *I'm not certain but I'm going to do it anyway.* Live with the uncertainty and stop asking yourself and your family members for reassurance. Tell your family that if you ask for reassurance, they should respond, *it sounds like anxiety is messing with you.* Instruct them not to reassure you. Explain to your loved ones why they must stop accommodating your compulsions and safety behaviors, including opening doors for you and preparing meals in specific ways.

I worked with a woman in her twenties who would not allow her mom to go on business trips because she was afraid she would get sick and panic while alone. I gave her mom permission to do what her employer required instead of following the demands of her daughter's anxiety monster. The first business trip was rough and my patient experienced anticipatory anxiety, crying, begging, as well as panic attacks the day her mom left. She never barfed despite being alone for a week. My patient improved with each business trip her mom took and by the fourth trip she was no longer fearful of her mom leaving.

If you need to be 100% certain and comfortable to live, you must retain your anxiety disorder. At this moment, as I am writing this chapter, I am on an airplane. There is no certainty that this plane will land safely. I cannot be 100% certain but I am certain enough. Perhaps I will get nauseous and puke from motion sickness. That will be unpleasant but I am certain enough that I will tolerate it. You must sacrifice 100% certainty to live the life you desire. If you want to rid yourself of anxiety then you must be willing to be uncertain. In fact, you must demand it.

While it is common for anxiety sufferers to have obsessions and compulsions, this does not mean there is a diagnosis of Obsessive Compulsive Disorder. For an accurate diagnosis you should be evaluated by a mental health professional. Because the treatment for OCD is the same for anxiety disorders, do not be overly concerned with the diagnosis.

STEPS TO FREEDOM

ERP: Make a list of your compulsions. Go on offense every day and conquer them, one by one, step by step, by doing the opposite of what your obsessions and compulsions demand. Expose yourself purposefully to what scares you. Do it quickly and then resist doing the response that would reduce your anxiety. Increase the intensity and duration of each exposure week by week.

Verbalize Fears Out Loud for Ten Minutes: Instead of engaging in a physical or mental compulsion, write a paragraph about what is worrying you and then read it out loud for ten straight minutes. This writing exercise is effective if anxiety lingers after you do an exposure. Be sure to read it out loud for ten minutes, including your best attempt with an accent. Here is an example:

After playing games on my cell phone at the doctor's office I did not clean it. Anxiety told me that it's covered with flu germs. I think the germs entered my mouth when I talked on the phone. Now I'm going to get the stomach flu. Sometime in the next 48 hours I will vomit uncontrollably. It's going to be disgusting and I won't be able to stop.

Chapter 32
Externalizing Panic: Healing the Past and Stepping into the Future

Because the roots of panic are the same as the roots of emetophobia (intolerance of uncertainty and distress), everything you learn in this book will apply to both, including the exercises in this chapter.

Many people who suffer with emetophobia also have panic attacks. The panic stems from a fear of vomiting or witnessing someone else vomit, but once you've experienced a severe panic episode, the fear of subsequent attacks is quite common. Panic attacks are not dangerous but they are terrifying and result in avoidance of anything that could trigger one. When your imagination perceives a possibility of danger (VOMIT! PANIC! TRAPPED!), your amygdala will fire off, sending signals to your adrenal glands resulting in severe symptoms – racing heart, difficulty breathing, chest pain, hot flashes, lightheadedness, jelly legs, sweating, nausea, depersonalization, etc. It might feel like you are having a heart attack, dying, our of your body, going crazy, about to pass out, or seconds away from puking. Panic can strike unexpectedly or be triggered by a thought or situation.

As I stated in the beginning of this book, adrenaline is dubbed the *fight-or-flight hormone* because when it secretes into the body, you have a choice: Fight through or flee but when you're captured by fear, another possibility is to *freeze*. When anxiety is high, it does not feel like a choice. There is a dominant impulse to escape to safety. With a lot of practice, you have learned that the most effective way to stop anxiety is to escape (and avoid). Your brain has learned that unless you flee, you are in danger. What you and your brain have not learned is that the urgency to flee creates **more** distress, while staying and pushing through **reduces** anxiety.

The most common situations panic sufferers avoid are places where they **feel** trapped. I emphasize the word **feel** because you are not actually trapped but it does **feel** that way. You will always eventually get out but it may not be immediate, which is what your amygdala requires. **Feeling** trapped implies being in a dangerous or scary situation. It might be scary but if it were truly dangerous, everyone would be fleeing. It's only scary to you because you believe that if you don't get out immediately, you will vomit or panic. Symptoms of anxiety will then escalate quickly when you can't escape as fast as you desire.

Places where it is difficult to exit quickly include underground parking, shopping malls, large department stores, elevators, subways, boats, buses, the back seat of a car or a taxi, highway traffic, trams, amusement park rides, the middle seat of a movie theater, cruise ships, hair salons, high buildings, and planes. Other triggers of panic include being alone, not having a cell phone, or being far from your home or car. I worked with a client who avoided making appointments because doing so gave her the feeling of being trapped. Being committed to meet another person at a specific time and day felt like being in an elevator.

Overcoming Panic Trauma

Earlier I discussed how to work through a vomiting trauma. What is important to understand is that a major panic attack is a trauma too. If you believe you are dying, going crazy, or are trapped -- that is traumatic! Memories of a trauma can plague your mind, weaken your confidence, cause avoidance, and prevent you from moving forward with the proper mentality. An intense panic attack can flip your mindset from offense back to defense. Instead of entering situations with a commitment to stay, you look for ways to flee as you desperately pray you don't panic. Approaching exposures with this outlook will result in failure as well as feelings of disappointment and hopelessness. It's not uncommon for the memory of a panic trauma to invade your mind as you attempt exposures.

Even when doing milder exposures, the terror of a past panic attack can flash in your mind and trigger an instinct to flee.

To help you process and move beyond a traumatic panic attack, write the trauma in the present tense with as much detail and emotion as you can. Tell the story from beginning to end. Highlight the terrifying images that still plague you. Then, read it **out loud** five times. Record the story and listen back. Share your story with a therapist or a supportive person. Allow yourself to cry and experience the anxiety. Take a few breaths and then tell it again and again. You will notice that your anxiety lessens as you verbalize your story repeatedly.

As I mentioned previously, working with a therapist who uses EMDR is a powerful way to reduce the intensity of a trauma. If you cannot find a therapist who utilizes EMDR, *The Anxiety Solution Series* at QuietMindSolutions.com has an Image Reprocessing exercise that works in a similar fashion and will help you decrease the intensity of traumatic images and sensations. Taking action to move beyond a panic trauma is a necessary component to overcoming panic disorder.

Worry Scripts: Externalizing Panic and Practicing Your Response

Similar to preparing for an athletic endeavor, a presentation, or anything challenging, you should prepare to face your fears. One method is to **write, record, and listen** to worry scripts for any situation or exposure you fear. I will use underground parking as an example. Apply these steps to any challenging situation:

Step 1

Identify a situation that causes anxiety and create a worry script. Write all the thoughts you would experience if you were in that specific situation, in this case, underground parking. Write in the second person, your worries, what-if thoughts, questions, threats, orders, and confidence busters. Here is an example:

> *There are so many cars. What if you get trapped?*
> *This is too big of a step. You shouldn't do this.*
> *It's really dark and creepy and the ceiling is so low.*
> *What if you have a panic attack?*
> *Who's gonna help you?*
> *You're a loser. What's wrong with you? Why can't you do this?*
> *Make sure you know how to get out.*
> *You're not ready for this. Maybe you should turn around.*
> *The ceiling is getting lower.*

You're feeling anxious. Go back. Turn around.
Your heart is racing! You've gone too far
What if this anxiety turns into a full-on panic attack?
You're so far from home. You should leave now.
You can't do this. It's too hard.
Where's the exit? Make sure you know how to get out.
No one can help you. You're all alone. This is not good.
Your heart palpitations and shaking are getting worse.
You're trapped. You're really trapped.
You're starting to feel nauseous. This is it!
How do you get out of here? You're lost.
You're about to have a PANIC ATTACK!
If you don't get out now, you're gonna VOMIT!
Where's the exit! Get out of here.
Hurry. Get out now!
Get out!

Step 2

Record your worry script into your phone with urgency, angst, and desperation. Don't read the thoughts with a monotone voice. Say it like you're trapped and anxious: how you hear it in your head. Also, and this is important, pause five to fifteen seconds between worries. Sometimes pause five seconds and other times for ten or fifteen.

Step 3

Record your worry script again this time with an accent (Irish, Russian, Jamaican, etc.).

Step 4

Take a picture of your anxiety monster.

Step 5

Practice responding to the recording at home. As you look at the photo of your monster, listen to the recording of your worry script with headphones. This is your opportunity to practice your responses as the executive: the one in charge. As you hear each anxious thought, respond back with a competing emotion (anger, amusement, excitement, love, sarcastic, nurturing). Amplify the competing emotion. Express it with your voice, body, and facial expression. Your responses should be short and to the point. Do not fill the silence in the recording with a long response.

Keep the lies coming, big mouth.
Give me more (flex your muscle). *I can handle it.*
This is exactly the feeling I need right now to be free.
I'm not leaving so give me what you got. (shake your fist)
F-Off! (crush him in your fist) *I got this. You're not going to win.*
I'm not going to panic. I refuse!
I'm not answering the question, asshole. (slap the passenger seat)
I'm excited to be anxious because I'm excited to be free.
I'm excited to choose faith over fear.
I see you. I love you. We got this.
Welcome back, sexy. Now flick off. (flick him off your shoulder)
Give me a panic attack. I want to panic. Bring it on! (growl)

Use no more than three different responses within each practice session. This will simplify the process and prevent you from engaging in a dialogue. Practice responding out loud and in your imagination until your responses are programmed and automatic. Then, listen to the recording with your accent and do the same.

Step 6

After practicing at home listen to your worry script in the very situation you have been avoiding. As you drive into an underground parking lot, listen to your recording and respond just as you did at home. Practice responding out loud at first and then think your responses. When you respond in your head, imagine using the tone you desire (anger, excitement, amusement). Sit in a parking spot and play the recording again as you look at the picture of your monster. Listen to both recordings: the anxious one and the one with the accent.

Anxiety sufferers worry that listening to their recording while in the feared situation will cause them to feel more anxious and are pleasantly surprised when they feel less. Hearing thoughts outside of your head makes them sound less ominous and the recording with the accent will sound silly. Not only will you feel less anxiety, many patients report feeling empowered. Doing this exercise daily will improve your ability to recognize your thoughts as well as your skill at responding.

Create worry scripts for any scary situation or exposure, for instance, driving far from home. Then listen and respond to the recording first at home and then as you drive:

If you drive too far, you will panic – ***Bring it on!***
Are you sure you want to do this? – ***Not answering the question.***

What if you have a panic attack? – **Not answering the question.**
What are you going to do if you panic? **- Not answering the question.**
Don't do this today. You're not ready. **– F-off. I'll handle it.**
You're already feeling anxious. **– Bring it on. I'm rewiring my brain.**
If you feel bad you can always turn around. - **F-off. I'll handle it.**
You're too far. Turn back and go home. **– F-off. I'll handle it.**

Writing, recording, and responding to worry scripts can be done with every phase of every exposure – looking at vomit videos, walking in the mall, riding on a subway, driving, and eating at a restaurant. In public places, listen with headphones and respond in your head. There is no need to look at the photo of your anxiety monster while in public. Instead, do what you would normally do with anxiety talking to you in the background. One of my patients recorded two worry scripts to overcome his fear of eating in restaurants: one worry script for driving to the restaurant and another for when he was eating. Every day, as he would drive or take an Uber to a different restaurant, he would listen to the first recording. Then, while eating his food, he would listen to the second. After two months he was able to eat comfortably at any restaurant.

Exposures for Panic Disorder

Any of the following exposures can be broken down into small steps. For example, if you are too anxious to sit in the back of a moving car, first sit in the back of a parked car beside your home. If you are too frightened to drive in the back of a taxi, pay the driver to drive you one block. (I encourage you to share why you are doing this.) Too anxious to ride in an elevator? Stand outside and look in for twenty seconds. Increase the time and eventually go inside and hold the door open for greater lengths of time. You decide the order of exposures from least to most difficult.

- Drive in the back of a family member's car
- Drive in the back of an Uber or taxi
- Ride in a bus
- Ride a subway, train, tram, amusement park ride
- Drive in underground parking. Proceed one level down at a time
- Drive in traffic
- Walk to the middle of a mall or any discount warehouse store
- Stand in a closed elevator and wait for someone to summon it
- Take an elevator to the top floor of a tall building
- Jump while an elevator is moving
- Go to a place that is crowded

- Drive alone, slowly increasing the distance
- Drive aimlessly, get lost, and then use GPS to find your way home
- Stand in a long line
- Wait in line at a drive-through
- Stand in a small closet
- Try on clothes in a small dressing room
- Go to a high place
- Donate blood
- Sit in your car as you go through a carwash
- Make an appointment and follow through (haircut, movie, friend)
- Separate yourself from that which gives you comfort (house, car, cell, person). Slowly increase the distance and time apart.

Find your Motivation

Given the intensity of a panic attack, why would you do anything that might trigger one? You wouldn't. Unless you had a good reason. To face any difficult exposure, you must identify what you value. Find your motivation and let that be the focus of your attention. Instead of contemplating escape, focusing on your symptoms, or imagining a panic attack, remind yourself why it's so important that you face anxiety.

I treated a patient who suffered with panic attacks and a fear of being trapped. She shared her experience donating blood for her best friend who was in the hospital and required surgery. As she laid calmly with a needle in her arm, she suddenly realized she could not escape! She was trapped and began to panic. But then quickly thought, *my friend needs me. I'm not leaving.* She laid back down and her anxiety subsided. She found her motivation: a higher calling. It wasn't about her. It was about her friend in need. You too must find your motivation and be prepared with a motivational response: *I'm doing this for my friend. She needs me. I'm not leaving!*

Last September I was in Jerusalem in the ancient City of David. The last stop on the tour was Hezekiah's Tunnel, a water channel carved through the rock over 2000 years ago. The length of the tunnel is about one-third of a mile (1.2 kilometers) and roughly two feet wide (60 centimeters). Tourists can walk through the channel standing upright but periodically many people must walk hunched over because at times the height lowers to less than 5 feet, 8 inches (177 centimeters). It takes more than twenty minutes to walk through the dark tunnel which flows with water at ankle level. Once you enter there is only one direction to go. You cannot turn around because the tunnel is too narrow.

We were told not to walk through if we had claustrophobia. For a few minutes I wondered if being inside would make me anxious. I imagined people in front of me and behind me and envisioned myself panicking, not able to get out. What would I do if I panicked? I felt anxious thinking about it and I contemplated not going. I then thought, *I ask my patients to do hard things. Fuck it. I have to do hard things too. I'm going in!* At that moment I decided I was going into the tunnel, no matter what. I found my motivation. I made a firm decision. And that enabled me to stop engaging with anxiety and visualizing panic. I stopped trying to figure out what I would do if I became anxious.

Although having an escape plan seems like a good idea, it requires you to imagine the worst and think defensively. Anticipatory anxiety is a terrible predictor of what happens when you face your fears. Once inside the tunnel I had no anxiety. Nothing my monster predicted occurred. I enjoyed chatting with the other tourists inside. In fact, the woman in front of me said she suffered with claustrophobia until she was treated in therapy. Obviously, the therapy worked.

Prior to facing an exposure, do not prepare for an escape. This not only puts you in a defensive mindset, it requires you to imagine the worst, which will escalate your anticipatory anxiety. The only preparation needed are the items outlined in this book.

Hezekiah's Tunnel was one of the many highlights of my trip. The goal is to live your life, not to be certain.

STEPS TO FREEDOM

Panic Story: Write your panic trauma in the present tense in detail. Read it out loud four times in a row. Record the story with and without an accent and listen to both. Repeat daily until it is no longer upsetting.

Worry Script: Write a long list of your worries about a specific feared exposure. Record the worries with urgency. Listen in the safety of your home to practice responding. Then listen and respond while facing the feared situation.

Focus on your Motivation: Review chapter 11, read your Statement of Determination daily along with the letters you have written to yourself.

Chapter 33
Conquering Panic with a Winning Mindset

A key component to overcoming panic attacks is your mentality. Because panic attacks feel horrific, the natural instinct is to not want them. That's basic human nature. Here's the problem: not wanting a panic attack increases the likelihood of experiencing an attack, especially if pursued with urgent desperation. Therefore, the necessary mentality to overcome panic attacks is to WANT to have panic attacks. What? I know that sounds crazy but stay with me.

The more you worry about having a panic attack, the more likely it is that you have one. Conversely, as your odds of having an attack reduce, the less you care about having one. In other words, to be successful, you must want what you don't want. You're playing a mental game against a tricky opponent and to win you must take him off guard with a strategy he does not expect.

Remember the paradox of the Chinese Finger Trap? To escape you must do the opposite of what is instinctive. As your anxiety rises, demand it rise more. *Give me a panic attack! I can handle it.* Be the voice in charge. Match your opponent's intensity and then elevate it. This will increase the belief in what you are saying. One of my patients responded to her symptoms by affirming, *I'm a mom. I can do anything. Give me more bitch!* These words convey power but only when said with intensity.

Imagine for a moment that panic is like a wave in the ocean and you are a surfer. In order for an inexperienced surfer to master the skill of surfing, there must be waves to practice. If a surfer shows up at the beach day after day and there are no waves, he cannot get better. Like a novice surfer who needs waves to practice, you need to experience waves of anxiety to improve your ability to ride out your symptoms. And like a new surfer, this takes a lot of practice. You must show up at your feared destination (underground parking, mall, elevator, etc.) **wanting** to experience waves of anxiety. *I want to be anxious. Give me a panic attack. I need the practice.* Say it like you mean it, even if you don't. Show your opponent you will not be intimidated. Put on your game face, have an offensive mindset, and view these moments as opportunities to practice, improve, rewire your brain, and advance in the game. Want what you don't want.

Commit to a Predetermined Goal

When a surfer goes to the beach, his goal is to ride the waves, not try to stop them. He attempts to stay above the waves and ride them out to the end. This must be your goal as well. An anxiety wave is temporary and can subside if you respond correctly. Once you feel a wave of anxiety rise within you, be committed to staying, riding out your symptoms, and reaching your predetermined goal. For example, if driving out of your comfort zone causes anxiety, identify an attainable destination and commit to driving there. You must decide this ahead of time because when anxiety builds, there will be a powerful reflex to flee.

Although committing to a goal can be scary, here is the good news: staying and riding out anxiety produces less anxiety than fleeing. A predetermined goal prevents ambivalence and a dialogue with your monster about when to turn back. Fleeing exacerbates symptoms because in an emergency your brain must give you adrenaline to get you out fast. When you can't escape fast enough, your anxiety monster becomes threatening and your symptoms and fear escalate quickly.

When you commit to achieving a predetermined goal, that goal becomes your focus. When you obligate yourself to ride out anxiety, you train your brain that there is no emergency.

To overcome the fear of panic attacks, do daily exposures. For each exposure, identify a specific goal, i.e., ride an elevator to the third floor, five times. Make the goal mandatory. No matter how you feel, you will stay on the elevator until you reach the third floor and you will do it five times. You will not get off on the second floor or stop after you doing it twice. Committing to a goal prevents ambivalence and a conversation with your anxiety monster about when to get off or stop. Make your goals realistic and attainable. You can always do more, but never less. Having a predetermined goal that is mandatory and having strong motivation to succeed are crucial to success.

With frequent repetition, you learn that you can tolerate discomfort and uncertainty and do not have to flee to calm yourself. As you rewire your brain, what was once terrifying, becomes relatively easy. Riding elevators, trains, and buses, daily, for longer periods of time will help prepare you for a subway and an airplane.

One major difference between air versus ground transportation is the ability to exit at each stop. Although there is less anticipatory anxiety knowing that you can disembark at the next subway station, the ability to exit gives your anxiety monster an opportunity to engage you in a conversation and insist that you get off. As you contemplate what to do each time the subway approaches a station, you lapse into a defensive mindset and become more anxious. As a passenger on a plane, there is nothing to contemplate; therefore you are 100% committed and all of your effort can be devoted to riding out anxiety. This is why identifying a predetermined goal for each exposure is important. No matter how many times the subway doors open, act as though you cannot disembark until you arrive at your preplanned destination.

Breaking down exposures into small steps is a good strategy but at some point you will have no option but to take a giant leap onto a subway or plane. Utilize all the tools in this book to push through your fear and ask a supportive person to help if needed.

One of my patients was able to get on a subway with the support of her husband and a compelling motivation. She realized, *I will never be able to fly to see my grandchildren unless I can get on a subway first.* She repeated, *I'm excited to do hard things because I'm excited to see my grandchildren.* This motivated her to face her fears. When the doors opened, she looked at a photo of her grandchildren, and as the buffalo, she forcefully headed into the storm.

That first step, which is usually the hardest, was a bit easier with her husband present. Once inside, her husband kicked his foot into the air towards the open subway door as it was closing. My patient was puzzled by his behavior. He explained, *I just kicked your anxiety monster off the subway.* She smiled, thanked him, and off they went -- one stop which is what she decided. She did not panic, but her anxiety fluctuated from high to moderate as they continued to take four more short rides, which was her predetermined goal.

As they road she periodically exclaimed, *Make my heart race. Give me a panic attack! I dare you. I'm excited to do hard things because I'm excited to see my grandchildren.* The more she invited panic with ferocity, the less anxious she felt. She also used *3 by 3 Breathing* and got her mind off of her anxiety by conversing with her husband. On the final ride she began to cry and her husband worried, *Are you okay?* She was more than okay. *I'm just feeling emotional because I'm finally beating anxiety.*

Another patient of mine had the same fear but we devised a different plan. He asked his girlfriend to ride ahead to the next subway station. With her waiting at the next stop, he felt a responsibility to meet her. It gave him motivation. He adjusted his headphones, cranked up the volume of his favorite song, and when the train arrived, he got on quickly. He sat down, closed his eyes, and fully immersed himself in the music, drumming his thumbs to the beat. He imagined hugging her at the station which is exactly what happened. Pride and excitement motivated him to do it again and again. After repeating this exposure three weekends in a row, he was ready to book a flight. He flew one hour to Las Vegas with high anticipatory anxiety and no anxiety the last 30 minutes of the flight.

Mentally and Physically Prepare Before an Exposure

Usually there is anticipatory anxiety before doing an exposure and with physical symptoms comes the worry that a panic attack is looming. This is just the anxiety monster in your imagination threatening you. Expect anxiety to apply as much pressure as possible to prevent you from doing exposures.

Any time you are not feeling well, have anxiety, or the weather is bad, your opponent will encourage you to take the day off. On the contrary, this is the exact time to do an exposure. If you wait until you feel good, you might be waiting a long time. You must learn to live your life and view these difficult days as opportunities to practice. When it's raining, you're menstruating, or suffering with indigestion, it's go time. If you're feeling anxious, *give me more please*, and then push through.

Before a basketball game, players warm up on the court and listen to a pep talk in the locker room. You, too, can prepare yourself mentally and physically before doing difficult exposures. There are several ways you can prepare. Try them out and see which combination works best for you.

- Write and record a worry script. Play it and practice responding.

- Listen to a relaxation exercise or do *3 by 3 Breathing* without putting pressure on yourself to relax. If you are unable to decrease your anxiety, that's okay.

- Do physical exercise while listening to music. Run, ride a bike, do yoga, etc. The combination of music and physical activity will prepare your mind and body for doing something difficult.

- Do an easy exposure that you've done previously to warm up and build your confidence. Focus only on the present exposure, not on the one ahead.

- Verbalize your worry out loud with an accent. *My monster is messing with me by telling me...*

- Be prepared for how you will respond when you feel symptoms or have worrisome thoughts. Write it down and memorize it. Identify the competing emotion will you utilize.

- Declare why you are doing this. What is your motivation? What do you value? What is driving you to beat anxiety?

- Identify a predetermined goal and be resolute to succeed.

- Imagine yourself on the other side of anxiety, feeling triumphant that you succeeded. If you fear riding a bus to the beach, envision yourself at the beach enjoying the day. If you are worried about having a panic attack while getting a haircut, focus on how you will feel and look afterwards. If you are afraid to drive to a friend's home, picture the embrace upon your arrival. Focus past the anxiety to the other side.

- Do none of the above. If you feel as if preparing makes the exposure bigger than it should be, do it quickly without preparation. Simply identify what you are going to do and be determined to do it.

What to Do When Anxiety Rises Unexpectedly

Small and moderate levels of anxiety do not have to lead to panic. Learning to tolerate moderate levels will give you confidence and reduce your fear of panic attacks. Retraining your brain that you can stay in optional situations (movie theater, mall, hair salon) will help prepare you for situations where you do not have an option to leave immediately (planes, trains, subways, boats, elevators).

To conquer anxiety, one hundred percent of you must be focused on what you need to do. If even a part of you is looking to flee, you are only using a fraction of your power, which is insufficient. One hundred percent of you must be focused on using your tools and staying on offense for the duration. This is why having a powerful motivator is key.

Once you have a powerful motivator and are one hundred percent committed to staying and riding out anxiety, implement the following interventions when you feel anxiety rising and your monster threatening. This applies to when anxiety builds gradually, comes out of nowhere, or is triggered by a specific situation or thought. Most people use a combination of these strategies:

Respond with a Winning Remark and Competing Emotion

When you face a fear, assume that you will feel strong symptoms, see images of being trapped, hear messages to *get out*, and have an intense urge to flee. The messages you tell yourself when you do an exposure or when anxiety hits unexpectedly are not meant to replace your anxious thoughts. Dr. Wilson writes, *Again and again and again, as you keep stepping forward, you'll hear a voice that says, "Step back!" Our new messages are designed to come immediately after any instruction to run. At that moment, mentally detach from the instruction and give yourself the "step forward" message.... We're not removing your obsessive voice. We are bringing up a parallel voice and then elevating it so that it becomes the executive voice, the one in charge.* If your anxious voice is the one in charge, it is likely that your symptoms will escalate. To contain your symptoms, your voice needs to be more forceful. Relegate your anxiety to that of an opponent and be determined to win. Have your responses memorized so they are programmed in your mind. Employ a competing emotion and physically dispose of your opponent in a creative manner. Accept your physical symptoms, reject the lies, and refuse to engage.

Quickly Turn Your Attention onto an Activity

Play a game on your phone, scroll through social media, talk to someone, do a puzzle, read this book, etc. By fully engaging in an activity, and not your thoughts or symptoms, your anxiety will eventually settle. Accept your symptoms and then focus on whatever you would be doing if you were not anxious -- continue shopping, eating, socializing, working, etc. When I was a student at UCLA, I was temporarily stuck in an elevator in one of the university libraries. Because this was the late

1980s and there were no cell phones, I used the emergency call system for assistance. Since my original plan was to find a quiet place to study in the library, I figured this was as good as any. I sat down on the floor, opened a text book, and started studying. Fifteen minutes later the elevator was fixed and I continued on my way. Getting stuck in an elevator is unlikely but it can occur. It's happened to me one time in my entire life. Planned exposures will prepare you for such moments.

Do 3 by 3 Breathing with Self-Directives

Because symptoms of anxiety are difficult to tolerate, people often flee the scene before their anxiety diminishes, never experiencing the relative calm while in the place they fear. Be determined to stay and ride it out. Like a surfer who wears a wetsuit to help ride out the waves, you can use *3 by 3 Breathing* to help you ride out anxiety. Breathe to help you through the anxiety, not to stop it. As you perform *3 by 3 Relaxation Breathing* (review chapter 15 if you need a reminder), you will think statements of strength, self-direction, and encouragement, as you **slowly** inhale and exhale. Try some of these:

Inhale....... **Exhale**
Ride it......... out
I will............ win
I can............ handle it
This will.........pass
Stay...............strong
Not going......anywhere
Iron stomach... man
Fuck off........ asshole
Give me........ more
I'm excited.... to win
I'm excited.... to be free

If you feel anxiety rising and an urge to flee while in the middle of a mall, find a comfortable place to sit and then breathe (you can also listen to a relaxation exercise). It takes time for adrenaline to subside, so breathe for as long as it takes to reduce the anxiety to a manageable level and then continue shopping. If you begin to feel a second wave of anxiety building, instead of feeling discouraged, thank your monster for another opportunity to practice. *Welcome back. Stay as long as you like. Thanks for the opportunity to practice and rewire my brain.* Sit down again and breathe. Remember, whatever phrase you use, think it slowly. Do not wish or rush the symptoms away. If they don't subside, it's an opportunity to practice enduring and tolerating anxiety by using one of the other interventions.

To help you disengage from your thoughts and symptoms, try *3 by 3 Breathing* with a theme: animals, colors, famous people. For example, as you inhale, think the name of an animal slowly (el-e-phant) and then think of a different animal as you exhale (kan-ga-roo). Or think the first name of a famous person as you inhale slowly (George) and as you exhale, slowly think the last name (Wash-ing-ton). This will help you disengage from your thoughts.

Having treated thousands of anxiety sufferers over the years, I often hear from patients that it can take between five minutes to two hours for high levels of anxiety to subside. With practice, you will improve and the length of time will reduce.

Be Mindful

In addition to repeating self-directives, as you breathe, you can practice mindfulness. As you patiently ride out anxiety, mindfully notice your environment and your symptoms without judgment. **Slow** your mind down and start each sentence with ***My mind is noticing***...

...my heart racing fast
...I'm feeling nauseous
...I am holding my breath
...I am making myself breathe slowly
...my anxiety monster wants me to leave
...the smooth surface of this tile table
...a man with a long, grey beard
...how my pants feel soft when I touch them
...that woman scolding her child
...a lady with a lip piercing
...the taste of this apple, the sound of the bite, the feeling of chewing

With the goal of creating discomfort and tolerating it, you teach your brain that anxiety does not require you to flee and that there are more efficient and healthy ways to respond. You must be willing to experience this to fully understand it. Sit with your anxiety and observe it **without judgment**, instead of attributing meaning to your symptoms and beating yourself up for having them.

In the beginning and middle of treatment, success is measured by how well and how frequently you practice implementing the strategy and tools, not on how you feel. Refrain from evaluating your progress via your symptoms. Why? Because the short-term goal is to purposefully want to feel anxious, nauseous, and uncertain. That's how you know you are headed in the right direction. It's your compass. You're not changing your behavior and attitude to make anxiety go away in the short run. Eliminating debilitating anxiety, panic, emetophobia is the long-term goal. Be kind to yourself when you experience anxiety. It's not your fault. Being harsh with yourself will prolong your recovery.

Medication

Benzodiazepine/anti-anxiety medication is taken on an as-needed basis, primarily when having a panic attack. Many panic attack sufferers never take their anti-anxiety medication but just having it with them at all times provides comfort, reduces anxiety, and gives them more security to face their fears. If you are too anxious and fearful to do exposures correctly or sufficiently, then medication might be needed. If your panic attacks are out of control despite your best efforts, then seek out the services of a psychiatrist who can evaluate you for an anti-depressant or anti-anxiety medication.

STEPS TO FREEDOM

Learn the material: Reread the last two chapters to fully grasp all the information before tackling difficult exposures.

Exposures: Begin to rewire your brain by taking small, brave steps into areas of the maze that might trigger panic. Prepare yourself mentally before facing each exposure and start off with easier challenges. Be committed to stay until anxiety subsides by at least 50% if not more. Repeat exposures multiple times a day and record your victories. Refer to the previous chapter for a list of exposures for panic attacks.

Chapter 34
Challenging the Illusion of Control: The Game Changer

I shared this joke in the beginning of the book but it's worth repeating:

Two men are sitting on a bench reading in New York's Central Park. Periodically one man pats the top of his head three times in a row. The other man is perplexed.

Excuse me. I'm curious as to why you are patting your head.

It's a trick I learned in Africa. It keeps the elephants away.

But there aren't any elephants around here.

Yes. Works quite well, doesn't it!

As I discussed previously, the illusion of control is an overestimation of the ability to control events. It occurs when people believe they can control or influence outcomes which they cannot. The man who is tapping his head is expending a lot of time and energy to make sure elephants stay away. He is afraid that if he does not continue to tap, disaster will ensue. The only way for him to fully comprehend that his efforts are an illusion and that he is not in danger is to take a risk, stop tapping, and see what happens. When elephants don't appear, he will begin to question the logic of his tapping. If he continues to resist his compulsion to tap, his brain will come to understand that his safety behavior is pointless and then, and only then, will his worry about elephants cease to exist.

Most emetophobia sufferers rarely vomit and they believe that this is a direct result of their efforts. They believe they have successfully prevented themselves from vomiting because of their avoidance, hypervigilance, safety behaviors, compulsions, and defensive tactics. There is a sense of victory when they make it through the day without throwing up. This sense of victory comes at a high price, however, since it requires a life of subjection, restriction, and subordination: essentially, a self-imposed imprisonment.

Like the man who believes that tapping his head keeps away elephants, you too have been taking extraordinary efforts to control your life and yet your life feels very out of control. Whether it's chewing gum after a meal or eating only at certain times of the day, you believe it's necessary to do these behaviors to prevent vomiting. This is an illusion. Your efforts are unnecessary because you will not puke whether you do them or not.

None of your safety behaviors prevent vomiting but they can prevent nausea. These efforts are **not** an illusion. One of my former emetophobe patients needed to eat slowly or she would become nauseous. This was true. Each time she sped up she became nauseous. Emetophobes, therefore, **can** institute measures to reduce the likelihood of becoming nauseous but this comes at a price. What's the price? Curing yourself from emetophobia!

You have learned that to free yourself from this debilitating phobia, you must be willing to be anxious. When you eliminate a safety behavior, you are driving your bus down the road of uncertainty. That uncertainty will result in anxious thoughts and physical symptoms of anxiety, including nausea. My former patient became nauseous when she ate more quickly because she feared doing so would cause her to become nauseous and vomit. Her worry triggered her nausea. To cure herself of emetophobia, she had to **accept the nausea** while simultaneously **reject the lie** that being nauseous would cause her to vomit.

Another patient believed that after she ate, she could prevent vomiting by waiting two hours before she drove. Her belief, that she would puke if her food was not fully digested, was false and her efforts, therefore, were unnecessary. However, this safety behavior did spare her from becoming nauseous and anxious. If she did drive after she ate, she would experience nausea and anxiety. The problem was that her efforts to exert control caused so much disruption to her life, it actually caused more anxiety overall. How? Because the struggle to vigilantly maintain safety behaviors is stressful!

She desperately wanted freedom and was willing to do whatever it took. To reduce the likelihood of intense nausea, she took measured steps, beginning with the smallest one possible: Licking a popsicle and sitting in her car. When she discovered that this did not trigger anxiety or nausea, she took a few licks and drove her car ten feet. She continued with more brave steps into anxiety's territory, by eating one cracker and then driving down the street and then two crackers and driving around the block.

Every day she worked diligently, increasing the intensity and risk. It wasn't easy. Each time she made an uncertain move, her anxiety monster threatened she would vomit. When she took her thoughts seriously, her brain signaled her adrenal glands which resulted in nausea and more worries about vomiting. She was prepared with an offensive mindset (*Bring on the nausea. I can handle it*) and calculated responses (*I'm excited to be nauseous because I'm excited to be free*).

She eventually worked her way up to a bowl of cereal and a drive around her neighborhood. With each successful step, she realized that her attempts at control were an illusion: a lie. With unwavering determination, she eventually was able to eat a meal and drive across town.

Other illusions of control include eating only familiar foods and taking anti-nausea medication throughout the day. These behaviors are burdensome, do not prevent vomiting, and strengthen emetophobia. To fully comprehend that your efforts to control are an illusion, you must embark on an exposure hierarchy. For example, slowly reduce the dose and frequency of your anti-nausea medication. Step by step, increase the portion size of "unsafe" foods, beginning with one bite.

When you choose these uncertain roads, expect to feel nauseous but don't be fooled by the nausea. You're nauseous because you are anxious, not because the food is unsafe or you didn't take anti-nausea medication. Adrenaline is causing the nausea. Be prepared to dismiss the lie, respond with an offensive mindset, and back up your words with action.

Want What You Don't Want

Ask yourself these questions and circle your answers:

Is it possible that everything you are doing to prevent vomiting is pointless? Yes or No

Are you willing to take risks by stopping safety behaviors to see what happens? Yes or No

If you could snap your finger one time and your emetophobia and panic attacks would be gone forever, would you do it? Yes or No

If you could vomit one time and your emetophobia and panic attacks would be gone forever, would you do it? Yes or No

Consider the last question. After puking once, the rest of your life would be anxiety free. No more fear. No more missing out. Just a full, productive, happy life. Would you take that deal? On an intellectual level, you might, but your barf prevention instincts have been perfected over the years due to your staggering determination and work ethic. Hour after hour, day after day, year after year, you have focused all of your energies on avoiding all vomit-related situations and running from panic. Your brain circuitry is wired this way and the urge to flee and avoid is automatic and reflexive. You have been forcefully driving in one direction with full conviction that this is the only way**...**

...and now you must change course and head in the opposite direction. What does this require?

Drop **ALL** efforts to run away from vomit. Let go of your determination to stop yourself from vomiting. Discontinue all energies to control something you can't control. And then go a step further – want to puke and mean it!

Because of the wiring in your brain, this will be unnatural and seemingly impossible, which is why overcoming emetophobia and panic attacks is a lengthy process. It begins by saying to yourself out loud, *I want to vomit. I want to panic!* To want what you don't want. Every time your opponent asks, *what if you puke*, you respond, *I want to puke*! Why is it important to **want** it? How does this make sense? How do you train your body and mind to want something it does not want?

A former patient who grew up in Canada and played hockey as a defenseman in college shared his experience as we talked about *wanting it*. He said there is an instinct to move out of the way when a hard rubber puck is flying at you at 100 miles an hour. As a defenseman you have to learn to stand there and block it. With practice, hockey players train themselves to block the puck with their body.

The analogy is perfect. To become a good defenseman, you must train your mind and body to do the opposite of natural human instinct. You must practice taking the hit and the best way to do this is to **want** it and **lean** into it. Forcing yourself to lean into the hit with your game face and doing the opposite of what is instinctual, rewires the brain and reduces the fear. Wanting to block the puck is the equivalent of wanting to puke in the toilet.

Soccer players must practice taking the hit as well. There's a natural, reflexive instinct to avoid getting hit in the head with a ball. Yet to be a good soccer player, hitting the ball with your head is exactly what you must do. You must practice heading the ball correctly. If you **attack** the ball with force, with your forehead, it does not hurt but if you make a tentative attempt, with your eyes closed, the ball might hit you on the top of the head or on the face, which is painful. Forcing your head to do what is unnatural, repeatedly, rewires the brain and eventually becomes natural.

Want what you don't want to be successful on the soccer field, on the ice, and in your life.

When I learned to rollerblade decades ago, I had to force myself to do what was unnatural. The natural instinct when learning to skate is to look down at your feet. Doing this throws off your center of gravity and your balance. You must force yourself to keep your head up and eyes looking forward. This is not natural but by doing it repeatedly, it becomes natural.

In his book, *Stopping the Noise in Your Head,* Reid Wilson talks about *loving the mat*, a slogan he learned from the world of martial arts:

If you're training and competing on a regular basis, it's a given that you're going to end up on the mat over and over and over again. If you hate the mat—if you step into the ring thinking, "Don't get hit! Don't get knocked down! Don't lose!"—then you're chewing up consciousness that could be attending to your skills. You're devoting your attention and energy to bracing against the mat.

The mantra, *love the mat*, is akin to *love to vomit.* Wanting to vomit will not be easy and will feel inauthentic. Although you might understand intellectually that this is what is needed to win your freedom, your brain and body is wired NOT to want it. You will need to force yourself to do what is unnatural. Like Adam Sandler in *Happy Gilmore*, you will be putting on your game face, taking the hit, and responding with toughness.

You would never try to stop a bowel movement. Similarly, you should not try to stop vomiting if that is what your body needs to do. Giving yourself permission to vomit will take courage and practice. To reprogram your brain to counteract years of programming to **not** want to puke, declare with passion, *I WANT TO PUKE,* anytime you face a fear or do an exposure.

> *I WANT TO VOMIT BECAUSE I WANT TO BE FREE!*
> *I WANT TO PUKE BECAUSE I WANT MY LIFE!*
> *I DON'T CARE IF I PUKE. I DON'T CARE IF I'M NAUSEOUS.*
> *MAKE ME VOMIT! I DARE YOU!*

I capitalized the statements above because it's important to express these words with passion and determination, like you mean it, even if you don't. To make the words feel more believable, declare these statements out loud, in a LOUD voice, with the fury of someone yearning to be free. And if you are in the presence of others, say them silently with ferocity.

Now here's the tough part: you must back up your statements with action, otherwise these words are meaningless. Short of making yourself vomit, how do you do this? By going on offense and doing what you don't want to do. Prepare yourself for the game changer.

The Game Changer

Each time you do an exposure by eliminating a safety behavior, you will feel fear. Whether fear is triggered by an exposure or symptom (loose stools, indigestion, nausea), there is an immediate and a reflexive reaction to make it stop. This is you in defense mode. To win you must go on offense. When you feel anxiety, stomach distress, or nausea, it is your opportunity to respond like the buffalo and run towards the storm. This bit of Native American folklore is a great metaphor but how is it applied practically?

When the storm is approaching, when you feel nauseous and your monster is threatening a vomit emergency, run towards the storm by pretending to vomit, the opposite of your instinct to run away. Put water in your mouth, get on your hands and knees, and give the performance of a lifetime. Do this every time you worry about puking, feel nauseous, have diarrhea, or any stomach distress. Like a hockey player leaning into the puck, you will be leaning into the toilet. And like a soccer player attacking the ball with the head, you will be attacking the toilet with yours -- and a mouth full of water. This is the *game changer.*

If it sounds like a horrible idea, I have great news. Emetophobes actually feel **better** after they pretend to puke. Time after time, patients tell me that when they feel nauseous and pretend to puke, they feel empowered and their acute anxiety dissipates and often vanishes completely. Additionally, the cumulative impact of pretending to puke each time you feel nauseous or worried, will result in a diminished fear of vomiting overall. To beat emetophobia you will not have to make yourself vomit but you will need to pretend to puke when you feel sick and worried.

Planned Vomiting Exposures

In order to successfully accomplish this *game changing* intervention, you must first pretend to puke as a **planned** exposure when you are NOT feeling nauseous or symptomatic. Begin with baby steps by spitting water without making vomiting sounds. Simply spit in the shower, then move to the sink, trashcan, and finally the toilet. Slowly transition from spitting water to pretending to vomit water, unrealistically. Enhance your performance each step of the way with the goal of loud, realistic vomiting sounds, as if you were performing in a movie. Then replace water with challenging liquids: milk, juice, and soup, followed by something distasteful. Finally combine exposures: Before pretending to puke, put liquid in your mouth and make yourself dizzy. As you pretend to barf into the toilet, listen to vomiting sounds on You Tube.

Once you are able to perform vomiting exposures at home with minimal distress, ask yourself these questions: Do you find vomiting embarrassing? Do you imagine what people will think if they see you barf? Do you worry about vomiting in public and does it impact your behavior? Do you ever feel nauseous at restaurants, parties, or other public places? If you answer yes to any of these questions, it's essential to do vomiting exposures in public. YIKES! These exposures target the fear of public humiliation and are vital to your recovery and freedom.

Pull your car into a parking lot or the side of a road, put water in your mouth, open the car door, and hurl onto the cement. Drive to a park for the sole purpose of pretending to vomit in a trashcan. Pretend to puke in a friend's bathroom. Go to a business with a single stall restroom and puke loudly into the toilet. Fake vomit in a restroom with multiple stalls, first alone, and then with people inside. Your goal is to fool the strangers who hear you. If someone asks if you're okay, then you know your performance was Academy Award worthy.

If these exposures sound awful, then that's a good indication you need to do them. To eradicate emetophobia, you must face what you fear. What you will discover is that these exposures are not as horrible as you imagine. Once you've done them in various locations multiple times, you will no longer fear vomiting when away from home.

You will then be prepared to apply the *game changer*. The next time you are outside your home and you feel nauseous or worried about vomiting, pretend to puke. If you're at a party and suddenly feel worried about what you just ate, put on your game face, go to the bathroom, and fake vomit in the toilet. Whenever you feel anxious sitting at a restaurant, excuse yourself, walk into the restroom, and pretend to vomit. Then return to the table as if nothing happened. This often eliminates the fear and symptoms, enabling you to enjoy the rest of your time.

Planned vomiting exposures will prepare you for how to respond when you feel nauseous and terrified. See these moments of nausea and fear as opportunities to heal and free yourself. Pretend to puke at home and in public **every time** you feel worried about vomiting. Do it quickly before anxiety convinces you otherwise. Want what you don't want and do what you don't want to do. When the storm approaches, run towards it. *I want to vomit! Make it happen. I dare you!* And then back up your statements with action. What you will discover is that you don't vomit, and instead come away feeling empowered and confident.

One of my current patients experienced elevated anxiety and fear each time she had loose stools. I instructed her to put a cup of water and an empty bucket in her bathroom. Whenever her bowel movements were loose, she had to pretend to puke in the bucket as she sat on the toilet pooping. OMG! NO WAY! She thought I was joking. I wasn't.

My patient was making a critical error by focusing her energy on trying to stop her bowel movements from being loose. Gastrointestinal symptoms are extremely common if you suffer with anxiety and the chance is high that these symptoms will remain a periodic presence throughout life. Therefore, her focus and effort needed to be on accepting loose stools and learning to be unafraid. To rewire her anxious brain so that her GI issues no longer triggered fear, my patient had to experience loose stools and then practice responding with an offensive mindset. Her focus shifted from trying to stop her symptoms, to wanting them.

The irony is the more she wanted loose stools, the less it happened. Each time it occurred was an opportunity to rewire her brain by pretending to puke in a bucket. Soon loose stools did not trigger anxiety and because she was no longer afraid, she did not experience them as often.

Instead of falling for the illusion of control, take genuine control over your disorder by applying the *game changer* to planned and spontaneous exposures. Giving in to the illusion will worsen emetophobia, while taking actual control will lead to freedom. Do NOT stick your finger down your throat. That is not necessary or recommended. Instead, do ALL the exposures in this book. Repeated practice will prepare you for the day when you have the flu, food poisoning, or are pregnant.

This video depicts the battle between an emetophobe and his anxiety monster and how to successfully implement a planned *game changer* with an offensive mindset and competing emotions.

STEPS TO FREEDOM

Planned Vomit Exposure: Purposefully pretend to puke at least three times in a row, twice a day. Begin with unrealistic vomiting or spitting and then make it sound realistic. Begin in the shower then move to the sink, trashcan and toilet. Once you can do this with mild anxiety, progress through the exposure hierarchy with other liquids: milk, juice, soup, and then beverages that are unpleasant. Do these exposures without cleaning the toilet first. Then pretend to puke in public.

Spontaneous Vomit Exposure: After working on planned vomiting exposures, pretend to puke every time you feel nauseous, experience stomach distress, or become fearful of vomiting. Begin with water and unrealistic barfing and work your way up to loud and intense puking using various liquids, inside and outside of your home.

Slowly Reduce your Safety Behaviors: Step by step choose the uncertain path and challenge your illusion of control. Reduce the frequency of your safety behaviors, including your use of medication with the goal of taking it only when needed.

Listen to this former emetophobe share how she conquered her anxiety by bringing intensity and an offensive mindset to her exposure work:

Chapter 35
Interoceptive Exposures

Interoceptive Exposures are exposures meant to create physical symptoms of distress with the goal of gaining greater distress tolerance. Like the other exposures in this book, they will test your expectations and disconfirm incorrect beliefs about the sensations they produce. Tackle them one by one and practice on a daily basis.

Once you can do two exposures with relative ease, combine them. This is analogous to a weight lifter building muscle by adding more weight. By combing two exposures together, you will strengthen your tolerance and confidence muscles. Begin with the least distressing and least uncertain. Work your way up the hierarchy step by step, every day. You are driving the bus so you create the order. Find your motivation and drive down these roads of discomfort and uncertainty, despite your opponent threatening disaster. With each exposure, your anxiety monster will predict you will vomit. It's uncertain. Let's see if he is right.

INTEROCEPTIVE EXPOSURES

- In a standing position, bend over, put your forehead on the end of a baseball bat (or something similar), and move your body around it 5 times as fast as you can. (This will help build tolerance to dizziness).

- Eat or drink something that is unappealing. (This will build your tolerance to disgust)

- Eat more food than usual. (This will build your tolerance to bloating)

- Drink a carbonated beverage quickly to induce burping (This will build your tolerance to gassy noises spewing from your mouth)

- Eat a meal quickly (This will build your tolerance to indigestion, heartburn, acid reflux)

- Ride on a boat, roller coaster, Ferris wheel, Merry Go Round (This will build your tolerance to motion)

- Make yourself gag by **carefully** sticking a lollipop/Dum Dum towards the back of your throat. **Do not place it far. Only enough to cause a slight gag reflex – not to make yourself vomit.** (This will build your tolerance to gagging)

- Obtain **vomit** flavored Jelly Bellies and eat one every day for two weeks. (This will build your tolerance to the taste of vomit) Go to jellybelly.com and call the factory directly to place a custom order.

- Eat a vomit flavored Jelly Belly while in the back of an Uber (Combining two exposures will strengthen your tolerance and rewire your brain)

- Put disgusting food and liquid in your mouth, spin around five times, and then pretend to vomit in an unclean toilet. Make it sound real. Stick your head into the toilet and look at the pretend vomit for one minute. (This will strengthen your tolerance to dizziness and disgust)

- Smell something that will make you gag. The goal is to gag. (This will build tolerance to noxious smells and gagging)

- Make fake vomit (see recipes below) and dump the vile concoction in a toilet. Put your head inside the toilet. Look at it and smell it for 30 seconds. Increase gradually to three minutes. (This will strengthen your tolerance to disgust)

• Two recipes for fake vomit:

VOMIT RECIPE #1	VOMIT RECIPE #2
-Oatmeal	-Cooked lentils
-Stinky cheese	-Pea soup
-Beef barley soup	-Parmesan Cheese
-Tomato soup	-Mustard

When you do these exposures, you will feel anxious and there will be a part of you that prays you don't puke. That's the old mindset. The new mindset is to *want to vomit*. Why? Because that's your ticket to FREEDOM. **Acceptance of nausea and vomiting is the key that unlocks your self-imposed prison. Trying to make yourself puke opens the door immediately.**

Before doing these exposures declare, *I don't care if I vomit. Make it happen. I can handle it.* Say it loud, like you mean it. Declare, ***I'm excited to vomit because I'm excited to be free!***

You do not need to induce vomiting to conquer emetophobia but you will need to stop caring about vomit. Practice all exposures with the mindset of trying to make yourself puke — *Make me puke. I dare you!* — and when you don't, you will feel empowered and confident. On the off chance you do hurl, seize the opportunity and unlock the gate of your self-imposed prison. Maintain an offensive mindset — *Give me more! I can handle it!* — Think these statements with ferocity and toughness and you'll see that vomiting is not as horrific as you imagine.

Robin Arzon is Vice President of Fitness Programming at Peloton, an ultramarathon runner, an author, a former lawyer, and a hostage survivor. She motivates people, not only to embrace the discomfort of running and biking, but to embrace the discomfort of life and push through. When I ride my Peloton in her cycling classes, I hear her inspiration and passion: *The pain you feel today will be the strength you feel tomorrow! -- If you can name it, you can claim it! -- Sweat with swagger! -- Chin up, crown on, be proud of your struggle!* When the cycling gets gritty, she periodically puts on her game face and growls. When I mirror her growl, I can generate intensity and determination to push through the tough stretches and reach my predetermined goals. When you confront terrifying exposures, put on your game face and GROWL! Recall the story of my son on Halloween, growling at the monsters with chainsaws, as he walked through the haunted yard. When your anxiety monster tries to scare you with lies, growl back! When you feel an urge to flee, growl, and keep moving forward.

STEPS TO FREEDOM

Interoceptive Exposures: Make you way through the exposures in this chapter, tolerating the discomfort and uncertainty, while wanting to vomit.

Planned Vomit Exposures: Purposefully pretend to puke at least three times in a row, twice a day. Begin with unrealistic vomiting and progress through the exposure hierarchy with water, milk, juice, chunky soup, and then beverages that are unpleasant. Do these exposures without cleaning the toilet first. Pretend to barf in public restrooms, parks, and other people's homes.

Spontaneous Vomit Exposures: Pretend to puke every time you feel nauseous, experience stomach distress, or become fearful of vomiting. Begin with water and unrealistic barfing noises and work towards realistic, loud, and intense vomiting, inside and outside of your home. This is the *Game Changer.*

CHAPTER 36
Setbacks and Your Push To Freedom

After working hard for months, you will notice that you begin to do more and feel better. Perhaps after several more months a new self begins to emerge. An internal battle for supremacy wages as your healthy self yearns to break free and your unhealthy self resists. This battle can be scary as you observe and feel the change taking place very slowly. You might fear what freedom means, what you will be like, and new expectations from others. Remember not to dwell on these questions. Instead, process them with a therapist, a close friend, or family member.

When you're out of the crisis stage and functioning has improved, there is a natural tendency to ease up. It's common to feel tired from doing exposures and worry that doing more could trigger a setback. This work is not complicated but it is hard and the thought of doing more difficult exposures is daunting. Yet, the goal is to gain complete freedom from emetophobia and panic. Your monster will declare that you've done well enough and claim that complete freedom is not possible. This is a trick. Applaud yourself for the steps you have accomplished thus far and keep going, even when freedom feels far away and progress is slow.

Firefighters combating a forest fire don't stop until the fire is 100% out. They don't walk away after 50% containment. In a similar fashion, press on until the fire of emetophobia and panic is extinguished. This does not mean an absence of anxiety. It means that anxiety no longer has power and control over you and you are living the life you desire.

Believing you will **not** get better will make your journey harder. A firm belief that failure is inevitable will erode your grit and effort. On the other hand, a belief that you will prevail (or at least a belief that it's possible) will motivate you to push through the setbacks.

Anxiety sufferers often ask, *How long will it take to get better?* In my experience, those who work hard every day, view the problem from a mental game perspective, change their beliefs, shift their focus from defense to offense, and use the tools and strategies correctly and frequently get better faster. Even if an emetophobe with panic disorder does everything correctly, significant progress usually takes a minimum of four months and sometimes closer to two years when cases are severe. The speed of progress varies widely.

Why does it take so long? There can be external stressors (financial stress, unsupportive family, living in a stressful environment, oppressive work situation, family obligations, recent changes, loss of a loved one, inability to find a therapist who specializes in anxiety or inability to afford one). Co-occurring mental health issues will complicate and extend recovery (major depression, bipolar disorder, substance abuse, personality disorder). There are often medication issues (fear of trying or taking medication, side effects, multiple medication trials). The fear of taking medication for medical issues (acid reflux, IBS, heart burn, etc.) will delay your recovery. You might also be experiencing medical issues which may or may not be caused by your emetophobia. Fear of doing exposures, a lack of self-discipline, and self-sabotage are also common and delay improvement.

Responding to Setbacks

The healing journey is challenging and this often results in pessimism and minimal effort. With years of practice at being anxious your brain is wired to impulsively flee when you feel trapped and constantly on guard to prevent vomiting. The moment you experience nausea, symptomatic distress, or any other physical symptom, there is an explosion of fear. Rewiring the brain to respond differently takes time. As I've stated, after six months of lessons, you wouldn't expect to play piano like a virtuoso or know a foreign language fluently. Similarly, you shouldn't expect freedom from anxiety to happen quickly. There will be many setbacks and missteps along the way. This is normal.

I currently have a patient who has had countless setbacks through her journey of overcoming her emetophobia and panic disorder. In the beginning of treatment, she repeatedly took two steps forward and one back. On many occasions she took five steps forward and five back which always eroded hope. But she was persistent. After a year and a half she was taking on high-level exposures and has not experienced major anxiety, obsessions, or panic for two months.

A few weeks ago, she re-experienced loose stools, a decade long trigger. Her amygdala hijacked her entire brain and she forgot everything she had learned and practiced. She reverted into a defensive mindset and regressed into obsessions, believing the lies of her imagination. Her voice was no longer in the dominant position. Her anxiety monster was now in charge and she was terrified of vomiting.

Similar episodes have occurred dozens of times since she started treatment. The duration of each relapse (in days and weeks) has shortened but they continue to occur. This is common. Because of the strong neuronal connections of the anxious brain, it's normal to lapse into old behaviors.

After two days of suffering she spoke to me. She was disappointed with herself because she thought she had beaten emetophobia and panic and she worried she would never be free. Anxiety was able to lure her to the back of the bus and engage her in a dark conversation. My job was to get her back into the driver's seat. I told her to congratulate her opponent for the victory, learn from the experience, and try again. Her biggest mistake was being upset when her symptoms of anxiety returned. These are opportunities to rewire the brain by responding differently. She needed to **want** loose stools and anxiety, instead of being upset when they occur.

Her second mistake was beating herself up when anxiety won. There will be countless times when you're defeated by anxiety, but like an Olympic figure skater that falls, you must quickly rise up, and continue on. If you understand that setbacks are a normal part of the healing process, you will not dwell on them for as long. Like all baseball players that fail to get on base 70% of the time, expect moments where anxious thoughts and symptoms get the best of you.

Use Your Symptoms to Your Advantage

I reminded my patient of the winning strategy and prepared her for the next time she experienced loose stools, which usually took place in the morning. I instructed her to write a letter to herself to serve as a reminder of how to proceed when anxiety returns. I also reminded her that physical symptoms (loose stools, heart burn, nausea, stomach discomfort) are common and will be a regular part of the rest of her life or at least for the immediate future. I told her: *Your symptoms aren't going away anytime soon.*

I explained how she can use her symptoms to her advantage. *I know your goal is to visit your family and on the morning of your flight, do you think you're going to be anxious? Absolutely. Very anxious. You are well aware that when you have anxiety you have loose stools, correct? It's how your body experiences anxiety. That's what's going to happen on the morning of your flight whether you like it or not, so you must be prepared for that day. The best way to prepare for loose stools is to have them. Each day you have loose stools and anxiety is an opportunity to practice. View loose stools and anxiety as an opportunity to prepare for the day you fly home.*

She understood the logic and had the motivation but she needed maximum effort and an offensive mindset. I instructed her to put a bucket in the bathroom along with a cup of liquid. The next time she had loose stools or diarrhea she had to pretend to puke at the same time. That's right: liquid scream from both ends. This was terrifying. She had been successfully pretending to vomit for two months. Now it was time to practice with the same ferocity at the exact moment when fear seized her mind and body. For the first time she wanted to have loose stools. She understood that practicing repeatedly would rewire her brain and at some point, loose stools would not elicit fear. The first step was to want loose stools and that is what she did.

For the next three mornings, however, no loose stools, no anxiety, and no opportunity to practice. She was actually disappointed. When you stop being afraid of symptoms, they are less likely to occur. On the fourth day, in the afternoon, she finally had her opportunity and she took full advantage. She used her anger at anxiety and pretended to vomit as realistically as possible as she sat on the toilet. Her anxiety disappeared and she felt empowered and confident. By repeating this exposure each time she had loose stools, her fear diminished significantly.

It takes months to heal the mind and cultivate a new relationship with anxiety. You are in the process of rewiring your anxious brain to tolerate uncertainty and distress and this must be done one step at a time. You will stumble as you take those steps. Accept the missteps and setbacks as part of the process and learn from those experiences.

Frequency of exposures is key but you must do them with the correct attitude. Remind yourself why you are doing this and push forward on a daily basis, doing as many exposures as possible, particularly when symptoms of anxiety hit hard.

As I have stated previously, you do not need to make yourself vomit to beat emetophobia. I do not advise drinking Ipecac or sticking a finger down your throat. Several risks are associated with inducing vomiting repeatedly (e.g., dental damage, esophageal damage) Boschen (2007). Instead, complete all the exposures in this book, including the ones that trigger uncomfortable physical sensations. These exposures will rewire your brain to not *react* when you feel nauseous, bloated, disgusted, lightheaded, or have loose stools. No one likes to feel these symptoms but the goal is to not feel anxious or worried when you experience them.

The exposures are necessary to win complete freedom because they will condition you to ride out waves of anxiety, believe that you can handle it, and understand that nothing catastrophic is happening. Then, after months of repeated practice, nausea will just be nausea, stomach distress will just be uncomfortable, and indigestion, diarrhea, and menstrual cramps will not cause worry or fear -- they will just suck.

The Role of Others on Your Team

Although *The Emetophobia Manual* is your roadmap to freedom, it's always easier to take a journey with the help and support of others. That's where a good therapist and supportive family and friends come in. All therapists treat anxiety and depression but they all don't do it well. I recommend an anxiety and OCD specialist who uses CBT, ACT, and ERP. If these therapeutic modalities are highlighted on a therapist's website, that's a therapist worth contacting.

Below is a list of websites with a *Find a Therapist* section to help you identify therapists in your hometown. If you live in a remote area (or even if you don't), search for a provider in your state who does treatment via secure video conferencing. Almost all therapists do.

- Anxiety and Depression Association of America – ADAA.org
- International OCD Foundation – IOCDF.org
- Association for Behavioral and Cognitive Therapies – ABCT.org

Supportive family and friends can also play a role in your recovery. They can participate in certain exposures, encourage, cheer you on, and remind you of important concepts, but they should not push you faster than you are willing to go. Although you will work as a team, your teammates need to understand that you are the one in charge. You are driving the bus. If you are doing an exposure with a partner and want to stop the exposure or leave the situation, your partner must respond *you're in charge* – without argument. There is enough inner-struggle going on in your head. Pressure from a partner will cause reluctance to do exposures together due to a lack of trust. Likewise, your teammates need to trust that you are working hard to get better. If they witness you making maximum effort, they will back off and let you take charge of your treatment. If they believe you are slacking, conflict will ensue. Keep them informed of your progress, be honest, and let them know how they can help.

Emetophobia sufferers often lose friends. Canceling plans, not returning calls, and turning down invitations are common and can destroy even the closest of relationships. I highly recommend reaching out to the people you have lost and being honest. Apologize and explain what you have been going through. Educate them on your disorder and you will see how supportive and compassionate people can be. Since 18% of adults have an anxiety disorder, don't be surprised when they disclose their own anxiety or tell you about the struggles of a close relative. Ask for their forgiveness and to keep the conversation confidential. Then ask them to dinner with an opportunity to start over. This might seem like a scary idea, but you've learned that uncertainty is the winning path, so go for it.

What Does Victory Look Like?

Since you have anxious genes, you will always have some anxiety. So when can you claim victory over your opponent? You are victorious when you no longer avoid situations, engage in safety behaviors, or try to prevent vomiting. You win when your brain stops searching vomit disasters and stops reacting with fear to physical symptoms and external triggers. At that point, drive your bus into the Land of Freedom! You have successfully navigated the maze and freed yourself from your self-imposed prison. Finally, you can enjoy a happy, productive, and full life.

Part of having a full life, however, means getting the flu or food poisoning and when this happens, the chances are high you will vomit. Because vomiting is rare and infrequent, this might not occur for many years, which means you will need to continue to do vomiting exposures periodically for years. To maintain your gains, prevent slipping backwards, and to be prepared for the moment you do puke, I recommend doing challenging vomiting exposures once a week. Alcoholics who have been sober for years go to weekly AA meetings to prevent relapse, and athletes who want to remain strong and fit, exercise regularly. To maintain your gains and prepare for the inevitable, you must continue to practice. Then when you do barf, you will feel the same level of discomfort that everyone experiences but it won't be accompanied by high levels of anxiety. It'll just suck.

CHAPTER 37
Summary of the Strategies, Tools, and Key Concepts

Look at the problem of anxiety from a different point of view. Externalize and personify anxiety. View your struggle as a mental game against a tricky opponent whose goal is to make sure you are miserable. If you fall for his tricks, you will lose. If you are determined, take risks, and use the strategies in this book, you can win. Put yourself into the game by using a tally counter app and earn a point for each victory.

Understand your opponent's strategy. Your opponent has two strategic moves: A) lie, B) engage you in a conversation. The quicker you comprehend this and implement a counter strategy, the quicker you win.

Refuse to believe the lies in your imagination, including long-held core beliefs and the illusion of control. All of your efforts to prevent yourself from vomiting are not preventing anything except a life of happiness. Demand reality. Drop all efforts to control. Reject what your opponent predicts. Refuse to believe that nausea and stomach distress will lead to vomiting. Do the opposite of what your opponent demands.

Respond to physical symptoms with acceptance. Accepting physical symptoms is key to reducing them. Respond in a paradoxical fashion: *Welcome back. Stay as long as you like.* Or *This is exactly the feeling I need. I can handle it.* Mean what you say. Don't say, *Riding the wave. I can handle it* with the hope that your symptoms go away.

Seek roads of discomfort and uncertainty to get through the maze and win your freedom. If you are anxious, uncomfortable, and uncertain, you are winning. If you seek comfort, certainty, and safety, you are on the losing path.

Don't try to stop anxiety. That's the end goal. Your immediate goal is to seek it out and create anxiety thereby giving you opportunities to practice responding correctly and rewire your brain.

Stay motivated and be persistent, particularly when you falter. This is a long process with many setbacks. Work hard every day and don't give up. Beware of your monster's attempts to deflate your efforts: *You'll never be able to do it. This is too hard. There's no point in trying.* Read your statement of determination, play your fight song, read your motivational letter, and keep track of your victories in your Victory Journal. When your monster wins, congratulate him, figure out what you did wrong, learn from your mistakes, and try again.

Do not put your attention on your thoughts and symptoms. Like a garden that grows when you tend to it, giving your thoughts and symptoms attention will cause them to grow. Worrying about having a panic attack will escalate your anxiety and increase the odds of panicking. Focusing on your nausea will make it last longer. The best way to reduce anxiety is to turn your attention away from your symptoms and thoughts, and focus on living your life.

Don't take the bait. Do not go to the back of the bus and engage with your anxiety monster. Don't answer his questions, reply to his comments, debate, reassure, or strategize. Instead, respond quickly and turn away. Otherwise you will be hooked.

Be ready to respond to anxious thoughts. Respond with something your opponent does not expect: *Thanks for sharing. Have a nice day.* Or *You're a liar. F-off.* I recommend keeping it simple by only using a few different responses. Making them easy to remember will automate your replies and prevent you from engaging with your anxiety monster. Verbalizing your worries out loud with an accent or silly voice will help you detach from your thoughts.

Respond with competing emotions. Anxiety is intense. To elevate your voice to the dominant position, use a competing emotion to help you face and push through anxiety. Verbalize your worries out loud with an accent to hear how silly they sound. Tell yourself repeatedly, *I'm excited to do hard things because I'm excited to be free.* Say it out loud with passion to make it feel more believable. Pound your fist and tell your opponent *F-off. I refuse to believe your lies.* After a while, maximum intensity will not be needed and you can quietly dismiss him with *whatever, that's not true.*

Shift focus from seeking comfort and certainty to living your life. Exercise, socialize, revisit old hobbies and start new ones, go to church, mosque, or temple, and spend time with friends and family. The goal is to live your life, not to be comfortable or certain. Go to the movies, skate at a rink, work out at a gym, get your hair cut, take a hike, go on vacation, attend a sporting event, get a massage, attend a concert, eat at a restaurant, take a class and see a play. Then do it all again. Make plans with people on a weekly basis and do not cancel. Find groups to join and do what you enjoy, every single day.

Maintain an offensive mindset when doing planned and unplanned exposures. Your choice is to fight or flee. Be like the buffalo and choose to run towards and through the storm. Be determined to stay and ride it out. When anxiety says to leave, go deeper into his territory.

Do exposures correctly. People don't make real change by *learning new information.* They change by *living new experiences.* Do exposures with a competing emotion and an offensive mindset. Have a predetermined goal and a vital reason to meet it. Do exposures one step at a time and then combine them for a more challenging experience. Doing them multiple times a day, for longer periods of time, will rewire your anxious brain.

Mentally prepare before doing exposures. Know your plan, anticipate what anxiety will do, and have your counter move ready. Identify a goal and be determined to push through anxiety to meet that goal. Remind yourself why you are doing this. Keep what you value in mind as you face your fear. Do an easier exposure as a warm up to build your confidence and then do a challenging exposure with ferocity and determination.

Ride out anxiety. Be steadfast in your resolve to stay and push through fear instead of flee. Your natural instinct to run is based on faulty wiring and a perception of danger. You will be rewiring your brain, teaching it that there is no emergency and no reason to flee.

Employ the Game Changer. Want what you don't want and do the opposite of what your opponent demands. Want to puke and then try to make it happen each day by doing planned and spontaneous vomiting exposures. Every time you feel nauseous and worry about vomiting, get on your knees, and pretend to puke in the toilet. *Good. This is exactly what I want. Keep it coming. I can handle it.*

Change your attitude to want symptoms. To rewire your anxious brain to not fear physical symptoms, you must experience physical symptoms and practice responding correctly. Like a novice surfer needs waves to practice, you need symptoms to practice.

Focus on where you have influence or control (your thoughts and behavior) and accept what you don't have control over (your symptoms). You can't stop your thoughts or symptoms from surfacing. They come too fast. Your task comes right after. Hit the thoughts hard and turn away from them while simultaneously accepting your body's physical sensations. Being upset about your symptoms and trying to make them stop will only worsen and prolong them.

Don't be fooled by nausea and stomach distress. Nausea, loose stools, stomach distress are common symptom of anxiety. If you don't vomit due to anxiety then you won't. Only when you accept symptoms without reacting to them will they subside.

Get out of bed immediately and take a walk. Do not lie in bed cuddling with your anxiety monster. Start your day with an immediate victory.

Try medication. If your symptoms are so severe you are unable to do exposures frequently or correctly, if you are not eating enough, or if you have not made progress despite your best efforts, schedule an appointment with a psychiatrist. Medication can make the journey easier and reduce suffering. Instead of walking up a sand dune with a backpack full of rocks, you'll be walking up a steep hill with a walking stick. Refuse to believe anxiety when it claims that medication will make you puke.

Use all of the tools and do all of the exercises:

- **3 by 3 Relaxation Breathing** – 5 to 10 times a day.

- **Mindfulness exercises** – at least once a day.

- **Relaxation exercises** – once a day.

- **Victory Journal** – record your successes on a daily basis.

- **Tally Counter App** – Each day is a new game you can win!

- **Horror Stories** – Compose horror stories about your worst fears (including exposures) and read them out loud repeatedly. Record and then listen to them.

- **Trauma Stories** – Write your trauma story in the present tense and read it out loud several times a day. Trauma stories might include past vomiting traumas, panic attacks, or other traumatic events.

- **Create worry scripts and practice responding** – Create a list of worrisome thoughts pertaining to a specific fear (e.g., eating at a restaurant, riding an elevator, etc.). Record these statements and questions onto your phone. Listen back and practice responding, first at home and then where you feel afraid to venture (e.g., restaurant, elevator, etc.)

- **Eradicate your monster** - Get rid of your opponent in creative ways. Crush him, flick him off your shoulder, microwave his ass.

- **Teamwork** – Use your entire team: family, friends, therapist, online emetophobia support group, dietitian psychiatrist, medication, secret identity, fight song. You are the team captain, the one in charge.

- **Reread this book! -** To strengthen concepts you have learned.

In my twenty-plus years treating anxiety, I have witnessed many amazing transformations. You just may be the next one. Work hard, use the strategies, and don't give up.

Thanks for allowing me to coach you to victory!

Accept what is, let go of what was, and have faith in what will be.
--Sonia Ricotti

References

Agoraphobia: Prevalence of Agoraphobia Among Adults. (2017, November) Retrieved from https://www.nimh.nih.gov/health/statistics/agoraphobia.shtml

Anxiety Disorder: Prevalence of Any Anxiety Disorder Among Adults. (2017, November) Retrieved from https://www.nimh.nih.gov/health/statistics/any-anxiety-disorder.shtml

Becker ES, Rinck M, Turke V, Kause P, Goodwin R, Neumer S, Margraf J ¨ (2007). Epidemiology of specific phobia subtypes: findings from the Dresden Mental Health Study. *European Psychiatry* 22, 69–74.

Boschen, M. J. (2007). Reconceptualizing emetophobia: A Cognitive Behavioral Formulation and Research Agenda. *Journal of Anxiety Disorders*, 21, 407–419

Bourne, E. (2003) *The Anxiety and Phobia Workbook.* Oakland, California: New Harbinger Publications

Brooks, A., (2013) Get Excited: Reappraising Pre-Performance Anxiety as Excitement. *Journal of Experimental Psychology*. Vol. 143, No. 3, 1144-1158

Carter, B., (2018) *Raw: My Journey from Anxiety to Joy.* Berkeley, California: She Writes Press

Clark, D.A. (1999). Anxiety Disorders: Why they persist and how to treat them. Behavior Research and Therapy 37, S5+S27

Clark, D.A. & Beck, A. (2010). Cognitive Theory and therapy of anxiety and depression: Convergence with neurobiological findings. *Tends in Cognitive Science*, 12(9), 48-24

Coles, N., Larsen J., Lench H., A meta-analysis of the facial feedback literature: Effects of facial feedback on emotional experience are small and variable. *Psychological Bulletin*, 2019; DOI: 10.1037/bul0000194

Duckworth, A.L., Peterson, C., Matthews, M.D., & Kelly, D.R. (2007). Grit: Perseverance and passion for long-term goals. Journal of Personality and Social Psychology, 92(6), 1087-1101.

Fredrickson, B., (2001) The Role of Positive Emotions in Positive Psychology: The Broaden-and-Build Theory of Positive Emotions. *American Psychologist*. Vol. 56, No. 3, 218-226

Gillihan, S.J., Williams, M.T., Malcoun, E., Yadin, E., and Foa, E.B. (2012). Common pitfalls in exposure and response prevention (EX/RP) for OCD. *Journal of Obsessive-Compulsive and Related Disorders, 1(4), 251-257*

Goldin, P.R., Ziv, M., Jazaieri, H., Hahn, K., Heimberg, R. & Gross, J. (2013) Impact of cognitive behavioral therapy for social anxiety on the neural dynamics of cognitive reappraisal of negative self-beliefs: Randomized clinical trial. *JAMA Psychiatry*, 70(10), 1048-1056, doi:10.1001/jamapsychiatry.2013.234

Holler Y., van Overveld M., Jutglar H., Trinka E., (2013) Nausea in Specific Phobia of Vomiting. *Behavioral Sciences* 3, 445-458

Jokic-Bergic, N. (2010). Cognitive-behavioral therapy and neuroscience: Towards closer integration. *Psychological Topics* 19(2), 235-254

Kalin, Ned (2018). Functional Connectivity within the Primate Extended Amygdala Is Heritable and Associated with Early-Life Anxious Temperament. *Journal of Neuroscience* 29 August 2018, 38 (35) 7611-7621

Kirkpatrick DR, Berg AJ (1981). Fears of a heterogeneous non-psychiatric sample. Paper presented at the Annual Conference of the American Psychological Association, Los Angeles, California

Kraft, T. and Pressman S. University of Kansas (2012) Grin and Bear It: The Influence of Manipulated Facial Expression on the Stress Response. *Psychological Science* 23(11) 1372–1378

Langer, E. (1975) The Illusion of Control. *Journal of Personality and Social Psychology*, Vol 32, No. 2, 311-328

Lipsitz J., Fyer A., Paterniti A., Klein D., (2001) Emetophobia: Preliminary Results of an Internet Survey. *Depression and Anxiety* 14:149–152

Mason, L., Peters, E., Williams S., et al. (2017) Brain connectivity changes occurring following cognitive behavioral therapy for psychosis predict long-term recovery. *Translational Psychiatry.* doi:10.1038/tp.2016.263

Morrow, K., Elizabeth, S., (2018) *CBT for Anxiety: A Step-by-Step Training Manual for the Treatment of Fear, Panic, Worry, and OCD*. Eau Claire, Wisconsin: Pesi

Norwegian Institute of Emotion-focused Therapy (2015, November 24) *About Emotions: How do you Change Them.* [Video file]. Retrieved from https://www.youtube.com/watch?v=f_yO-6zLG9k

Panic Disorder. Retrieved from https://adaa.org/understanding-anxiety/panic-disorder

Philips HC (1985). Return of fear in the treatment of a fear of vomiting. *Behaviour Research Therapy* 23, 45–52.

Porto, P., Oliveira, L., Mari, J., Volchan, E., Figueira, I., Ventura, P., (2009) Does Cognitive Behavioral Therapy Change the Brain? A Systematic Review of Neuroimaging in Anxiety Disorders. *The Journal of Neuropsychiatry and Clinical Neurosciences.* 21:114–125

Riddle-Walker L., Veale D., Chapmanc C., Ogle F., Roskoa D., Najmi S., Walker L., Maceacherng P., Hicks T., (2016) Cognitive Behaviour Therapy for Specific Phobia of Vomiting (Emetophobia): A Pilot Randomized Controlled Trial. *Journal of Anxiety Disorders* 43

Seif, M., Winston, S., (2019) *Needing to Know for Sure: A CBT Guide to Overcoming Compulsive Checking and Reassurance Seeking.* Oakland, California: New Harbinger

Stefan G. Hofmann, Alice T. Sawyer, Ashley A. Witt, and Diana Oh (2010) The Effect of Mindfulness-Based Therapy on Anxiety and Depression: A Meta-Analytic Review *J Consult Clin Psychol.* 78(2): 169–183.

TEDx (2015, December). *After Watching This Your Brain Will Not be the Same* [Video file]. Retrieved from https://www.youtube.com/watch?v=LNHBMFCzznE

TED (2013, May). *Grit: The Power of Passion and Perseverance* [Video file]. Retrieved from https://www.youtube.com/watch?v=H14bBuluwB8

Van Overveld M., de Jong P., Peters M., van Hout W., Bouman T. (2008) An Internet-based Study on the Relation between Disgust Sensitivity and Emetophobia. *Journal of Anxiety Disorders* 22, 524–531

Veale D., Murphy P., Ellison N., Kanakam N., Costa A., (2012) Autobiographical Memories of Vomiting in People with a Specific Phobia of Vomiting (emetophobia) *Journal of Behavior Therapy and Experimental Psychiatry* 44: 14-20

Wilson, R. (2016) *Stopping the Noise in Your Head: The New Way to Overcome Anxiety and Worry*. Deerfield Beach, Florida: Health Communications Inc.